The English Ideology

The English Ideology

George Watson

The Lutterworth Press
Cambridge

Published by
The Lutterworth Press
P.O. Box 60
Cambridge
CB1 2NT
England

e-mail: **publishing@lutterworth.com**
website: **http://www.lutterworth.com**

ISBN 0 7188 9156 2 paperback

British Library Cataloguing in Publication Data:
A catalogue record is available from the British Library.

First published 1973
First published by the Lutterworth Press 2004

Contents

Preface ix

1 Introduction 1

2 Ideology and the Victorians 10

3 History and Revolution 26

4 Ideas of the Good 48

5 *Laissez-faire* and the State 68

6 The Terms of Party Politics 91

7 Political Oratory 112

8 The Parliamentary Novel 133

9 Democracy and Equality 155

10 Class or Rank 174

11 Race and Empire 198

12 Socialism 219

13 The Sages 241

Index 265

Preface

This book describes the parliamentary idea in Victorian England – its terms, its literature, including fiction and oratory, and its most characteristic arguments. None of these, as it happens, are dead letters today, and I hope there are few spent cartridges here; though I am haunted by Bagehot's warning that 'the characteristic danger of great nations, like the Romans or the English, which have a long history of continuous creation, is that they may fail from not comprehending the great institutions which they have created'. But my main concern here has been historical, notably with the interpenetration of politics and literature in the Victorian age. Pioneer works like Humphry House's *The Dickens World* (1941) and Kathleen Tillotson's *The Novels of the 1840s* (1954) have eased my task, as well as historical studies by W. L. Burns, Asa Briggs, G. Kitson Clark and many others. I hope none of my Welsh or Scottish friends will be offended by the word 'English' in the title: as a literary historian, I prefer to use a word that describes a language rather than the name of a nation; and the book is subtitled 'studies' to suggest that the chapters, though related, are not continuous. Some of the findings concerning the relation between the study of a society and the study of its fiction I have already made available, in a more theoretical sense, in the chapter on sociology in *The Study of Literature* (1969). The present book, which is historically more specific than that, and more fully documented, attaches some of these principles to a single nation in a single age. My hope is that the theory and practice of parliamentary government, that most profound of all constitutional ideas, may be better respected and more intimately understood. Victorian England offers the supreme example of a civilization where the political and the literary are richly linked; and it is the nature of those links that is my theme.

Some of the debts I have contracted on my way will be seen in the range of quotation, especially to those recent editions that are now transforming the study of the Victorian age. These include, most notably, the *Complete Prose Works of Matthew Arnold*, edited by R. H. Super (Ann Arbor, 1960–77); the *Collected Works of John Stuart Mill*, edited by John M. Robson, F. E. Mineka and others (Toronto, 1963–); Gordon S. Haight's edition of *The George Eliot Letters*, 7 vols (New Haven, 1954–56); the Pilgrim edition of Dickens's letters, edited by Madeline House and Graham Storey, which began to appear in 1964; Bagehot's *Collected Works*, edited by Norman St John-Stevas since 1965; Gladstone's *Diaries*, edited by M. R. D. Foot (Oxford, 1968–); Walter E. Houghton's *Wellesley Index to Victorian Periodicals 1824–1900* (Toronto, 1966-89), with its abundant identifications of many anonymous articles; and Maurice F. Bond, *Guide to the Records of Parliament* (London, HMSO, 1971). My debt to the *New* (later *Oxford*) *English Dictionary*, for which editing began in 1879, is almost too obvious to record: but it is, after all, a Victorian book, and without it I could not even have considered such an undertaking as this.

Beyond the reach of books, I have been helped by librarians, institutions and friends. Some of these studies began as lectures for undergraduates in the University of Cambridge, and it was their active interest that prompted me to read more, and to question more of what I read. Edwin Muir, in his *Autobiography*, tells how when he taught Mill's idea of liberty to Prague students after 1948, some looked agitated, while many 'seemed to be fearfully enjoying a forbidden pleasure', as if 'coming to life again' (p. 272). I am above all grateful not to have known all of that experience. Others have helped too. David Holland, Librarian of the House of Commons, guided me to manuscripts in that collection, and Maurice F. Bond to those in the Record Office of the House of Lords. And John Gross and Henry Pelling were generous enough to read and criticize an early draft of the book.

G.W.

St John's College, Cambridge

Numerals in the text following a quotation refer to chapters; in footnotes to volume and page.

Though for no other cause, yet for this: that posterity may know we have not loosely through silence permitted things to pass away as in a dream...

HOOKER

1

Introduction

The English idea of government, which I shall here call the English ideology, is the idea of liberty expressed through parliamentary institutions. It has long attracted attention and emulation; but the study of its time of flowering, in the reign of Victoria, has also attracted some misunderstandings that need to be dispelled. Three such misunderstandings are pre-eminent, and will be dealt with here in due turn: that the Victorians believed democracy to be the best form of government; that they believed in economic *laissez-faire*; and that they conceived individual man to exist independently of his social and economic conditions.

The study of the salient political doctrines of a complex institution like the British Parliament in the reign of Victoria cannot be simple, and I shall attempt it in stages, assembling ideas in groups and dealing with the larger literary forms such as the political novel, oratory and the social critics or 'sages' in separate chapters. I make no attempt to chronicle the institution of Parliament itself, a task that still remains unattempted. Historians have always found it understandably difficult to isolate events at Westminster from the history of the nation and the lives of members of its two Houses. The Victorians themselves were conscious of that omission. Macaulay observed in his *History of England* that 'no writer has yet attempted to trace the progress of this institution, an institution indispensable to the harmonious working of our other institutions'.[1] A few

1. Thomas Babington Macaulay, *The History of England* (London, 1849–61) iv. 437. Sir Lewis Namier, John Brooke and others, *The History of Parliament* (London, HMSO, 1964) a work now in progress and so far confined to the eighteenth century, will eventually provide a biographical dictionary of members.

years before, Erskine May had done something hardly less difficult than that, but far more practical. He had produced the first edition of a famous handbook, *A Treatise on the Law, Privileges, Proceedings and Usage of Parliament*, which under successive revisions has remained the standard guide to matters of procedure; and a few years after Macaulay's death Alpheus Todd, librarian of the Legislative Assembly of Canada in Ottawa, issued *On Parliamentary Government in England* (1867–69)[1] to supply a guide to the new parliamentary organs of a united Canada. These were practical aids. By contrast, Stubbs's *Constitutional History of England* (1874–78), though it offered itself as a History of Institutions, amounts in effect to a far-reaching social and economic history of England from Roman times. Parliament still lacks a history of itself, and this study does not attempt to fill that gap, even within a single century. It is a work of intellectual history; it describes the idea of Parliament in the vital decades between the first Reform Act of 1832 and the end of the century, a period when an ancient institution skilfully absorbed the strains of democracy and of advancing industrial revolution; and its sources are in the widest sense of the word literary.

A literary historian, in the nature of things, is bound to see such questions in a more extended sense than a political or social historian, and the uniqueness that might most safely be claimed for the present inquiry lies in the continuous significance it attaches to literary evidence, especially the novel, in expounding what is of lasting interest in Victorian political ideas. The general status of fiction as historical evidence may still need to be defended, though there can be no point in defending it absolutely. That it is unreliable evidence, regarded as a whole, I take to be beyond question: but then so are all other considerable bodies of evidence unreliable – whether parish records, newspaper reports, government statistics or eyewitness accounts. The plain truth is that there is no large category of historical evidence which is totally trustworthy; if novelists are capable of

1. This was reissued posthumously in 1887–89, expanded and revised. For an admiring American view of the system, barely post-Victorian, see Abbott Lawrence Lowell, *The Government of England* (New York, 1908); and for a recent anthology of constitutional texts, *The Nineteenth-Century Constitution 1815–1914*, edited by H. J. Hanham (Cambridge, 1969).

bias, omission, honest misunderstanding and plain lies, none of which I doubt, then so is everybody else; and to grant that is only to grant that the information they provide is, in that respect, like all other kinds of historical evidence. That it needs to be used with delicacy, tact and a reasoned scepticism is equally to say something that could be said of other kinds of historical evidence. But to suppose that because it is fictional it is likely to be less accurate than the essay, the political treatise or works of cultural analysis is at once to overrate the reliability of the essayist and analyst and to misunderstand the serious descriptive purpose to which much Victorian social fiction was dedicated.

The Victorians themselves were clear that novels described both the facts and the aspirations of the world they lived in: so much so, indeed, that they sometimes exaggerated the documentary interest of their fiction at the expense of the artistic. 'Truth in art is so startling', George Eliot once complained to her publisher, 'that no one can believe in it as art.' Her own delicately balanced view that a novel is a work of art, however representational, and that it should never be allowed to lapse 'from the picture to the diagram' or degenerate into the purely didactic, was at times too subtle for some of her contemporaries.[1] They read novels, as the English read them to this day, to learn more about the world they lived in – where it had come from and where it was moving. Novels were social knowledge. When Carlyle suggested to Meredith that he should write history, Meredith replied that his novels were already just that.[2] Maria Edgeworth, writing to Mrs Gaskell after guessing her to be the author of *Mary Barton* in 1848, saw that novel as a contribution to the growing science of political economy, and notably to the problems of overproduction and overpopulation, 'both conjoined and acting as cause and effect'[3] –

1. *The George Eliot Letters*, edited by Gordon S. Haight (New Haven, 1954–56) iii. 185, iv. 300.

2. J. A. Hammerton, *George Meredith in Anecdote and Criticism* (London, 1909) p. 108.

3. R. D. Waller, 'Letters addressed to Mrs Gaskell by celebrated contemporaries', *Bulletin of John Rylands Library*, xix (1935). Extracts from Maria Edgeworth's exchange of letters with Ricardo in 1822–23 were first published in the *Economic Journal* xvii (1907); they have since appeared in full in David Ricardo, *Works and Correspondence*, edited by Piero Sraffa (Cambridge, 1952) vol. ix.

a flatteringly serious view of fiction from an old lady who more than twenty years before had corresponded at length, and on something like equal terms, with David Ricardo on the problems of food supply in Ireland and the economic function of the potato.

The Victorians did not merely expect novels to be accurate: they demanded that they should be so. This argues powerfully in favour of the general accuracy of their novels as social evidence, though many details may still be questioned: in a tradition in which the terms of operation are as widely understood as in English social fiction, a novelist cannot easily commit inaccuracy without a loss of credit and a loss of sales. Reviewers and readers insisted on the truth, nothing less and nothing other. George Eliot's first letter from a stranger about her first work of fiction, *Scenes of Clerical Life* (1858), admonished her in characteristic vein to maintain her fidelity to reality: 'You are natural and truthful now – will you always keep it so?'[1] She could hardly have afforded not to keep it so, even if she had wished. The limits of the activity and its procedures were widely known, and a novelist who tried to draw a prudent veil of fantasy or romance over the reality he described might still reveal more than he intended. Macaulay's biographer, with no exceptional knowledge of Dickens's career, perceived that, 'for those who could see between the lines' in *David Copperfield*, what emerged was no invention but 'the most delightful of autobiographies'; and that the novels of Thackeray could no less be seen as a picture of his life and times.[2] This is how such novels were read: they were seen, by their earliest readers, as direct sources of social knowledge.

The great ancestor in accuracy in that sense of the word was Scott, and he was an exacting model. 'The best writer of history we have', Ruskin called him in a lecture as late as 1884, more than half a century after his death: greater than any Victorian historian, he added, since he had shown in the Waverley novels how a historian can 'see all round a thing'. That view of historical fiction is no longer common. But it is not absurd to see

1. *The George Eliot Letters* (1954–56) iii. 154.

2. George Otto Trevelyan, *The Life and Letters of Lord Macaulay* (London, 1876) i. 2.

the novel, on occasion, as more informative than a factual account. It can be based on firsthand experience, and often is; whereas few works exceed in misrepresentation the writings of the heavily committed historian or of the social analyst with an axe to grind. And it can be based on scholarly research, as surely as any work of scholarship can be based on research. The difference between 'fact' and 'fiction' is not the same as that between truth and falsehood. Engels's study of Manchester poverty in the 1840s, *The Condition of the Working Class in England*,[1] once thought of as a serious contribution to social observation, has recently been shown to be spurious in its claim to direct knowledge and less than trustworthy in its details. This has not yet been shown of an exactly contemporary novel on a similar theme, *Mary Barton*. That novelists could be wrong as well as right is not, of course, in question; what matters is that when they were wrong they could be caught out. Their inquiry was objective in its nature, irrespective of whether their findings were true or false.

The social fiction of the nineteenth century begins in the past, with Scott, moves into that fascinating period of middle ground between past and present in Dickens's early novels of the 1830s – that recent era which the old and the middle-aged can recall, and which the young know because their parents and grandparents have told them of it – and achieves high contemporaneity by the 1850s and 1860s. Trollope is the master of the final phase, of the fiction of the here-and-now. His first successful novel, *The Warden*, appeared in 1855 when he was forty, and with a record of false starts in historical and regional fiction behind him. By that time practical men were already using novelists as indicators not just of large periods but of the brief span of a decade or less: reliability could shift as social reality shifted. An historian of the later century, James Bryce, noticed that Dickens's grasp of lower middle-class London life remained rooted in the 1830s, when he had been a reporter, and that the twentieth century would have to read Trollope to learn the

1. Edited by W. O. Henderson and W. H. Challoner (Oxford, 1958). In their introduction the editors expose Engels's dependence on unacknowledged sources, concluding that he 'can hardly be taken seriously as a historian' (p. xv) or, in the light of ensuing events, as a political prophet.

flavour of the years after 1850; what is more, life had changed again since then.[1]

But the modes coexisted. Mid and late Victorian fiction, though nowhere stronger than in contemporary analysis – in what Trollope called 'the way we live now' – never totally abandoned the historical, and it remained especially powerful in that middle ground between past and present with *Adam Bede*, *Silas Marner*, *Great Expectations* and *Tess*. The historical novel itself did not die, but it languished after the turn of the mid century under the competition of more immediate interests. Thackeray triumphed over these difficulties in *Henry Esmond* (1852) in a startling *tour de force*, achieving an Augustan style of language as well as of life; he demanded in his first chapter that history must now 'rise up off her knees and take a natural posture', one 'familiar rather than heroic', as if even the historical sense were now influenced by the demand for accurate social detail. That was the climax: a dozen years later George Eliot had to swallow defeat, both artistic and commercial, in *Romola* (1863); Blackwood had hoped that in that novel she would 'return historical romance to its ancient popularity',[2] but his hopes, and hers, were dashed. The trouble was not just that she had failed to capture the Florence of Savonarola. Her age, by then, had reached a point where it was too obsessed with its own century to find it easy to look steadily at another. 'Whatever you do,' remarks a publisher to an aspiring authoress in Trollope's *The Way We Live Now* (1875), 'don't be historical. Your historical novel, Lady Carbury, isn't worth a straw' (ch. 89). The word 'straw', adds Trollope, was pronounced after some hesitation. If he had not been addressing a lady, he would have used something stronger.

The social novel from the 1830s was a novel of reform; it rejected, by and large, both conservatism and revolution. As a mirror of the times it could hardly do otherwise. Scott had died in September 1832, three months after Bentham: the Reform Act he had hated and opposed was already law; and his successors noted with satisfaction the paradox of a conservative fathering so much that was analytical to the point of radicalism.

1. James Bryce, *Studies in Contemporary Biography* (London, 1903) pp. 123, 125.
2. *The George Eliot Letters* (1954–56) iii. 340.

Though 'a Tory of the purest water', as T. H. Green wrote half a century later, Scott had been 'a reformer against his will'.[1] To analyse is to perceive how things might be better; equally, it is to respect the state enough neither to wish it away entirely, nor to wish it entirely some other thing. Analysis tends towards reform: to that middle way between blind acceptance and the horrors of upheaval. This is largely true of all social analysis in that age, and not merely in fiction. But the novel was quickest and subtlest in its task. It was known to hear the note of distress earlier, on occasion, than other forms of discourse. 'The novelist catches the cry of suffering before it has obtained its strength or general recognition', as Green goes on. Newspapers only take up causes already familiar. 'The miseries of the marriage-market had been told by Thackeray, with almost wearisome iteration, many years before they found utterance in the columns of *The Times*.' Fiction is even faster than reporting. And the novel can inform, and with accuracy, not only about your own street and region, but about the street at the other end of town and a region at the far end of the kingdom. Englishmen learn of the totality to which they belong by watching the novelist 'merging distinctions of privilege and position into one social organism'. This remark of Green's is an apt comment on novels like *Felix Holt* and *Bleak House*; less apt as a comment on early Dickens or even early George Eliot, where distinctions of rank are not merged but presented in startling clarity. Status and distinction never lapse: no society could survive if they did. But the novelist shows that they matter less than might be supposed, that they are far from rigid, and that the common properties of human kind outweigh differences of birth and wealth. A good novel, as Green puts it memorably, 'does something to check what may be called the despotism of situations', and prevents 'ossification into prejudice'. Even if the world chooses to remain as it is, at least it perceives that it might be otherwise.

The fine balance of the social and the fictional in the Victorian novel is precarious and transitory. Its heyday follows the death of Scott and the emergence, four years later, of the precocious genius of Dickens in *Pickwick*. Its gentle decline, in the 1870s

1. T. H. Green, 'An estimate of the value and influence of works of fiction in modern times', in his *Works* (London, 1888) iii. 43.

and 1880s, follows the pursuit by new novelists after Dickens's death in 1870 of ever finer analysis and an ever more inward vision. Politics, which calls for a large view of human realities, is among the first victims of the new psychological realism. A telescope turns into a microscope. Henry James, like Jane Austen, was to confine his vision with rare exceptions to a single social rank. Hardy, who had tried to launch a literary career in 1868 with a revolutionary novel, *The Poor Man and the Lady*, a work rejected by Meredith as a publisher's reader and now lost, came later to believe that inner events are the more authentic sources of narration – 'not physical but psychical'. It is not adventure that the new novel handles, but rather 'the effect upon the faculties';[1] and a note written a few days later shows he had ceased to call himself either a Tory or a Radical. Henry James, from his earliest fiction in the 1870s to the last, could hardly view political ideas seriously, in any human context. They were too large to be real. Acton's ideas, he once told a friend, were mere verbal juggling: 'How unreal, how remote it all is from the realities of practical life!' And Parliament, so far as he could see, was an 'immense waste of talk and energy and solemnity'.[2] A precarious marriage between fiction and politics had already lapsed.

The mid century in literature, by contrast, is supremely a political age, and its coincidence of literary skill with high ideological ferment in the cause of a principal party of state is the subject of this book. Politics itself was a more strenuously intellectual endeavour than in previous ages. Mill, with an intellectual's exaggeration, called it 'thought in action'. That may never have been quite true, but it is not a naïve view. Those who pride themselves on the pragmatic notion that, in the real world of political action, men move only under the compulsion of events and reform only what they find intolerable should be invited to answer two questions: what initiates the events that compel change, unless men themselves; and what unless a shift in the world of ideas renders an existing situation intoler-

1. Florence E. Hardy, *The Life of Thomas Hardy* (London, 1962) p. 204, from a note written by Hardy in January 1888.

2. Leon Edel, 'Henry James and Sir Sydney Waterlow: the unpublished diary of a British diplomat', *The Times Literary Supplement* (8 August 1968).

able? It is what men think that counts. Foreign conquest apart, as Mill argued, 'all political revolutions . . . originate in moral revolutions'.[1] Thought is the primal force: events can only follow behind. The Victorian political mind, and especially in mid century, denied the cogency both of mere pragmatism and of lofty abstractions about historical inevitability. Both positions were familiar to intellectuals of the age, both were rejected. The note that is struck again and again is that of rational debate in open forum. Parliament is the summit, but many a house and many a club is a lesser debating ground. Even Bagehot, a cautious observer, emphasizes in the 1850s the 'total revolution of political thought' that had occurred in the forty years since Waterloo: an intellectual revolution that stood for minds open to ideas of reform. Where reform had once been resisted as a road to revolution, he argued, during and after the Napoleonic wars, it had since been accepted in differing measure by both parties of state since Peel's ministry of 1841–46.[2] The most favourable of all situations for a political literature had been achieved. Men knew they had the right to speak and publish freely; they also knew that what they wrote might be acted upon, and perhaps swiftly. If there were delays, as there often were, they were not inevitable: men can now ask for what they want, and Parliament can give it.

The impulse of the present study, then, lies in its assumption of a close and continuous relation between literature and events in the Victorian age, and I have used fiction as readily as other sources, and more readily than some, in pursuit of intellectual and political history. For my title, *The English Ideology*, I have adapted that of a well known treatise on the German ideology by Marx and Engels. However apt or inapt it may be thought, I find it hard to doubt that the parliamentary idea is at least as certainly English as socialism is German. Whether ideology itself is English must now be considered.

1. John Stuart Mill, review of Alison's *History of Europe*, *Monthly Repository* (August 1833).

2. Walter Bagehot, 'The character of Sir Robert Peel', *National Review* (July 1856); reprinted in his *Collected Works*, edited by Norman St John-Stevas (London, 1968) iii. 246.

[2]

Ideology and the Victorians

The British enjoy a universal reputation for pragmatism, and yet twice in modern times they have won for themselves another kind of fame: once in the seventeenth century, when they committed regicide and tried to justify it to the world on abstract political grounds; and again in the nineteenth, when they achieved a second ideological renown as the chief exponents of liberty with order in the exacting and unrehearsed circumstances of the first industrial revolution. Liberty is the English ideology, and its achievement within parliamentary institutions dignified by traditional and ceremonial forms – sometimes called 'the Westminster model' – is still the first image that springs to mind when most men hear the name of England. In this chapter I shall consider the nature of that commitment.

'Ideology' was, and perhaps still is, a tainted word. In the early and mid nineteenth century it was widely supposed to be a contemptuous coinage of Napoleon to characterize the light-headed revolutionaries he had replaced; and it never fully acclimatized itself into English as a favourable term. Even Mill, the principal liberal ideologue of the age, uses it ironically to signify something airily metaphysical or merely word-spinning.[1] But it is hard to see what other term could better be used here. Political theory may be purely descriptive, and often is. But the Victorian liberals were not just describing a society or diagnosing its ills. They proposed an ideal. Anyone who misses this characteristic tang of idealism, this zeal for righteousness, or who persuades himself that men like Mill, Gladstone and Acton were seeking mere idealistic pretexts for proposing and legislating as they did, has radically misconceived the temper of the

1. John Stuart Mill, *A System of Logic* (London, 1843) iv. 1.4.

time. That age has good reason to be called an ideological age – as good reason, say, as the Russia of Lenin and Stalin. Acton called it Government by Idea. It is a rare enough phenomenon anywhere in human history, but it is not totally foreign to the English temperament or the English mind.

The new ideologues of the 1830s approached their task, which must have borne a supremely difficult aspect, with a lively sense of the resistance they were likely to meet. Political theory was one matter, and one in which the British could boast a continuous tradition since Hobbes and Locke. Ideology is something else. Theory, in its traditional aspects, is rooted in observation and experience: it is the intellectual fruit of practical politics, and arises out of events. Ideology, by contrast, is rooted in morality; it arises out of a conviction of what is right, and demands by right to shape events according to the contours of a moral law. The American and French revolutions, with their open insistence that the rights of man take precedence over any existing state or government, are classic examples of ideology in action. So, though in a less cataclysmic sense, was the reshaping of the British political scene after 1830. To suppose that because it was not revolutionary it must be other than ideological is to miss a cardinal fact about the doctrine itself. It preferred reform to revolution in parliamentary states such as England, and on reasoned grounds that survive to be studied and meditated. Its distaste for revolution is part of the ideology itself.

The English liberals were fully aware that they were claiming power in a nation unused to taking abstraction seriously in the political field. Even radical ideas in the preceding generation sometimes gave them little reason to expect otherwise. Cobbett's contempt for abstraction was notorious. Bentham, in a withering clause-by-clause demolition of that 'great error' born of mob enthusiasm, the French revolutionary Declaration of the Rights of Man, had applauded the dislike of British parliaments for abstract speculations and declarative utterances.[1] His argument underlines the ultimate unfitness of Benthamism to serve

1. Jeremy Bentham, *Sophismes anarchiques*, published in French in *Tactique des assemblées législatives* (Paris and Geneva, 1816) ii. 271f.

as the main ancestor of Victorian liberalism: like much of what he wrote, it lacks in its bleak logic the essential tone of moral concern, of reaching for a truth in the human condition beyond the merely observable and classifiable – the sheer righteousness of the Victorian mind. The French Rights of Man may have been imperfectly formulated and inadequately grounded in institutions, but generosity of impulse, even in failure, is not to be so lightly set aside. The shift towards sympathy for the highly speculative is perfectly seen in John Stuart Mill, the son of Bentham's chief disciple. Temperament, and the feeling of the age, combined to loose him from the grip of a Utilitarian upbringing and make him the chief analytical conscience of the new faith.

But far deeper than the limitations of inherited radicalism lay, or was thought to lie, the traditional pragmatism of the Anglo-Saxon. That was why the task, when measured by the new ideologues, was felt to be awful. The English, wrote Mill ruefully to a French confidant, 'habitually distrust the most obvious truths if the person who advances them is suspected of having any general views';[1] and Tocqueville, in a tart note on the Whigs, noticed that by and large 'the English seem to me to have great difficulty in getting hold of general and undefined ideas', not least the Whigs themselves, who perhaps needed their illusions as much as anyone. He reports that Mill had made a similar charge, but in a more hopeful vein, in a conversation of 1835. The inevitable growth of the powers and functions of government, Mill then believed, or centralization, would drive Englishmen into a wider tolerance of pure intelligence in politics, in spite of ancient and parochial suspicions.

> Our habits or the nature of our temperaments do not in the least draw us towards general ideas; but centralization is based on general ideas; that is, the desire for power to attend, in a uniform and general way, to the present and future needs of society. We have never considered government from such a lofty point of view. So we have divided administrative functions up infinitely and have made them

1. J. S. Mill, *The Earlier Letters 1812–48*, edited by F. E. Mineka (Toronto, 1963) i. 48, from a letter of 9 February 1830 to Gustave d'Eichthal.

independent of one another. We have not done this deliberately, but from our sheer inability to comprehend general ideas on the subject of government or anything else.[1]

On balance, this is a hopeful and affirmative view. There is an historical tendency, so Mill cheerfully felt as he approached his thirtieth birthday, which could easily prove too strong for the celebrated stolidity of his countrymen. The break-up of local aristocratic administration and the decline of squirearchy might easily create a new sort of political curiosity. But complaints of stolidity still go on. Arnold and Ruskin utter them often. As late as 1876 Bagehot is bemoaning the intellectual inertia of the English in the realm of ideas, 'their want of intellectual and guiding principle, their even completer want of the culture which would give that principle, their absorption in the present difficulty'.[2] But then complaint is part of the journalist's task. In a more generous mood Bagehot might have agreed that the intellectual progress he demanded was already well advanced.

Broadly speaking, there are three kinds of political intellectuals in the age. First, there are ideologues or doctrinaires like Mill and Acton, whose passion is for general principle and whose interest in the minute functioning of the electoral and party system is slight. Second, there are the close observers like Dickens, Thackeray, Bagehot and Trollope, who may momentarily enter the political scene to fight a cause or contest a parliamentary seat, but who are largely content to stand in the wings and report on it. And thirdly, there are the men of power, like Gladstone and Disraeli who, though themselves authors, seek and achieve high office through a professional knowledge of the parliamentary system. This classification is over-simple. Oddly enough, both Acton and Mill sat briefly in the House of Commons, whereas Thackeray, Bagehot and Trollope, for all their close observing of the scene, all stood without success as parliamentary candidates. Their powers of

1. Alexis de Tocqueville, *Journeys to England and Ireland*, edited by J. P. Mayer (New York, 1968) pp. 66–7.

2. Walter Bagehot, 'Lord Althorp and the Reform Act of 1832', *Fortnightly Review* (November 1876); reprinted in his *Collected Works* (1968) iii. 202.

observation may not have been as remarkable as they hoped, or they may have lacked staying power in the race for office. But Mill and Acton are pure ideologues, none the less, and of their election to Parliament it can best be said that it was more surprising that they should attain membership of the Commons than that they should lose it.

The visible achievements of the English ideology by the end of Gladstone's first ministry of 1868–74 were large: larger, it may safely be guessed, than many men who had embarked on the legislative uncertainties of the 1830s can have expected. Victorians are more inclined to exclaim at the speed of change than to bewail a lack of progress. They had widened the suffrage in 1832, freed the slaves and passed the first effective Factory Act in the following year (though neither of these were party measures), and in 1834 they had adopted the new Poor Law. By 1835 many Englishmen besides Mill must have felt that the ground was rocking beneath the feet. A concern for the merely practical, for what Tocqueville called 'the facts of today', could not alone explain what was happening or what now seemed likely to happen. The new speculative urge, which was not solely liberal, was fed from many streams. A revived Hellenism, in Newman and Arnold, was soon to entice the intellectual mind with the prospect of a loftier notion of educated leisure, of knowledge acquired and enjoyed for its own sake, 'considered irrespectively of its results', as Newman told a Dublin audience in 1852. 'This is how it comes to be an end in itself; this is why it is called Liberal. Not to know the relative disposition of things is the state of slaves or children; to have mapped out the Universe is the boast of Philosophy.'[1] This was spoken by an extreme enemy of liberalism, both in Church and state; but it sums up a craving of the age wider than any denomination or political allegiance. As prosperity grows, knowledge and understanding become ends in themselves. Even Dickens, whose own mind was less than highly speculative and whose readership was far wider than the intellectual, finds Gradgrind a boor and Podsnap a joke.

1. John Henry Newman, *Discourses on University Education* (Dublin, 1852) no. 6; reprinted in *Newman: Prose and Poetry*, edited by Geoffrey Tillotson (London, 1957) p. 465.

The death of Palmerston as an octogenarian premier in 1865 was felt by many to mark the end of an era. Things must change; the old school of British statesmen were finished at last, or so it seemed. They had been shrewd and skilful, and they had served the nation well according to their aristocratic lights. But those lights had dimmed. Now the nation expected something different: personalities more public, and more oratorical, to satisfy the mood of an expanding electorate in search of leadership and faith; and minds at once more speculative and more zealous than those of the knowing old Whigs who had presided with mixed motives over the reforms of the 1830s and after and the muddles of the Crimean War. The new temper of politics which Gladstone and Disraeli at once exemplified and exploited, when they took the helm in the late 1860s as party leaders, was both more public than the old, and more principled. 'The politics of the salon', as someone wrote on the death of Palmerston, must now give place to 'the politics of a creed' – to 'narrower doctrine, more scrupulous conscience, more anxious temperament'.[1]

That demand was met, and the intensity of the response is most clearly marked in the half century between the first Reform Act of 1832 and Gladstone's second ministry of 1880–85. By then some sense of fatigue is to be felt and seen. The Irish Home Rule crisis of 1885–86 shook the liberal hegemony of the intelligentsia and helped the Conservatives to escape the charge of tardy imitation. Mill, in his *Autobiography*, had called them 'the stupid party'; but they were soon to find some intelligent support. Henry Sidgwick, hitherto a Liberal, reports a shift at Cambridge from a Liberal to a Tory preponderance at the High Table of Trinity in 1886.[2] The pendulum did not cease to swing, but the first era of liberal intellectualism was closing. By then, and notably in the name and personality of Gladstone, it had made itself the symbol of a movement that was seen to be worldwide.

The doctrine that held such sway in England had grown to

1. *Pall Mall Gazette* (19 October 1865), an anonymous article perhaps by James Fitzjames Stephen.

2. A. and E. M. Sidgwick, *Henry Sidgwick* (London, 1906) p. 450; see John Roach, 'Liberalism and the Victorian intelligentsia', *Cambridge Historical Journal* xiii (1957).

political maturity between two extremes, both of them archaic by the last years of Palmerston's office. On the one hand, there was the world of the old Whigs which Palmerston had prolonged, by a miracle of longevity, to far beyond its natural span; and Whiggism, though possessed of its own historical myth in the Glorious Revolution of 1689 and splendidly served by Macaulay as its public advocate and spokesman, was a technique of government rather than a doctrine. 'The Whig governed by compromise,' as Acton put it, 'the Liberal begins the reign of ideas.'[1] The other extreme is remoter and harder to characterize. There is a residual memory in the Victorian liberal mind of distant Godwinian speculations, immortalized in the poems of Shelley and belonging to that far fringe of libertarian doctrine where it shades into anarchism. Such survivals as these might smack too much of the age of George III to provide a doctrine. Still less could they provide a platform. But Byron could still be quoted by Victorians, and often was, on the rights of small nations, Paine and Bentham were viewed inquiringly from a distance, and Shelley was felt to touch a deep chord of nature. Victorian liberalism is not the creation of a single generation, and its assurance would have been less firm if it had felt itself without an ancestry. Bertrand Russell's mother, Lady Amberley, tells in her journal how once in his last years Mill had read to them from Shelley's 'Ode to Liberty' one evening after dinner, till 'he got quite excited and moved over it, rocking backwards and forwards and nearly choking with emotion', and murmuring 'It is almost too much for one'.[2]

Between these polar extremes the Victorian reforming mind moved, and it continued to feel the demands of both. That 'union of theory and policy' which, in Acton's view, characterized the genius of Gladstone, embodied the exacting ambition of the age. Other lands and other ages had achieved one or the other: the English ideology of government attempted both. Gladstone alone, in his disciple's view, could combine guile with vision, demonstrating 'all the resource and policy of the heroes of the Carlyle's worship' while yet moving 'scrupulously along the

1. Acton, Additional MS 4,949 in the University Library, Cambridge.

2. *The Amberley Papers*, edited by Bertrand and Patricia Russell (London, 1937) ii. 375.

lines of the science of statesmanship'. Burke, in Acton's view the finest political genius of England before the nineteenth century, had lacked ideological consistency, and 'loved to evade the arbitration of principle'.[1] This is from a letter of 1880, and it rings confidently in the new atmosphere of Gladstone's second ministry and the moral fervour evoked by his Midlothian campaign a year before. Gladstone's own estimate of his political consistency was not much different. 'In theory at least,' he had written years before, in his *A Chapter of Autobiography* (1868), 'and for others, I am myself a purist with respect to what touches the consistency of statesmen.' But that is a matter for instant qualification: 'Change of opinion . . . is an evil to the country, although a much smaller evil than their persistence in a course which they know to be wrong. It is not always to be blamed. But it is always to be watched with vigilance; always to be challenged, and put upon its trial.' In a fast-moving situation, consistency is plainly not the same as always thinking the same thing. But those who listened to Gladstone, and read his extensive works, were probably right in recognizing a deep underlying faith. 'Whatever may have been the vacillations of Mr Gladstone's political career,' wrote a reviewer of his collected essays, *Gleanings of Past Years 1845–76* (1879), 'there has been but little change in his more inward and higher thoughts. We do not know any other writer of the day who has remained more steadfast through a generation and a half to the same central principles.'[2]

This is the accepted view of political consistency, and it is compatible with changes of policy and even of party allegiance. A more abstract consistency than that might deprive a statesman of some degree of credibility. Acton once apologized to Newman for such an excess, and it haunted his political career. 'I have studied politics very elaborately', he wrote shamefacedly, 'and more as a science than people generally consider it, and therefore I am afraid of writing like a doctrinaire, or of appearing zealous to force a particular and very unpalatable system

1. Acton, *Letters to Mary, Daughter of W. E. Gladstone* (London, 1904) pp. 48–9.

2. 'Mr Gladstone as a man of letters', *Fraser's Magazine* (November 1879), from an anonymous review.

down people's throats.'[1] The inhibition was uncharacteristic, and it did not last: however much the doctrinaire in Acton might fail to engage the attentions of an English audience, it was too powerful an obsession to be concealed. In 1877 he lectured to his former constituents in Shropshire on the idea of liberty in antiquity and in the Middle Ages; and soon afterwards, according to Bryce, late one night in his library at Cannes, he spoke of that projected History of Liberty which was to remain unfulfilled to the end of his life – a history of Western man with liberty as 'the central thread':

> He spoke for six or seven minutes only; but he spoke like a man inspired, seeming as if, from some mountain summit high in air, he saw beneath him the far-winding path of human progress from dim Cimmerian shores of prehistoric shadows into the fuller yet broken light of the modern time. . . . It was as if the whole landscape of history had been suddenly lit up by a burst of sunlight.[2]

The portrait is touched with fanaticism. And if ideologies are to be broadly divided into two kinds, the hard and the soft – in the sense of those that are rigorous as opposed to those which are easy and lax – then the English ideology was at its most intense a hard ideology. To later ages this fact has been much misunderstood and much underrated, but the Victorians did not underrate it. To friend and enemy alike, liberalism was a political doctrine with a hard edge. Let its enemies speak first. Disraeli, in one of the earliest of his fictions, an attack on the new political economy entitled *The Voyage of Captain Popanilla* (1828), saw the new political faith as the most extreme of doctrinaire absurdities, credulous in its abstraction and hopelessly deductive in its logical processes. 'What he said must be true,' Disraeli observes sarcastically of his hero, 'because it entirely consisted of first principles' (ch. 4); and his footnote is even more withering in its sarcasm: 'First principles are the ingredi-

1. Acton, *Selections from the Correspondence*, edited by J. N. Figgis and R. V. Laurence (London, 1917) i. 33, from a letter of 9 June 1861.

2. James Bryce, *Studies in Contemporary Biography* (London, 1903) pp. 396–7. Mary Gladstone reports a similar outpouring, of 'a whole hour or more', in the Piazzetta at Venice in 1879, with her brother Herbert; Mary Drew, *Acton, Gladstone and Others* (London, 1924) pp. 9–10.

ents of positive truth. They are immutable, as may be seen by comparing the first principles of the eighteenth century with the first principles of the nineteenth.' This accurately represents the substance, though not always the tone, of hostile views of liberalism by English intellectuals beyond its pale. It is a narrow doctrine, as they depict or caricature it: the squinting leading the squinting, Ruskin called it: 'The modern Liberal politico-economist of the Stuart Mill school is essentially of the type of a flat-fish – one eyeless side of him always in the mud, and one eye, on the side that *has* eyes, down in the corner of his mouth.'[1] Arnold's attack on Hebraism in the fourth chapter of *Culture and Anarchy* (1869) is similar in the scope of its accusations, though far blander. Hellenism is flexible and spontaneous; Hebraism, which afflicts the English middle class as the diseased inheritance of Puritanism, is close, restrictive, morally legalistic and strenuously obsessed with sin. This was no soft doctrine. Its enemies thought it all too unbending.

The English ideology is about the liberty of man. Acton summed up the doctrine in its most extreme and memorable form: 'Liberty is not a means to a higher political end. It is itself the highest political end.'[2] The epithet 'political' is of more than perfunctory interest here: the question whether liberty is the highest end of man, absolutely and without qualification, is one that lies outside the range of political debate. Religion, for example, would commonly forbid one to suppose that it could be so; so would aestheticism or hedonism. But within the wide yet finite range of political decision, liberty stands immutable as man's choice and man's dilemma, regardless of place and time. The dilemma lies in the social bonds of man, which require him to cede his own liberty to others while yet insisting that he must remain free. All these are practical difficulties: difficulties of great moment, indeed, but not so great as to alter the fact of choice itself. Man would always wish to be free, independently of whether or not freedom is possible in a given circum-

1. John Ruskin, *Fors Clavigera* letter 10 (October 1871); reprinted in his *Works*: library edition, edited by E. T. Cook and A. Wedderburn (London, 1903–12) xxvii. 180.

2. Acton, *The History of Freedom and Other Essays* (London, 1907) p. 22, from one of his Bridgnorth lectures of 1877, 'The history of freedom in antiquity'.

stance. This is the point from which the political argument begins, and to which it unfailingly returns.

Liberty is a doctrine of thought, of inclination and of opinion. It begins not with the study of how matters stand in society, but with what individual men hope and fear. The doctrine of liberty explains society – why men do what they do, and how they might do otherwise. Society, by contrast, cannot explain the doctrine of liberty; if men could be socially conditioned into servility and acceptance, they would have forgotten the doctrine of liberty long ago, or would never have known it. But this has not happened. They desire it *as men*, however rare its achievement, and never so much as when they are tyrannized. 'The delicate fruit of a mature civilization', Acton called achieved liberty in the opening sentence of his lecture. Seldom known, it is seldom forgotten. This primacy of thought over circumstance and condition guarantees to the English ideology a characteristic highmindedness, a lofty intellectual flavour. A reader has to pinch himself, on occasion, to recall that men like Gladstone were men of affairs and competent, in varying degrees, in the world of action and power. The link with that world is not neglected by the doctrine itself. But it is not its point of departure or its standard of judgement.

History is made by individuals, and that conclusion, though awkward and untidy to the historical theorist of deterministic bent, seems in the end inescapable. Men may toy with general laws of history like Comte's laws of social dynamics or the inevitability of class war, but they are toys that break in the hand. The Norman Conquest, so Mill argued in *A System of Logic* (1843), was 'as much the act of a single man as the writing of a newspaper article' (VI. xi. 4). Thought is the prime factor of change – what Mill called 'the state of speculative faculties' (VI. x); and the mass tendencies of an age, irresistible as they often look, are made and directed, or misdirected, by individual thinkers. Even dogmas of allegedly 'inevitable' historical laws, like the class war, are paradoxically examples of how very far from inevitable the laws of human history are. It was not inevitable that someone should think of them, or propagate them, or that they should be believed. But if they are powerful in the world, they are powerful as ideas, because someone once thought of them and wrote them down, or left them to be written by others. In this regard the very doctrines of determinism bear witness against themselves. They are counter-examples to their own case.

Only an individual can have an idea for the first time. This is a simple reality, not a matter of idealism; but it is a reality that fascinates the liberal mind. The primacy of thought, and its movement from individual to party and masses, is best described late in the period, in A. V. Dicey's Harvard lectures of 1898, *Law & Public Opinion in England during the Nineteenth Century* (1905). Individuals have ideas, he explains in his second lecture; apostles, eventually politicians, may be convinced by them, and the many some day come to accept them. This echoes, in a more analytical form, Mill's conviction that 'the order of human progression in all respects will mainly depend on the order of progression in the intellectual convictions of mankind'. As a young man, Mill was already clear that opinion is made by a few, and that political history considered in this light is a movement from 'the intelligent classes' to government, and from government to 'the stupid classes'.[1] The assertion is offered as an observation of how things happen, not as a prescription, and objections to Mill's 'élitism' are beside the point. Dicey refines the observation. Though not absolutely true, in his view, of all ages and nations, the primacy of thought is a fact of 'the peculiar conditions of an advanced civilization' (p. 4), of which general class Victorian England is an example. High civilization is vulnerable to ideas; and the more civilized the individual, the more vulnerable he is. The power of ideas predominates in the professional class, above all; for the millions who constitute public opinion, it must be admitted, opinion is formed rather than individually conceived. But this does not negate Mill's conclusion that thought controls legislation. Opinion is opinion, and thought is thought, whether original or secondhand. Men are influenced in their convictions by what they hear and read, and that fact is not altered or even modified by noticing the instances (by no means universal) in

1. J. S. Mill, *Earlier Letters 1812–48*, edited by F. E. Mineka (Toronto, 1963) pp. 27–8, from a letter to Gustave d'Eichthal of 11 March 1829, when Mill was twenty-two.

which men merely vote according to their interests. In 1830, as Dicey notes, most country gentlemen were against reform and most manufacturers for it; but the Reform Act of 1832 was still a victory of opinion and of nothing else. To try to shift the responsibility or the credit from opinion to 'interest', as a Benthamite might do, or to 'social conditioning', like a socialist, is only to reveal how imperfectly the nature of opinion itself is understood. Opinion is not a position taken up in a void; it is about something specific; and it includes highly 'interested' questions like 'Shall I be the better off for it?'

The vital area of opinion is the moral, and morality in this ideology is an objective standard which underlies political knowledge and political action. The complexity of events may momentarily obscure this truth; but it is the enduring task of political leadership to remind men that it is so. Acton, in his lecture of 1866 on the American Civil War which had just ended, called it grandly 'the light of that political science which resides in serene regions, remote from the conflicts of party opinion; a science whose principles are clear, definite and certain, and not more difficult to apply than the principles of the moral code'. This, in Acton's view, is not to say that private and public morality are the same thing. 'The principles of public morality', he once wrote to Mandell Creighton, 'are as definite as those of the morality of private life; but they are not identical.'[1] The moral censor does not lower his standards in contemplating the sins of statesmen in the public domain, though he does not confuse their choices and dilemmas with those of a private man. Public morality exists. Even the relations between nations and peoples are not merely a jungle. Treaties bind, conventions of behaviour survive, and beyond all treaties and conventions of behaviour the voices of subject peoples are heard and heeded.

It would only be to indulge a paradox to doubt that so imposing and so formal a political doctrine deserves the name of ideology. By any ordinary use of language, England was ruled by ideologues for much of the reign of Victoria. The characteristic completeness of dedication is there. 'All that I am now,

1. Acton, *Historical Essays & Studies* (London, 1907) pp. 125, 506.

all I hope to be' is the expectation of liberty in Browning's sonnet.[1] The doctrine demanded, and received, the total loyalty of millions. Those millions were led by statesmen, poets, novelists, historians and political theorists who, regarded as a creative leadership, form a political army of unexampled talent: Mill, Dickens, Gladstone, Acton, George Eliot, Browning, Thackeray and Trollope. A comparison with its evident rival in modern history, the Russia that followed the October Revolution of 1917, is plainly inadequate: Marxism, however imposing in its political interest, is by comparison a backward and impoverished doctrine in what it has inspired of enduring literary concern; and Fascism is still more impoverished, in the same terms, though the brevity of its heyday between 1922 and 1945 makes that comparison less safe and less apt.

It is the literary richness of the English ideology that makes it at once so seductive a theme and yet so elusive in its breadth and depth. Such a study is easy to begin and hard to complete. The very closeness of the doctrine to the events it helped to shape forces the intellectual historian to keep social history well in view; but I am primarily concerned here with an idea, and with a nation, a period and a people only as these formed the circumstances in which it became a dominant idea of state. That emphasis is inevitably precarious. No one acquainted with the Victorian political mind could fail to notice that novelists and poets as well as statesmen and theorists are working along a grain of history, and that they know it – that they can see events moving, though not without checks and setbacks, in a direction that is hoped for and desired. Talk meant action. Parliament, as the aged Gladstone remarked, was 'not mere debate, but debate ending in work'. Whoever works in that great arena 'is continually tested by results, and he is enabled to strip away his extravagant anticipations, his fallacious conceptions, to perceive his mistakes, and to reduce his estimates to the reality. No politician has any excuse for being vain'.[2] That puts the notorious optimism of the Victorians in critical perspective, and

1. Robert Browning, 'Why I am a Liberal', in *Why I am a Liberal*, edited by Andrew Reid (London, 1885).

2. W. E. Gladstone, *Autobiographica* (London, 1971) from a manuscript of 9 November 1894.

suggests what the grounds for that optimism were. They saw a future in the making; they were not spinning theories or dreaming dreams. The political refugees who crowded into London marked the contrast sharply enough for those who met them, and many a French, German and Italian ideologue found an English sanctuary where thought was free. Their condition was indeed something other; while the French, as it was often noticed, carve for an emperor three abstractions in stone on their public monuments, the English conceive ideas that might soon be made real. Weeks after Louis Napoleon had seized absolute power in Paris, George Eliot met a French refugee in London, and her comment is characteristically arch: 'He belongs neither to the school of Proudhon which represents Liberty only, nor to that of Louis Blanc which represents Equality only, nor to that of Cabet which represents Fraternity . . . [He] combines all three.'[1]

That sly comment leaves one asking whether the English ideologues were wiser than their fellow Europeans, or merely luckier. Whatever the cause, their fortune was good, and they knew it. They saw slight barriers, or none, between opinion and action. 'What we want to see', Stubbs told his Oxford audience at his inaugural in 1867, 'is men applying to history and politics the same spirit in which wise men act in their discipline of themselves.'[2] A moral imperative might alone suffice, if energetic, in a state so advantageously placed. Political institutions were subject to alteration but not subversion; an ocean and a fleet protected the land from the very thought of invasion; and men could reflect on a two-hundred-year tradition of advanced political inquiry. That tradition was already concerned with freedom, as a human if not as an institutional property. The history of England, as Erskine May boasted in his *Democracy in Europe*, was 'the history of liberty, not of democracy' – of reforms, not of revolutions. Her thinkers fear neither execution, imprisonment nor exile: 'English reformers, however bold and adventurous, never broke with the past: it

1. *The George Eliot Letters* (1954–56) ii. 5, from a letter of 21 January 1852 on the subject of Pierre Leroux.

2. William Stubbs, *An Address Delivered by Way of Inaugural Lecture* (Oxford, 1867) p. 30.

was ever their mission to improve and regenerate, rather than to destroy.'[1]

This defines the peculiarity of the enterprise with great precision. It combines a confidence in tradition with a determination to change, and a certainty that change can happen through rationality and persuasion. That is its oddity. It is always unusual to witness rational argument, at least at length, where politics or religion are at stake. 'Let no one think that it is nothing', as Mill wrote in 1840, in his essay on Coleridge, 'to acccustom people to give a reason for their opinions, be the opinions ever so untenable, the reason ever so insufficient.' The nineteenth century did not think it nothing, and for good reason; and the twentieth may with justice feel itself even more astonished at the spectacle.

1. T. Erskine May, *Democracy in Europe* (London, 1877) ii. 334, 474–5.

3

History and Revolution

Nations are as happy in what they forget as in what they remember, and an age may reveal its deeper instincts by what in the records of the past it chooses to preserve. For the Victorians, like others, history was a storehouse of lessons and examples. They had absorbed the significance of Scott's novels: an age and a nation possesses a spirit of its own, and time and place change not only institutions, manners and costumes, but thought and sentiment as well. The temptation to moral relativism in that view, once seen, had to be resisted. The moral law changes, indeed; but it does not follow that it is not law. Men misunderstand, and only slowly learn to understand, and then have to relearn the lessons of history by their own experience. But learning and understanding the truths of private and public life are still processes which are rightly described as that. The Victorians selected their history, but they did not merely fabricate it. If they came to see it as the history of liberty, of Wordsworth's 'flood of British freedom',

> which to the open sea
> Of the world's praise from dark antiquity
> Hath flowed, 'with pomp of waters, unwithstood',

they also believed that the evidence for that assertion was there in the documents, and could be shown to be there. It was not myth. 'The strong man and the strong nation', wrote one academic historian, 'feel the pulsation of the past in the life of the present: their memory is vital, long and strong', and he compared neglect of the past to a form of moral decrepitude.[1]

1. William Stubbs, *Lectures in Early English History* (London, 1906) p. 1.

What did an educated Victorian see in the past? In some ways the answer to that question is better apprehended from the historical novel than from historiography. The heyday of that novel is far from precisely Victorian: it stretches from Scott's *Waverley* (1814) to Thackeray's *Henry Esmond* (1852); after that astonishing triumph, the artistic possibilities of the form seem to shrink, and readership grows either more sceptical or less sophisticated. But if one adds to the masterpieces of the early nineteenth century some consideration of historical novels of the long decline, like Charles Kingsley's *Westward Ho!* (1855), Charles Reade's *The Cloister and the Hearth* (1861) and a mass of fiction for the young stretching down to the First World War, then a highly formal pattern of historical expectation emerges. History to the Victorians means anything earlier than Napoleon, since fiction set in the French wars, like Charlotte Brontë's *Shirley* (1849), belongs rather to that fascinating borderland of parental reminiscence than to history, being wedged between the world of one's own recollection and knowledge acquired from books. But beyond the French wars, realities all look simpler. The French Revolution and the Terror that followed it are the most recent event of real history. Behind that, there is the eighteenth century, an age of manners and even of mannerism, its refinements contradicted by a strong-stomached tolerance for the violent and the rankly sexual. The Restoration is dissolute; the Civil War pregnant with the Victorian future and groping violently towards a modern tolerance of religious variety and a party system. The Elizabethans are frank and manly, strong against papistry and the devildoms of Spain. Then the picture begins to fade, and the later Middle Ages, though brave with pageantry and tournaments, are viewed with a weaker historical eye. This is the panorama of the past which many a Victorian novel-reader knew and accepted. If he were to try to sharpen that view by reading Macaulay or Froude, he might enrich it in detail, it is true, but he would find little there to contradict or annul what he already knew.

But then the professional historians of the age saw little occasion to reject anything here, though much to refine. History is in any case an interpretative art, as surely as fiction: the historian views what he sees as a man of his age; and what he sees, and how, may aptly influence the political climate of his own time. This was candidly stated. 'There must always', wrote Buckle, 'be a connexion between the way in which men contemplate the past, and the way in which they contemplate the present.'[1] But historical interpretation is necessarily a subtle matter, and political solutions cannot be transferred unthinkingly from one nation or age to another. History, as Mill wrote in 1835, assists rather than creates an understanding of one's own society: 'It corroborates, and often suggests, political truths, but cannot prove them.'[2] It must be used, even though it can so readily be misused. It is a matter of being careful. Bryce, writing in support of the extension of manhood suffrage in 1867, quoted from Mommsen's *Roman History* with approval, but emphasized that the past, in instructing the present, cannot be allowed to operate 'in the vulgar sense', 'as if we could by merely turning over the leaves discover the conjectures of the present in the records of the past; collecting from them the symptoms for a political diagnosis and the specifics for a prescription'.[3]

Roman history cannot do that; neither can any other, since the lessons of history are never simple. What needs to be done is to study 'the organic conditions of civilization'; and this study should lead to no mere 'unreflecting reproduction', but to 'independent reproduction'. This is a view that combines high historical curiosity with an abundance of caution. And behind that caution lay something important: a sense of confidence in England as a unique state in a unique time.

That uniqueness was a matter of observation. The English ideology was neither indifferent to foreign influences nor philistinely insular, as some hostile zealots have complained then and since. But it was certainly buoyed up by a sense of national confidence – a confidence which, it was possible for an intelligent man to believe, was on the whole justified by the

1. Henry Thomas Buckle, *History of Civilization in England* (London, 1857–61) i. 267.

2. J. S. Mill, 'Professor Sedgwick's *Discourse on the Studies of the University of Cambridge*', *London Review* (April 1835).

3. James Bryce, 'The historical aspect of democracy', in *Essays on Reform* (London, 1867) pp. 275–6.

facts. The subject is an uncomfortable one, and is only to be broached with embarrassment. Broadly speaking, English superiority was based on two convictions: first, a matter of character derived from an ancient tradition of liberty with order, Wordsworth's 'flood of British freedom' pouring in from a dark antiquity; and second, a modern superiority in the technical efficiency that naturally accrued to the first industrial nation in human history. Such confidence was sometimes felt to be recent, and it is probably true that among the Victorians it was deeper and genuinely more assured than in the boastful and self-assertive claims that eighteenth-century Englishmen had made over the French. Dickens, who shared it, thought it a fact of his own lifetime: it was in his own boyhood, so he suggests in *Great Expectations* (1860), or in the 1820s, where the action of that novel is set, that the British had settled that they owned and were 'the best of everything' (ch. 20). Macaulay, in his essay on Hampden (1831), cast it all backwards into time, and believed that this superiority existed, and had been seen by Europe to exist, as early as the reign of James I, when parliamentary opposition had first begun to take shape:

> From a very early age, the English had enjoyed a far larger share of liberty than had fallen to the lot of any neighbouring people. How it chanced that a country conquered and enslaved by invaders. . . . should have become the seat of civil liberty, the object of the admiration and envy of surrounding states, is one of the most obscure problems in the philosophy of history. But the fact is certain. Within a century and a half after the Norman Conquest, the Great Charter was conceded,

and he quotes Froissart in support of English superiority in the fourteenth century. Such confidence inevitably showed, and foreigners observed and reported it. Tolstoy, in *War and Peace*, remarked that while the German is confident in his abstractions and the Frenchman in his personal attractions, the Englishman 'is self-assured as being a citizen of the best organized state in the world' (IX. x). Many visitors to England, notably Emerson, speak in similar terms. The claim to superior advancement in government and technology was internationally noticed and widely, if not universally, conceded.

More than that, Victorian England was the testing-ground of history and the land where the future was being made. Disraeli in *Coningsby* had admonished his young hero to visit Manchester: it would teach him more than Athens. Engels had already taken that advice. A tourist in search of the future, in the present century, might visit Los Angeles in a mood of similar curiosity. England offered the world a shape of things to come: disturbing or stimulating, according to predilection, but in any event a fateful spectacle. It was the prime example on earth of a nation progressing towards a notion of human liberty undisturbed by revolutions or foreign conquests. English history demonstrated how events could be self-engendered, 'due to causes springing out of itself', as Mark Pattison put it in his review of Buckle. England was 'the illustrative country'.[1]

The balance of ideas, then, was heavily favourable to the English: they gave more than they received in politics, in social science and above all in economics, and they knew it. But intelligent Victorians were still fond of acknowledging foreign debts and corroborations in the intellectual sphere; and in moments of indignation against themselves they could proclaim, and perhaps even believe in, the superior virtues of other nations. The grass on the far side of the Channel sometimes looked greener. Cobden announced in 1838 that, for the masses, Prussia might well enjoy the best government in Europe.[2] Mill and Matthew Arnold often declared French civilization the superior of the English: more democratic as a culture, better mannered, more 'possible'. Carlyle's enthusiasm for German philosophy and letters, the wide burst of literary applause for the Italian Risorgimento of 1860 in the poems of the Brownings, Swinburne and many others,[3] George Eliot's cultivated attachment to Goethe and Heine, Ruskin's boyhood passion for William Tell and Swiss liberty – these are all myths of significance to English intellectuals as individuals. But they refine and widen self-comprehension rather than render it possible. The colour of some Victorian literature would be different

1. *Westminster Review* (1857); reprinted in his *Essays*, edited by H. Nettleship (Oxford, 1889) ii. 397–9.

2. John Morley, *Life of Richard Cobden* (London, 1881) i. 130–1.

3. See *Songs of Italian Freedom*, edited by G. M. Trevelyan (London, 1911).

without them; its ideological substance, in all probability, much as it is.

The ancient Germanic theory of the origins of the British constitution, which may seem an omission here, is omitted on sufficient grounds. That theory, which finds its way into academic history hardly earlier than the 1870s, concerns local government rather than Westminster. The forests and plains of north Germany and Jutland, out of which the Anglo-Saxons invaded and conquered England in the fifth century, were held to have nourished a character favourable to self-reliance and independence; but as Stubbs, Freeman and John Henry Green understood the matter, the first Englishmen knew little or nothing of national unity or organization, and failed to create stable forms of central government in six hundred years. What praise the Anglo-Saxons find, in a work like Green's *History of the English People* (1877–80), which is dedicated to Freeman and Stubbs, is limited to the hypothesis that some of the rude forms of tribal justice and local representation practised by the Anglo-Saxons may derive from their dark Germanic past; but kingship and the new nobility were to be created only on the soil of England. The political debt to ancient Germany was seen as local, not national; and the remote Germanic origins of the English hardly merits more than an occasional reference in the constitutional debates of the Victorians.

There are many private enthusiasms for other lands and ages. But idiosyncrasy apart, the Victorian view of the past centres upon three great spheres of history: the ancient world of Greece and Rome; the European Renaissance and Enlightenment; and two great revolutions, the English of 1688 and the French of 1789.

GREECE AND ROME

Byron had made Greece a symbol of liberty by writing of it in youth and dying there before middle age; and Elizabeth Barrett Browning, even before his death in 1824, had written as a thirteen-year-old a poem on the Battle of Marathon. Greece was a political symbol for many peoples, but above all for the English. The historiography of ancient Greece, as it is now understood, was a British invention, and attempts before Mitford's *History of Greece* (1784–1818) or Grote's (1845–56) were largely confined to commentaries on the ancient historians. Both historians of Greece were Members of Parliament. But Mitford had been a Conservative, bitterly antidemocratic and eager to see in the collapse of Athens a timely warning against trust in the people. Grote, who had reviewed his predecessor in the *Westminster Review* in 1826, was a radical who annexed the whole history of ancient Greece to its more natural symbolism as the first dawning place of freedom. But this was to lay a weighty judicial interpretation on a mass of knowledge and sentiment that was already there, and there long before Thomas Arnold reformed Rugby in the 1830s, in the classical training common to statesmen at the time.

Such statesmen had met Greece before Grote; they had met it at school and university. As Rome was to the Elizabethans, so was Greece to the Victorians: the analogy works powerfully as an outline, though it underrates the intensity of Victorian hellenism. Rome, for Shakespeare's contemporaries, had been vast, alien, even terrible; Greece, for Gladstone's, was the birthplace of liberty after Marathon and, in Plato and Aristotle, the scene of a refined moral sensibility independent of the Christian religion. Benjamin Jowett's translation of the Platonic dialogues (1871), the first complete version in English, was followed in the 1880s by his Thucydides and the *Politics* of Aristotle; these are the late fruits of a very Victorian blend of public conscience and ethical discrimination. The sources run back early into the century in the nurture of statesmen. Martin Tupper, in his autobiography, describes how as an undergraduate at Christ Church, in the Oxford of about 1830, the Aristotle class he had attended numbered among its pupils Gladstone, the Duke of Newcastle, and three future governors-general: Canning and Dalhousie of India, and Elgin of Canada; along with Abercorn, a future Viceroy; the Duke of Hamilton; and two future heads of Oxford houses, Liddell and Scott, 'even then conspiring for their great Dictionary'; half a dozen professors-to-be; and George Cornewall Lewis, whom Palmerston in 1855 was to prefer to Gladstone as Chancellor of the Exchequer in his first administration. Members of other colleges, including Sidney Herbert of Oriel, the future minister of war and colleague of Florence Nightingale, also appeared in the class. The book they all read together was Aristotle's *Rhetoric*, which each member of the class illustrated with his own quotations.[1] That room by the great staircase at Christ Church must have witnessed one of the most memorable acts of cultural semination in all political history.

Byron and Grote triumphed easily over the conservative Mitford, and Greece remained ineffaceably a liberal symbol. Mill, who in his first review of Grote hailed Marathon as a more important battle in English history than Hastings, noted with satisfaction how often the Athenian Republic was belaboured by the Tory *Quarterly*, though he cautiously perceived an ultimate absurdity in the spectacle of a Radical idealizing any ancient people. 'A Radical who finds his political *beau ideal* still farther back in the past than the Royalist finds his', he remarked in his review of Vigny, 'is not the type of a Radical poet.'[2] That proved to be too sensible a view. Many a radical poet had already done so, and thirty years later a prime minister was to find in what he called the World's Youth an inspiration to power. Gladstone, in the parliamentary recess of 1867–68, composed his fourth study of the Homeric poems as *Juventus mundi* (1869) with an explicit view to elucidating the modern equivalences of Homer. These equivalences are all libertarian:

> the power of opinion and persuasion as opposed to force; the sense of responsibility in governing men; the hatred, not only of tyranny, but of all unlimited power; the love and the habit of public in preference to secret action; the reconciliation and harmony between the spirit of freedom on the one hand, the spirit of order and reverence on the other; and a practical belief in right as relative, and in duty as reciprocal (ch. 11).

The comment is more perspicuous as a political than as a literary judgement, and not all readers of the *Iliad* or the *Odyssey* will find them illuminating. But it was written by a man who, weeks or

1. Martin Tupper, *My Life as an Author* (London, 1886) pp. 55–7.
2. 'Writings of Alfred de Vigny', *London and Westminster Review* (April 1838); reprinted in J. S. Mill, *Dissertations and Discussions* (1859) i. 297.

months later, became the first Liberal prime minister of Britain, and it lingers in the mind as a declaration of faith.

Rome counted for something less. The Horatian ideal of a country retreat is too abiding a notion in England to be seen as especially Victorian; and for a nation with a world mission, the imperial moralizings of Virgil's *Aeneid* counted for surprisingly little. The real influence of Roman history was in the realm of social analysis, but it was only a fitful influence. Mill, as he relates in the *Autobiography* (1873), wrote under his father's encouragement histories of Rome around the age of eleven and twelve, an interest in Roman government pushing out an earlier bent for wars and conquests. Written in total ignorance of Niebuhr, it would have made a whole octavo volume, mainly on 'the struggles of the patricians and plebeians', and it upheld the Roman democratic party; but he later destroyed the manuscript. If his recollection is correct, he was already, a few years after Waterloo, within measurable distance of some of the characteristic concerns of the new German historiography and its emphasis on the social and economic forms that lay behind the texts of Livy and Tacitus. Niebuhr, in the 1826 preface to his *Roman History*, complains shortly afterwards of the 'prostration of the understanding and judgement to the written letter' which had pervaded classical scholarship in the sixteenth and seventeenth century; in fact, he held, the analogy between the ancient plebs and the modern poor is closer than a literal reading of Livy would allow. They were not mere clients, but a modern 'commonalty' like the Irish Catholics: 'The despair of the poor among them is the strongest weapon of their leaders.'[1] The uneasy Victorian foreboding of a class war had been anticipated, years before the new reign, by a precocious boy and a Prussian historian of Rome. By the time it seemed to grow close, however, in the 1840s, no historical parallels, Roman or otherwise, were felt to count for much. The Hungry Forties were an experience all their own.

1. From the English translation of 1828, i. 518. Niebuhr adds that Livy's mistake in supposing the poor to have been mere individual clients of patricians was the more surprising since 'elsewhere he abounds in passages which place the difference between the two classes, nay their opposition, in the clearest light' (p. 521).

RENAISSANCE AND ENLIGHTENMENT

The Revival of Learning, or the Renaissance (as it came to be generally called in England only as late as the 1840s and 1850s) was too fully identified with despotism to figure largely in the political, as opposed to the cultural, mythology of the Victorians. In Ruskin and Pater its attractions are severely aesthetic. When the Renaissance happened, and where, and whether it happened at all, all remained matters for learned debate. John Addington Symonds, as a young Fellow of Magdalen College, Oxford, found it puzzling to identify at all. 'I toil daily for an hour or two at the Renaissance period', he wrote to a friend in 1863, 'but I have not yet come to understand what it is. Each day carries me a step back, and I put the time of reawakening earlier by a century . . . In fact there is no such thing as the Renaissance . . . There is nothing like a clear definite all-including movement.'[1] Ten years later Pater abandoned the historical problem in favour of an aesthetic concept, as he explained in his preface to *The Renaissance* (1873), 'giving it a much wider scope than was intended by those who originally used it to denote that revival of classical antiquity in the fifteenth century'. But there is no discernible political influence there.

The Enlightenment, stretching from Locke and Hume to the French *philosophes*, Gibbon, Rousseau and the younger Burke, was more demanding of attention. Theirs was a movement of mind with numerous, if confusing, implications for political thought. It raises with it the total question of the attitude of the nineteenth century to the eighteenth: an uncomfortable and correspondingly complex attitude, and one that would some day repay a study in greater depth.

That attitude is admittedly cool; but then much of the Victorian response to the Enlightenment is towards its tone rather than its substance. Conservatives, in a general sense of the word, might still regard it as dangerously sceptical and morally corrupting. Elizabeth Barrett, so she once wrote to her future husband, was forbidden by her father to read Gibbon

1. J. A. Symonds, *Letters*, edited by Herbert M. Schueller and Robert L. Peters (Detroit, 1967–69) i. 377, from a letter of 21 January 1863.

or *Tom Jones* for fear, as an unmarried girl, of taking moral harm from them.[1] But sexual morality apart, much of the Augustan world of letters must have remained congenial to backwoodsmen in many a country house far into the Victorian age. Trollope's account of Squire Thorne and his sister in *Barchester Towers* (1857) is offered as representative of a cultural remnant that many readers would recognize, and he views them with a confident and amused indulgence: 'May it be long before their number diminishes.' Miss Thorne, who never opened a modern journal or newspaper, 'spoke of Addison, Swift and Steele as though they were still living, regarded De Foe as the best known novelist of his country, and thought of Fielding as a young but meritorious novice in the fields of romance' (ch. 22).

Such were the remoter rural survivors. For a more modern Victorian taste, at once more romantic and more moral, the Augustan world was inclined to look a picturesque but irrelevant fribble, overcast by what Dickens, in *A Tale of Two Cities*, called bluntly a 'leprosy of unreality', where a French aristocrat needed four footmen to serve his morning chocolate. Thackeray ends his history of *The Four Georges* (1861) with opposing tableaux of the future George IV, the First Gentleman of Europe, in a 'lovely pink coat' at his twenty-first birthday ball in March 1784, and General Washington laying down his triumphant command before Congress in the same month of the same year, and demands rhetorically: 'Which is the noble character for after-ages to admire – yon fribble dancing in lace and spangles, or yon hero who sheathes his sword after a life of spotless honour, a courage indomitable, and a consummate victory?'

Whatever the intellectual interest of the Enlightenment, the age that produced it could not easily be sympathetically handled: the note struck is condescending at the best, at the worst chastising. Carlyle thought the eighteenth century had found its justification only by destroying itself in the French Revolution; by the time of his hero Frederick the Great, it was already 'opulent in accumulated falsities' – so much so that it has no

1. Letter to Robert Browning, 15 January 1846; *Letters of Robert Browning and Elizabeth Barrett Browning 1845–46*, edited by Elvan Kintner (Cambridge, Mass., 1969) i. 392.

real history, and can have none; it 'had no longer the consciousness of being false, so false it had grown'.[1] This has the ring of dismissive impatience, but more patient minds than Carlyle are only slightly less scathing. The young Mill thought the French *philosophes* hardly more helpful to his own radical interests than the Church and dynasty they had opposed; the Bourbon Catholic tyranny raised up 'counter-prejudices', the human mind oscillating ever since between the extremes of belief and disbelief 'before it can settle quietly in the middle'. No wonder, then, if the greatest genius of his time preferred the condition of a naked savage;[2] but Rousseau's age is not ours, as Mill knew, and the extremism of his views rang false to the reformers of an industrial state. Stubbs, in his inaugural at Oxford as Professor of Modern History in 1867, could find nothing better to say of the founder of his chair, George I, than that he was honest and harmless. Even Acton, after a profound study of the documents, saw the eighteenth century as 'poor of character' in its capacity for writing history, neglectful of historical individuals and concerned only with shallow generalizations. It limped forward on intellectual crutches: 'Its incapacity made it make an advance in the science as an invalid may devise ingenious contrivances.'[3]

Why did one century learn so little from the other? The life of the eighteenth century, after all, was more than a dance, its historians better than shallow, and its political theory and practice abundant in lessons. That so many Victorians could see none of this is a warning example of malcomprehension. But two shadows lay between them: romance and reform. The romance of the past left the eighteenth century its prettiness, but it left it little else; and the literature of the dead age failed to satisfy a livelier taste for sentiment and lofty action. Leslie Stephen complained of the 'confined atmosphere' of *Clarissa* and *Tom Jones*; when he read Richardson and Fielding, as he did with admiration, he could not resist the sensation that 'there

1. Thomas Carlyle, *History of Frederick the Great* (1857), Proem.

2. J. S. Mill, 'The right and wrong of state interference with corporation and Church property', *Jurist* (February 1833); reprinted in his *Dissertations and Discussions* (1859) i. 25.

3. Lord Acton, Additional MS 5528,70, University Library, Cambridge; quoted by Herbert Butterfield, *Man on his Past* (Cambridge, 1955) p. 66n.

are regions of thought and feeling which seem to lie altogether beyond their province'.[1] The vacuum is first and last an emotional one. Thackeray managed to fill it ingeniously in *Henry Esmond*, where his age of Queen Anne mixes high sentiment with a mannered elegance; but the novel is a terminus, not a point of growth. Victorians admired it hugely – Trollope, in his study of Thackeray (1879), called it his greatest work: the novel that, beyond all others, illustrates the creative forethought that great fiction requires, 'the elbow-grease of the mind'. But all that was like rubbing an old mahogany table to make it shine, and the effort hurt. Nobody in later Victorian fiction was to try anything just like it.

Reform, after the 1830s, was a practical barrier to understanding, or at least to interest. By then the legislative way forward was clearer and simpler in outline, though taxing in its details. Democracy was seen to be inevitable, like it or not: the question was not how to prevent it, but how to ensure against the worst dangers it might bring. As Whiggism decayed, the interest that Macaulay had felt for Burke and the old oligarchical constitution of England could not be kept up. Gladstone, who was never a Whig, remarked at the end of his life that, in his historical imagination, he was a Pittite down to 1793:[2] the Tories of that century had little to do, in his view, with the Conservatives of his own. The political assumptions of the old century had all drifted into disregard. The last of them, and the closest to Victorian memory, is Benthamism, and Mill in *Utilitarianism* (1863) tried valiantly to patch up the faith of his upbringing and make some of it work. But Bentham is not an active name or reputation in Victorian dialectics: Acton bluntly calls his doctrine an 'error' – an error as elementary as Communism, he argued, or the confusion between lawlessness and freedom.[3] Past deeds like Marathon and Missolonghi may

1. Leslie Stephen, *English Literature and Society in the Eighteenth Century* (London, 1904) p. 168.
2. W. E. Gladstone, *Autobiographica* (London, 1971) p. 30.
3. Lord Acton, *The History of Freedom and Other Essays* (London, 1907) p. 17, from his Bridgnorth lecture of 1877, 'The history of freedom in antiquity'. On Bentham's alleged influence on Victorian administration see Oliver MacDonagh, 'The nineteenth-century revolution in government: a re-appraisal', *Historical Journal* i (1958).

inspire: past dogmas possess at best the antiquarian charm of ancient monuments. Locke, Voltaire, Burke and Bentham: such men had lived and reflected before the world had come to know the new promise and threat of modern industry and popular government. Their answers could only be to other questions, their certainties were forever lost.

REVOLUTION 1689, 1789

The English people, as George Orwell once remarked, have no tradition of revolution. Their rulers, however, have. When William and Mary were offered the throne by Parliament in January 1689, their acceptance was hailed as a revolution by that 'Whig oligarchy' which, as Disraeli was to complain, ruled England in its name down to his own times. This was the first modern revolution to be hailed as such by the men who made it and at the moment they made it. For many ruling spirits of the eighteenth and early nineteenth centuries, England was already a revolutionary state, and the revolution was an event that had already happened. 'The great and glorious revolution was complete', wrote Dickens in *A Child's History of England* (1851–53), ending his story in 1689; and Dickens was no Whig. But he accepted a view of English history which was simply a national one. The best thing that could ever happen had already happened.

A hundred years after the English revolution came the French, and between those extremes of good and evil the Victorian imagination of political change hovered. The American Revolution of 1776 was barely a rival: to call it such at all, in the usual English view, was a trick of the American mind, since a war of independence is a disagreement about sovereignty rather than about power within the state. In historical fiction between *Waverley* and *A Tale of Two Cities*, novels on North America are easily outnumbered by novels on the Reign of Terror in the Paris of the 1790s, and that number could be swelled still further with novels on the royalist revolt in La Vendée and its sanguinary suppression by the revolutionaries[1].

1. See E. A. Baker, *A Guide to Historical Fiction* (London, 1914), especially pp. 276–84.

Official prose in the period confirms the conclusion that the French example counted for more than the American. It was nearer, and it was more dramatic. The struggle of the colonies for independence was viewed without warmth, though sometimes with a degree of distant respect. Macaulay in 1831 ended his essay on Hampden with the reflection that in human history only Washington equalled his subject in self-command, judgement and rectitude. But these are cold words for a cold theme. They do not touch that sense of the theatrical, the antic or the macabre that were richly fed by the names of Robespierre or Marat.

The English and French revolutions, then, lacked active competitors in the Victorian imagination. The English civil war, though it counted for much, did not count under this head: hardly anyone called it the English Revolution before the twentieth century, though Macaulay and others sometimes speak of it as belonging to the general class of revolutions. In this the Victorians were content to follow the usage of the seventeenth century itself. Before any political application, 'revolution' had often been used to describe the return of a heavenly body to its starting-point, as in Copernicus's *De revolutionibus* (1543); Cotgrave, in his dictionary of 1611, called revolution 'a full compassing'. Its common use in English to describe a political event is essentially post-1689, though Clarendon had used it to describe the restoration of Charles II in 1660 in his *History of the Rebellion* (xi. 209). The Puritans had made rebellion; the Royalists, in restoring monarchy, later made a revolution or full compassing. So much of the rhetoric of change in the seventeenth century took the form of demanding ancient rights, real or supposed, that it is often difficult to distinguish the language of change from the language of tradition.[1] Revolution restores: Locke, in his *Two Treatises of Government* (1690), written before the Revolution of 1689, insisted that the people commonly seek traditional forms of government, and that monarchs who flaunt the established rights of the people are themselves rebels. 'This slowness and aversion in the people to quit their old constitutions has, in the

1. See Vernon F. Snow, 'The concept of revolution in seventeenth-century England', *Historical Journal* v (1962).

many revolutions which have been seen in this kingdom, in this and former ages, still kept us to or, after some interval of fruitless attempts, still brought us back again to our old legislative of Kings, Lords and Commons' (ii. 223). But the century after 1689 was to change that emphasis, and much of the eighteenth-century use of 'revolution' frankly connotes innovation. Burke, in his *Reflections on the Revolution in France* (1790), does not doubt that the dangerous mood of the French National Assembly is for novelty in the purest sense.

Henceforth conservative revolution is a paradox, though at times a lively and fertile one. The Victorian historiography of 1689 shows how the events of James II's fall could be brought into harmony with the reform of 1832. The myth is of sudden growth. Hume, as a Tory, had been on the wrong side, and his *History of England* failed to fuel the reforming cause. But Henry Hallam, in his *Constitutional History of England* (1827), had furnished a libertarian interpretation of 1689 twenty years earlier than Macaulay's *History*. The Revolution, in Hallam's view, had been no mere personal triumph of William III over James II, but 'rather the triumph of those principles which, in the language of the present day, are denominated liberal or constitutional, over those of absolute monarchy' (ch. 15). The Glorious Revolution had always been the prize possession of the Whigs; now it was liberal too, even radical, though its mythic energy faded gently after the Reform Act of 1832. Sir James Mackintosh, a Benthamite Whig, had died in that very year, a few days before Bentham himself; and the editor of his *History of the Revolution* (1834) remarks in his Advertisement that the book had already slightly dated: Mackintosh had been a Whig of the Revolution, an event now 'more dispassionately, more correctly, and less highly estimated' as a result of recent events. For the Whig it had been the great event of English history. For the Liberals and Radicals who were usurping power in the party, it was certainly less than that; it was more like an oligarchic prelude, oddly prolonged for nearly a century and a half, to the attainment of power by the people. It had brought the Crown into harmony with Parliament, as Macaulay wrote six years after the Reform Act, planning his *History*. But 1832 counted for as much or more: it was 'the

Revolution which brought the Parliament into harmony with the nation'.[1] For the mid-Victorians, the myth of 1689 was of a fading significance. 'Our revolution has long since run its round', wrote T. H. Green. 'The cycle was limited, and belonged essentially to another world than that in which we live.'[2]

Such considerations dominated the prospects of any revolution still to come. A revolutionary future for England was, after all, a natural probability. The first industrial society on earth might readily be thought likely to prove the first to suffer the violent shocks that the unrehearsed problems of industrialism must bring. All thoughtful Victorians knew that their society was riding a tiger. Whether industrialism – the factory system, or manufacturing system, as they commonly called it – was strictly speaking a revolution or not, it certainly bore some of the gravest marks of one. Oddly enough, the phrase 'the industrial revolution' is not known to have been used by an Englishman before about 1880, when Arnold Toynbee (1852–83) used it in his Oxford lectures, borrowing it from the French economist Blanqui. The French have had their own revolution; the English, in their quieter way, have been achieving another even more momentous in the field of production. Toynbee's lectures *The Industrial Revolution* (1884), published by his friends soon after his early death, is a striking acknowledgment of a truth many had already guessed. To the Revolution of 1689 and the constitutional reforms of 1832 and after must now be added a third irreversible process of history, an event without a date.[3]

In a continuing industrial revolution like the Victorian, political revolution of the classic kind can always occur; and since most European states had suffered and were suffering revolutions, it seemed natural to suppose that the most advanced of all should not be exempt. 'Since I have been in the world', Lady Charlemont remarked to Tocqueville in 1835, 'have heard it said each year that we are going to have a revolution, and at the end of the year we always found ourselves in the same place.' A listener found the remark complacent, and countered:

1. George Otto Trevelyan, *The Life and Letters of Lord Macaulay* (London, 1876) ii. 13–14, from a letter to Napier of 20 July 1838.
2. T. H. Green, *Works* (1885–88) iii. 277.
3. See G. N. Clark, *The Idea of the Industrial Revolution* (Glasgow, 1953).

'We have heard it said all our lives that we must die, and we do not die. Does this mean that we are immortal?'[1] But Lady Charlemont was right, after all. England did not suffer a revolution, in the classic sense of the word, after 1689, and the first industrial nation proved by the most improbable of paradoxes the most stable. How that happened was a question that puzzled the Victorians themselves, and which may well puzzle their inheritors. Perhaps Disraeli had the answer, or the outline of one, when in *Coningsby* he makes the leader of the Tory Party accept the consequences of democracy: 'I believe after all that with property and pluck, parliamentary reform is not such a very bad thing' (IV, xi). Property, it is true, might only have excited envy and destruction, as in France; but pluck is an outstanding attribute of the British oligarchy in the age of reform. They obstinately refused to panic. And to pluck may be added skill: the devious skill of the general who knows how best to preserve his forces while retreating under fire.

Reform was retreat, for some, but it was after all by reform that revolution was frustrated. These were the alternatives that were open to Englishmen in the 1830s and after, and enough of them saw it to be so. Macaulay's appeal to the Commons in March 1831, 'Reform that you may preserve,' is an echoing cry in the age. By stretching language, reform and revolution might even amount to the same thing: revolution only means 'speedier change', as Carlyle put it in *The French Revolution* (1837), since in a general sense 'all things are in revolution, in change from moment to moment . . . There is properly nothing but revolution and mutation' (VI, i); in fact 'nothing else is conceivable'. But the vast majority of Victorians could see perfectly well the vast chasm that separates progressive change from revolution: it is the key to their political choices. Reform is the guarantor of continuity. It offers a chance, even a probability, of moderating the shock of change and controlling its tempo. That was the prudent, even the conservative view. But liberals and radicals too came to see how lucky they had been to adopt legislative rather than revolutionary methods. The antithesis between reform and revolution is sharpened by hindsight. Revolution is at best a counsel of despair: the last

1. Tocqueville, *Journey to England and Ireland* (1968) p. 65.

terrible appeal to truth, as Dickens reveals it in *A Tale of Two Cities*, when the blind obstinacy of rulers allows for nothing better. England, as a parliamentary state, had something better already, and delay is a price worth paying. 'There are some rare cases', Cornewall Lewis concedes in *A Dialogue on the Best Form of Government* (1863), 'in which a nation has profited by a revolution. Such was the English revolution of 1688.' But that had been 'the very minimum of a revolution', changing merely the person of the sovereign without drawing a vindictive reaction upon itself. The Italian Risorgimento had also proved admirable, in Lewis's view, because of the moderation of its leaders. But by and large the record is unfavourable: 'the history of forcible attempts to improve governments is not, however, cheering', and men would be far better advised to work for reform than to buy 'a ticket in the lottery of revolution'. By the 1860s, at least, hardly any Englishman would have denied this. Macaulay, as a Whig, had always been a gradualist; but by 1876, when his nephew collected his letters, the profundity of that view seemed to him confirmed by events. Only 'defensive revolutions' turn out well, like 1689 or the July Revolution in France in 1830: 'What good have the revolutions of 1848 done? Or rather, what harm have they not done?' That is a conclusion his nephew, describing the passage of the Reform Bill in 1831–32, is glad to accept. After Waterloo,

> when the passion and ardour of the war gave place to the discontent engendered by a protracted period of commercial distress, the opponents of progress began to perceive that they had to reckon not with a small and disheartened faction, but with a clear majority of the nation led by the most enlightened and the most eminent of his sons. Agitators and incendiaries retired into the background, as will always be the case when the country is in earnest; and statesmen who had much to lose, but were not afraid to risk it, stepped quietly and firmly to the front.[1]

This is the legacy of Whiggism to the cause of reform. The conservative fears revolution: the percipient reformer despises it, since it means a loss in the control of events. Ruskin, in his lecture on Protestantism in 1884, begged his audience not to

1. G. O. Trevelyan, *Life and Letters of Macaulay* (1876) ii. 433, i. 158.

confuse Reformation with Revolution: 'They are each other's exact negatives. Reformation is of a broken square into a steady one; Revolution the blasting of a tower on a rock into its own ditch, head downmost.'[1] And you cannot build on a ruin.

Again, revolution is conservative, in the sense of being rigid in its effects. Dicey, in his lectures of 1898, noticed that, whereas in popular acceptance France is the land of revolution and England of conservatism, 'a glance at the legal history of each country suggests the existence of some error in the popular contrast'. In France a Napoleonic Code has remained essentially unaltered since its publication in 1804, and the United States has been equally averse to rapid legal change; whereas hardly a single part of the British statute book has survived intact from the beginning of the century to the end.[2] Revolution ossifies. That is hardly a lesson that the English reformers knew from the start; but some events suggested it, and the accumulation of events seemed to confirm it. No neighbouring European state offered a seductive example of revolutionary success. Revolution, as Bagehot noted gaily in 1876, 'is as much a term of reproach to Mr Bright' as to any arch-Tory.[3] The line between reformation and revolution, after two French failures and a host of lesser ones, was forever drawn.

The failure of 1789 was admittedly a qualified matter. The French Revolution, in some accounts, is the shadow under which the whole nineteenth century lived. All modern historiography, according to Acton, must start afresh, beginning at Burke and 'piecing together' what that great event had snapped.[4] On the other hand, it is a fading popular memory which excites ardour, as a political analogy, of an increasingly factitious kind. Carlyle, who was born in 1795, was writing of events almost contemporary to himself in *The French Revolution*, and his excitement and horror have the authentic note of war fever and of haunted fear. But Dickens, who borrowed from the book in *A Tale of Two Cities*, was only a three-year-old at the

1. Ruskin, *Works:* library edition (1903–12) xxxiii. 518.
2. A. V. Dicey, *Law & Public Opinion in England* (1905) p. 7.
3. *Economist* (29 April 1876); reprinted in his *Collected Works* (1968) iii. 320.
4. Lord Acton, Additional MS 5437.18, University Library, Cambridge.

time of Waterloo. If the *Tale* is an awful warning, it is a warning that has little to do with the England of 1859; only a feverish imagination would compare the incompetence revealed by the Crimean War five years before with the iniquities and vacillations of Louis XVI and his ministers. Most English views of the Revolution itself, though not of the Terror that followed it, are relaxed to the point of acceptance. Macaulay, who revered only one revolution in human history, proposed in his review of Sir James Mackintosh in 1835 that 'the French Revolution, in spite of all its crimes and follies, was a great blessing to mankind'; he already thought it a vulgarity of conservatism to try to use it as a bogey. The young Mill, more expectedly, took a similar view in a sharper tone. To forbid revolution in all circumstances is to concede the conservative case. The liberal task is to try to avoid revolution by legislation, not to deny in advance to others the right to act when events leave no choice between revolution and subjection:

> A political convulsion is a fearful thing: granted. Nobody can be assured beforehand what course it will take: we grant that too. What then? . . . Men are not to make it the sole object of their political lives to avoid a revolution, no more than of their natural lives to avoid death. They are to take reasonable care to avert both those contingencies when there is a present danger, but not to forbear the pursuit of any worthy object for fear of a mere possibility.[1]

The bogey of revolution was never accepted as an argument by educated Victorian opinion: earlier, in 1831–32, as Bagehot observed, it had been 'a kind of intellectual shuttlecock'[2] between the two sides of the House, the Tories invoking the French Terror as the outcome of rash change, the Whigs as the outcome of changes made too late. It was slowly to lose even that ambiguous significance, and 1848 was soon to provide more contemporary examples both of rashness and of delay. For 1859, *A Tale of Two Cities* is already an old-fashioned book. But its purpose, if curiously overlaid, still holds. A

1. J. S. Mill, 'A few observations on the French Revolution', *Monthly Repository* (August 1833); reprinted in his *Dissertations and Discussions* (1859) i. 58–9.
2. Bagehot, *Fortnightly Review* (November 1876); reprinted in his *Collected Works* (1968) iii. 218.

Radical is after all right to fear revolution, and he may have more in reason to fear from it than a Conservative. That revolution should happen at all is an admission on the part of history that radicals have failed; and when it happens, it may destroy for a generation, or forever, the profoundest hopes of change.

[4]

Ideas of the Good

The English ideology is a moral system. It is not ultimately based on practical considerations, that is to say, or on alleged 'laws' of history or of social change, but on a perceived difference between right and wrong. Its hallmark is a zeal for righteousness. 'Never to debase the moral currency'[1] – when Acton admonished his audience of historians at his Cambridge inaugural in 1895 in these terms, his summons to virtue had the true Victorian ring. This is the root, and all else the flower. And cynical observers as surely as the committed could sense morality as the note of the new age. The past, by contrast, was carefree, the present as different from that past as the Queen from her notorious uncles. Bagehot in 1864 noted the 'haunting atmosphere of reflection . . . around and about us', and observed how well the rising genius of Gladstone, not yet prime minister, summed up the new spirit, his speeches demonstrating a 'grave intensity which marks the man and marks his time'. Palmerston, whose age was nearing its close as the last Whig premier of England neared his eightieth birthday, belonged in moral atmosphere to the time of the Georges, 'born before *earnestness* was thought to be a virtue'. But then in the Regency, when Palmerston was young, social science had hardly been born: 'men ate and drank, and married, and gave in marriage, and no intellectual care troubled them. It is not so with us.'[2] The care and the trouble lie in the Victorian passion for discrimination. From Mill to Acton, from Dickens to George Eliot and her successor novelists, is a process of refinement in moral

1. Lord Acton, *A Lecture on the Study of History* (London, 1895) p. 63.
2. Bagehot, *Economist* (13 August 1864); reprinted in his *Collected Works* (1968) iii. 282.

choice, an increasing ethical awareness of the delicate and the borderline. Bagehot called the mood of reflection haunting, and indeed a ghost seems to walk the Victorian mind. Dogmatism is pursued by a fear of dogmatism, certainty by an awareness that, in the end, the totality of man's duty in society must always elude. The evangelical God had been exigent, the God of the Tractarians no less so; but no god ever demanded more of men than he who, for atheists like Mill and Arnold and George Eliot, had only recently ceased to exist. The duties which that sudden demise threw upon his survivors was felt by some as almost too heavy to be borne.

Escape towards fulfilment was through work, and liberal morality has its immediate actualities to comfort and enliven the devout. This was a world which, innocent of utopianism, saw itself to be moving somewhere, and somewhere better, at an accelerating pace. 'We hurry onwards to extinguish hell', as Elizabeth Barrett Browning put it with brisk confidence. And that confidence could be justified on the facts. Reform was happening, men starved less and worked for less long, the age-old abuse of child-labour was being legislated out of existence, and millions were winning the suffrage. Victorian optimism is not fatuous; it knows what it is about. On the other hand, work can be an anodyne to the soul-sick as much as a crying duty, and for those who regret the vanishing of God it may ease the pangs of a cosmic bereavement. 'We are here, however we came', as Clough once wrote, 'to *do* something – to fulfil our *ergon*. The world is here, however it came here, to be made something of by our hands. Not by prayer, but examination; [by] examination not of ourselves, but of the world, shall we find out what to do, and how to do it.'[1]

What decisively places the political ethics of the age in a secular sphere, above and beyond religion, is the coincidence of view between believer and non-believer. A Christian like Gladstone may believe that in effecting social reform he is fulfilling God's will, and the diary he kept for over seventy years from his Eton schooldays leaves no doubt that he did think that. An atheist, no less dedicated, might feel that since

1. Arthur Hugh Clough, *Selected Prose Works*, edited by B. B. Travick (University, Alabama, 1964) p. 285, from a review of J. H. Newman written *c.* 1850.

the world is all he has, he had best make the most of it. In the Cabinet Room or in committee the distinction was not a difference, unless a difference in rhetoric. In ordinary weekday life, and in the social novel that mirrors that life, religion matters surprisingly little. Of how many characters in Victorian fiction, or in public life, could it be said with much probability that their behaviour would have been different if they had believed in a religion, or not believed in one? The difference between the Christian denominations, it is true, and notably that between Anglican and nonconformist, powerfully affected voting habits between the first Reform Act of 1832 and the First World War, and it often affected styles of life as well. But the wider gap between Christian and non-Christian, paradoxically enough, affects political ideology less. This is not a sectarian movement, though it is a movement which, in the mouths of many, can take on a strong sectarian note. It is one of the strengths of Victorian liberalism that it can excite the enthusiasm of those of great faith or of none.

This is a doctrine of virtue, not of gain. It is curious that the fallacy of the cash-nexus, as Carlyle called it derisively, should have won such currency; though less curious when one reflects how little the works of the classical economists and their Victorian inheritors have been read in this century, how much their critics like Carlyle and Ruskin, and how easily myths have encrusted a corpus of political literature which, when studiously examined, seems lucid and explicit beyond complaint. The Victorians said what they thought, and clearly, but they have not been heeded. They rejected *laissez-faire* in word and action, and yet they are widely held convicted of it. They hated a morality of mere calculation based on personal greed, and often said so; and these declarations have been misrepresented as being no more than minority protests. Dickens's *Hard Times* has often been misinterpreted in this way, and few pause to reflect that the greatest best-selling novelist of his age is unlikely to have held views widely divergent from those of the millions who devoured his books, and that the social evidence for supposing most Victorian employers to resemble Mr Gradgrind is still lacking. Much that is glibly interpreted in the writings of the Victorians as protest against the state of

Victorian society is something else: a confident protest by confident men against human vices and follies which they know their readers too are likely to condemn. It is one thing to detect a social symptom and even to prescribe a remedy, as Dickens, George Eliot and Trollope often do: another to suppose that the patient is dying of an incurable disease. Much of Victorian social literature, in the novel and elsewhere, is concerned with detecting and isolating symptoms; but it is to misunderstand that literature to suppose that general condemnation is its usual purpose. A doctor knows that most men are healthy. The Victorian reformers proclaimed the moral and social evils they saw: some men are shallow, some greedy, some excessively calculating. But it does not follow from this that they thought their society shallow, or greedy, or calculating. The scorn of the novelists for those who theorize too fast and hasten towards generalities on very occasional social evidence, much of it derived from textbooks of sociology, is a powerfully persuasive element in their case for the essential variety of man.

It is against these reflections that much of the social comment of the age needs to be judged. If the twentieth century has often felt the nineteenth to have been mercenary, it is largely because the nineteenth often attacked what it saw of the mercenary spirit in itself. But Dickens's portrait of Gradgrind is much better evidence for supposing that the Victorians hated greed than that they admired it – which is not to deny, of course, they may also have been guilty of greed, as men are often guilty of vices which they know to be vices. This interpretation is fully supported by that Bible of Victorian business morality, Smiles's *Self-Help* (1859), which appeared with acclaim five years after *Hard Times*. Smiles believed in perseverance, hard work, thrift and a reasonable and creative individual ambition. But he believed in all this as conduct formative of character; and it is character, not wealth, that the book glorifies as the end of human existence. Even more, he believes in public virtue, generosity and the goods of life that money cannot buy; he is even sceptical of excessive thrift:

> It is against the growth of this habit of inordinate saving that the wise man needs most carefully to guard himself: else, what in youth was a simple economy, may in old age grow into avarice . . .

It is one of the defects of business too exclusively followed, that it insensibly tends to a mechanism of character. The business man gets into a rut, and often does not look beyond it. If he lives for himself only, he becomes apt to regard other human beings only in so far as they minister to his ends . . .

Though men of persevering, sharp, dextrous and unscrupulous habits, . . . may and do 'get on' in the world, yet it is quite possible that they may not possess the slightest elevation of character, nor a particle of real goodness (ch. 10).

Self-Help was a hugely popular book, and is said to have been translated into seventeen languages and to have sold nearly a quarter of a million copies before the end of the century. There is no reason to doubt that Smiles's warning against 'mechanism of character' was widely accepted by the Victorians as uncontroversial; no published objection to it has yet been produced. If this is what the consensus of commercial opinion on moral questions was like, then there is every reason to suppose that *Hard Times* and Trollope's *The Way We Live Now*, and other novels of the age that protest against the dangers of the crudely mercenary spirit, are equally a part of that consensus.

The morality of the age is objectivist, and contemptuous of the view that moral choices are merely matters of personal opinion. The Victorians knew of moral subjectivism, indeed, but rejected it – rejected it, by and large, as a conservative heresy, since an objective morality was rightly seen as the necessary foundation of any doctrine of social change. 'Opinions alter, manners change,' Acton announced sternly in his Cambridge inaugural, 'but the moral law is written on the tablets of eternity.' That law, in his view, is 'the very root of revolution', and 'the principle of the higher law signifies Revolution'.[1] The discarded nostrum of Utility, as Mill saw, had a similar strength, and the Utilitarians were as clear as anyone that morality is a kind of knowledge:

The adherents of the principle of utility . . . contend that the morality of actions is perceived by the same faculties by which we perceive any other of the qualities of actions, namely, our intellects

1. Lord Acton, *Historical Essays and Studies* (London, 1907) p. 355; *Lectures on the French Revolution* (London, 1910) p. 2.

and our senses. They hold the capacity of perceiving moral distinctions to be no more a distinct faculty than the capacity of trying causes, or of making a speech to a jury.[1]

All this is a necessary precondition of reform. If change is to be recommended, seriously and in good conscience, then it cannot plausibly be demanded as a mere whim or momentary inclination, still less in a mood which proclaims or implies that the issue is one on which honest and informed men may reasonably differ. Social change, whether by reform or revolution, is in the short run costly, time-consuming and dislocating; unless the case is little short of certain, it is not a case. That is why, as Acton saw, subjectivism favours the conservative: if he can show that moral choices are merely matters of personal opinion, he is well on the way to showing that Parliament had just as well leave things as they are. The opinion of an individual statesman, of a political party, of the people itself – all opinion whatsoever, in fact – is radically devalued by subjectivism. Free men in a free nation use real evidence as bricks to build a fabric of argument; in politics as in scholarship, argument is argument, not just a spouting of words. In the intellectual atmosphere of England, as Bagehot observed proudly, instancing Grote's *History of Greece* as a work of scholarship that no servile German historian could have written, there is a 'constant sense of evidence – the habitual perception of tested probability which the atmosphere of a free country produces, and must produce'.[2] That draws all the elements together. The cognitive processes of morality, political reform and scholarship are equally founded on the rock of objective truth. This is not to imply that moralists, politicians and historians are other than partial and personal in their judgement. But then if the question were not an objective one, the verdict of partiality or impartiality could not arise. It is the inquiry itself that is objective: whether any individual has it right or wrong is another matter, and a matter

1. J. S. Mill, 'Professor Sedgwick's *Discourse on the Studies of the University of Cambridge*', *London Review* (April 1835); reprinted in his *Dissertations and Discussions* (1859) i. 139.

2. Bagehot, 'The tribute at Hereford to Sir G. C. Lewis', *Economist* (10 September 1864); reprinted in his *Collected Works* (1968) iii. 403.

to be sifted by what Bagehot calls the 'constant sense of evidence'.

The same considerations apply, though less obviously, to obliquely subjectivist doctrines such as any farreaching doctrine of social conditioning as the root of all conviction. Marx will serve as an example: in the introduction to his *Critique of Political Economy*, in a famous declaration, he put the view of 'scientific socialism': 'The mode of production of the material means of life determines, in general, the social, political and intellectual processes of life. It is not the consciousness of human beings which determines their existence, it is their social existence which determines their consciousness.' That did not seem a plausible view to the Victorians, and least of all to Victorian radicals. If men believe what they do only or largely because they have been conditioned by their society into believing it, then the possibility of adjudicating between one conviction and another cannot seriously arise, since any such adjudication is itself subject to the same reductive view. This is the dark abyss of subjectivism, and those who take an absolute stand on the social conditioning of thought save themselves from this abyss only at the cost of self-contradiction. But Victorian liberal morality condemned such shallow scientisms: Mill on Comtism, George Eliot on the German sociologists in her review of Riehl, Henry Sidgwick's *Methods of Ethics* (1874) are some among many refutations of moral subjectivism in the age. Acton's contempt for mere relativism in the moral judgements of the historian is the resounding theme of his essays and lectures. Gladstone shared that contempt in his speeches; though his opponents were quick to point out moments in his career as a party leader when the high consistency of his words was unmatched in action.

The eventual task of an objective morality – a task which, in an absolute sense, must remain forever unfulfilled – was seen as one of establishing a base of principle upon which such a morality may be securely built. Acton's 'tablets of eternity' are there; whether any generation of men can discover them in their entirety is another matter. The task of the age was twofold: to explore downwards towards the foundations of moral knowledge, while yet giving men enough hope and certainty to accept the challenges of daily life. In hurrying onwards to extinguish hell, it would be foolish to pause and ask why the hurry; none the less, it is fitting that some men at some time should ask and seek answers. There is no need of an answer in order to act, but it would be incurious not to ask at all. There are principles deeper than the principles we already possess. Mill's dissatisfaction with his father's utilitarianism is based on the recognition that behind the felicific principle must lie another: 'There is no meaning in saying that pleasure is good', he wrote in *Utilitarianism* (1863), 'unless good is something different from pleasure.' The concept of duty may be modified and deepened, but it cannot simply be displaced by facile generalizations like Marx's about the motives by which men act. The complexity of the undertaking might even drive an enlightened spirit back to a point perilously close to the theism it had abandoned. Sidgwick, in the preface to his *Methods of Ethics*, sets out to examine 'the different methods of obtaining reasoned convictions as to what ought to be done', and plainly speaks of ethical knowledge as 'cognition'. But by the end of a long inquiry, he is very close to the despairing conclusion that, in the end, only divine injunction will do. If the universe is godless, then 'the Cosmos of Duty is thus really reduced to a Chaos' (iv, 6). Others, like Tennyson, Arnold and George Eliot, settled into one or another of the many stopping-places on the long road that stretches from belief to unbelief, often into that ethical Christianity that saw Christ as only man, but as the best of men. Others, like Gladstone and Acton, thought the tablets of eternity simply that, given by God and revealed in his Word. Certainty and doubt exist in all degrees: what unites them all is the conviction that, however much or little one may know, the moral law is there and is to be known.

As a form of knowledge, morality is accumulative: to that extent the doctrine was cheering. Men may live in a darkness, or at best a twilight of understanding; but there is a fair probability that we know more of good and evil than our grandparents, and that our grandchildren will know more than we. 'Is it not cheering', wrote George Eliot to a correspondent in 1853, after a reading of American history had reminded her how recent many momentous events were, 'to think of the youthfulness of this little planet, and the immensely greater youthfulness of our race upon it? – to think that the higher moral tendencies of human nature are yet only in their germ?' When she read Darwin's *Origin of Species* six years later, shortly after it appeared, the progress of the species seemed to parallel what she had seen in human morality in the short span of her own lifetime: 'So the world gets on step by step towards brave clearness and honesty', she wrote joyfully.[1] From now on it is the mystery that underlies the processes of life that needs to be explained, and that is hardly a task for a scientist. It was rather a chance for novelists to seize and exploit.

The novel, in a new and more serious role, might probe deep into that mystery. This sense of moral progress is not an ironic element in George Eliot's novels, though it could be expressed ironically. The Warwickshire of her childhood, where much of her English fiction is set, is a morally untutored world in a sense relative to the generation for which she wrote, and heroically simple in its understanding of mankind. 'In those days', she wrote in *Middlemarch* (1871–72), speaking of the late 1820s when the Duke of Wellington was prime minister, 'the world in general was more ignorant of good and evil by forty years than it is at present' (ch. 19); it understood less of the history of Italian art, less of romanticism, and less – since the chapter treats of the honeymoon of Casaubon and Dorothea in Rome – of the complexities of love. Some may wonder whether forty years could make much of a difference. But the evidence of change since the 1820s seemed to justify a confident view, and the 'consolidation of opinion' of which Mill speaks in *On Liberty* (1859) includes an increasing host of moral certainties: 'As mankind improve, the number of doctrines which are no longer disputed or doubted will be constantly on the increase: and the well-being of mankind may almost be measured by the number and gravity of the truths which have reached the point of being uncontested' (ch. 2). A hundred years before that sentence was written, hardly anyone had supposed slavery to be wicked, so that the case for supposing that moral progress can happen seems unassailable. Whether it happens inevitably

1. *The George Eliot Letters* (1954–56) ii. 85, iii. 227.

is another matter. Less than fifty years after Mill's death, extermination became the policy of one European state, Lenin's Russia, and some twenty years later it became the policy of another. Mill may have underrated the extent to which moral problems, once settled, give rise to further problems hitherto unnoticed. But this reflection refines rather than demolishes the doctrine of moral progress, and it makes moral problems look more than ever like problems in other areas of knowledge. As in the natural sciences, as in history, so in morality: the answer of one generation is the question of the next.

General propositions like Mill's partly obscure the fact that the nineteenth century was unique in its moral situation, and felt itself to be so. George Eliot's remark in *Middlemarch* suggests an exceptional rapidity of change, a sudden and unprecedented pace to the *Zeitgeist*. As a small model of a vaster whole, Casaubon's career as a scholar tells the story: he has not read the Germans, who are the latest scholarly authority in the field, and the scholar's difficulties in keeping up with the flood of intellectual discovery parallel the subtler problem of keeping up with the pace of social and moral change. A population explosion of almost Asiatic proportions – the population of Britain almost quadrupled in the course of the century – is matched by an unprecedented intellectual advance in the arts and sciences and an advancing industrial revolution. In the moral sphere, it is not surprising that men felt the situation to be without precedent in its rapidity, the new moral subtlety new in kind rather than in degree. Analogies might be sought in the past: Grote, in his *History of Greece*, sees a model in Solon, who represented 'the best tendencies of his age', combined with much that was personally excellent; 'the improved ethical sensibility; the thirst for enlarged knowledge' (iii, 158). Arnold's first series of *Essays in Criticism* (1865) is a gallery of portraits, most of them of delicate if minor French and German talents, but including Marcus Aurelius and Spinoza: various visions of highminded virtue softened by sentiment, 'consoling and hope-inspiring marks'.

But an impression remains that the age saw its devotion to duty as unique – if not in intensity, at least in refinement and analytical verve. 'The notion and analysis of conscience', wrote

Acton to Creighton, 'is scarcely older than 1700; and the notion and analysis of veracity is scarcely older than our time, barring sacred writings of East and West.'[1] That is not because the moral code is new. Acton is certain that it is old, and 'the difference in moral insight between past and present is not very large'. But the Victorians are analytical in their moral concern. It is at once their puzzle and their pride.

The puzzle was twofold. It concerned both the manner by which a consolidation of moral opinion was to be achieved, and the nature of that opinion itself. On the first matter, a consensus could not be found. Education, of course; since morality is a learning process, it will arise naturally out of the spread of knowledge, which will itself increase the demand for more education still. More will mean more: 'As the people grow more enlightened', wrote the young Mill in 1833, 'they will become more able to appreciate, and more willing to pay for, good instruction; so that the competition of the market will become more and more adequate to provide good education, and endowed establishments will be less and less necessary.'[2] There, it can now be said, he gravely underrated the future of state provision in education, and the future power of the voter to convert an honest desire for knowledge into a scramble for qualifications. But his predictions were true for his own age.

Beyond that point, views are divided. Grote, in a view slightly improbable in a Radical, thought morality in the end to be socially formed rather than individually conceived:

> The foundation of morality lies in the collective opinions of the larger portion of society, not in the separate opinion of each individual agent with regard to his own good – just as the foundation of law lies in the command of the legislator who disposes of the force of society, not in the opinion of each individual as to the line of conduct which it may suit him to pursue.[3]

1. Lord Acton, *Historical Essays & Studies* (London, 1907) p. 506, from a postscript to a letter written in connexion with his 1887 review of Creighton's history of the Papacy.

2. J. S. Mill, 'The right and wrong of state interference with corporation and Church property', *Jurist* (February 1833); reprinted in his *Dissertations and Discussions* (1859) i. 32.

3. Grote, *Minor Works* (London, 1873).

But that sounds more like Hume than a Victorian reformer. Others, and notably Herbert Spencer, whose ethics were based on evolution, saw the movement of all existence as from the less to the more complex – a view that harmonized with, and even helped to explain, the ascending complexities of modern behaviour. Leslie Stephen, in his *Science of Ethics* (1882), sought for a post-religious age a sanction against evil in social ethics: virtue is an aspect of evolution, in his view, and especially family virtue, since it is necessary for the survival of the race; and in the rearing of children can be detected a delicate relation between morality and utility. T. H. Huxley denied the facile equation of the fittest with the best, in his *Evolution and Ethics* (1893), and tried to supplant the cosmic process described by Darwin and moralized by Spencer by an 'ethical process' controlled by man. The puzzle remained that, while the total process of existence can with ingenuity be represented as just, it cannot be represented as anything but unjust to many an individual case. Tennyson bewailed that cosmic truth in *In Memoriam* (1850); W. S. Gilbert mocked its philosophical agony in *The Mikado* (1885) with his 'happy undeserving A' and 'wretched meritorious B'. Nature is still a stepmother, and social reform, however imperative, cannot easily lay claim to be part of the grand process of the universe.

The foundations of morality, then, were variously conceived. Its certainty, however, was not in doubt: men know the difference between right and wrong, and are learning down the ages to know it better and better. It is through such knowledge, ever more complex and ever more certain, that freedom is to be achieved. Men grow more certain about more and more moral decisions, life and literature joining to teach them how to live better; and the case for authority and regulation grows weaker as the moral fibre of the individual is progressively toughened by a training in virtue. The classic mistake about Victorian freedom is to suppose that it was a simple conviction that the power of authority, and notably of central government, ought to be reduced. In fact it was a conviction and a hope that private discipline would render large areas of public discipline unnecessary. To the extent that men govern themselves, they do not need to be governed. All this puts the doctrine of liberty at the farthest conceivable extreme from mere permissiveness. Liberty is not the right to do as you please: it is the chance to do as you ought. This is a high, austere and self-abnegating faith. It demands domination by the will. A man is morally free, Mill argued in *A System of Logic*, 'who feels that his habits or his temptations are not his masters, but he theirs: who even in yielding to them knows that he could resist; that were he . . . desirous of altogether throwing them off, there would not be required for that purpose a stronger desire than he knows himself to be capable of feeling' (VI, ii, 3). That sentiment was borrowed and adapted by Smiles years later in the eighth chapter of *Self-Help*. In his seventh edition of 1868 Mill added a sentence that links his doctrine of self-discipline with ancient and classical theories of ethics: 'And hence it is said with truth that none but a person of confirmed virtue is completely free.'

The liberty of the individual, then, is a discipline he must learn for himself. A man wins the right to liberty by self-mastery; a society wins that right by creating within itself 'a national clerisy or clergy' – Mill borrows the phrase from Coleridge, and confirms its use in a new secular sense – which can lead the less disciplined and the less instructed to want discipline and knowledge for themselves. Mankind, wrote Mill in 1833, must depend 'on the unremitting exertions of the more instructed and cultivated, whether in the position of a government or in a private station, to awaken in their minds a consciousness of this want, and to facilitate to them the means of supplying it.' This training of mind includes formal education, but is not limited to it. A clerisy would be 'a grand institution for the education of the whole people: not their school education merely, though that would be included in the scheme; but for training and rearing them, by systematic culture continued throughout life, to the highest perfection of their mental and spiritual nature'.[1] All this is a world away from a social or moral free-for-all, and it is compatible with political democracy only in certain highly specific conditions. The Victorians did not confuse individual liberty either with the absence of regulation or with the right to vote. Liberty is a moral property: some

1. J. S. Mill, 'The right and wrong of state interference', *Dissertations and Discussions* (1859) i. 38.

men can live to deserve it through learning morality and mastering their own lives; they can teach it to others; and in certain circumstances, towards which nineteenth-century England saw itself to be moving, they may even dare to entrust power to the masses of the people. But not in any circumstances whatever. The prospect is selective and confined.

The doctrine is strenuous, and has little enough to do with the rights of man. Indeed it is not doctrine of rights at all, but of duties. The rhetoric of the French revolutionaries and of Thomas Paine has only a slight place in Victorian political debate. Bentham had poured scorn upon the 'Droits de l'homme' as a philosophical nonsense and a mere prescription for anarchy. Victorian liberalism is circumspect in such matters, hostile to utopianism and sceptical of democracy. 'Trust in the people qualified by prudence' – that is Gladstone's recipe of government. The mass of men have the right to be informed, even consulted, and the parliamentary system is an educative process which is a model of Mill's clerisy in action. But they do not have the right in all circumstances of seeing their advice followed. Man, simply as man, does not have a right to liberty. That 'right' is the rhetoric of revolution – and only its rhetoric, one may add, since no society based upon a revolution practises it, or has ever practised it. But man, as man, has a right to earn his liberty by learning virtue. We sacrifice authority to morality, as Acton put it in a letter of 1879, but to nothing less: 'To speak quite plainly, as this is a confession, not an apology, I carried farther than others the doctrinaire belief in mere Liberalism, identifying it altogether with morality, and holding the ethical standard and purpose to be supreme and sovereign.'[1]

Virtue is not merely social; even a Robinson Crusoe can behave well or badly. But in the world everybody knows, most moral issues are about relations between persons, and these relations are the heartland of political discussion in the age. Savages cannot cooperate, as Mill argues in his essay on 'Civilization' (1836); their communities are poor and feeble of necessity; they have not learned how to cede a degree of personal liberty in return for more: 'It is only civilized beings

1. Lord Acton, *Selections from the Correspondence*, edited by J. N. Figgis and R. V. Laurence (London, 1917) i. 54.

who can combine. All combination is compromise: it is the sacrifice of some portion of individual will for a common purpose. The savage cannot bear to sacrifice, for any purpose, the satisfaction of his individual will.'

In a civilized order, Mill argues, the individual knowingly exchanges elements in his personal liberty in return for larger elements. He learns to act in concert. That is the true mark of social advancement. In the Spanish struggle against Napoleon, Mill adds contemptuously, none of the leaders could act in concert together, 'no one would sacrifice one iota of his consequence, his authority, or his opinion, to the most obvious demands of the common cause'.[1] Alliances and combinations, including what Mill dubs those 'questionable' combinations called trade unions, are all signs of maturity. This is not an atomized view of society. On the contrary, it sees the complexity of human relations, the acceptance of an imperfect liberty, and the readiness to exchange a smaller liberty for a greater, as in themselves marks of progress.

But the perception runs far deeper than a mechanical recognition of the workings of a social contract. Man is a congenial being in his nature, a social animal who cannot fully learn and understand the world in the solitary privacy of his own mind. He must compare, exchange and communicate with others in order to become himself. One would hardly bother to think at all, in the extended sense, without the prospect of telling one's thoughts to others.

> Were we solitary beings in the universe, *immediateness* would be in its nature the same. We should or we might have our eyes and ears open, and fact and we would meet each other as well in solitude as in company. . . . But the great impulse to reflection would be wanting, namely the impulse to communication. Intelligence is really co-intelligence. . . . Thought, if it is to be true, must be not only derived from fact, but must satisfy, or be good thought for, other intelligences as well as our own[2].

1. J. S. Mill, 'Civilization', *London and Westminster Review* (April 1836); reprinted in his *Dissertations and Discussions* (1859) i. 165–6.

2. John Grote (1813–66), *Exploratio philosophica: part II*, edited by J. B. Mayor (Cambridge, 1900) pp. 212–13. Grote was the younger brother of George Grote, and was himself Professor of Moral Philosophy at Cambridge.

None of this confirms the view that the Victorian ethic was individualistic, and it would be hard to read the Victorian novel on the assumption that the moral ideal of the age lay essentially in private enrichment and self-advancement. There is plenty of 'wretched meritorious B' in the fiction of the age. Its heroes and heroines learn to live in a world that others have made; if they live purely for themselves, like Pip in *Great Expectations* or Thackeray's Becky Sharp, they are taught a severe lesson by their creators. No atom survives in Victorian society; all enter, if they live and prosper at all, into combinations, of which the smallest and most elementary is the family; and some of the most climactic moments in human action are those in which a bond of sympathy is seized as if it were a lifeline. The devotion of Little Dorrit for her father in and out of prison, or the strange moment of congeniality between Dorothea Brooke and Lydgate, both victims of unhappy marriages, in the seventy-sixth chapter of *Middlemarch*, are examples among many. To be a solitary in that world, like Dickens's Miss Havisham, is to be in torment, and heaven is in other people.

These are largely truths the age would have taken for granted. What seemed a matter for disagreement, or at the best puzzlement, were the demands that the new industrial age increasingly made on the moral life. Simple, saintlike perfection is of no application in conditions as multifarious as these; nor was the Goethean ideal of man 'rounded off and made symmetrical like a Greek temple and a Greek drama'. Mill saw the urgent need for a new virtue so far unsanctified by moral teaching and still unspecified in epic and in song: 'Not symmetry, but bold, free expansion in all directions is demanded by the needs of modern life and the instincts of the modern mind. Great and strong and varied faculties are more wanted than faculties well-proportioned to one another; a Hercules or a Briareus more than an Apollo.'[1] Briareus the giant had a hundred hands and fifty heads, and he warred against the gods themselves; such seemed the unprecedented challenge of the times. But a moral delicacy rather than a moral decisiveness was increasingly to characterize the intelligentsia of the later

1. J. S. Mill, *Letters*, edited by H. S. R. Elliot (London, 1910) ii, Appendix A, from a letter of 8 February 1854.

century. As manners grew milder, so did moral discriminations grow finer and more analytical. George Eliot, reading *The Times* of 1832–33 as a preparation for writing *Felix Holt*, told her publisher how amazed she was at the strong language used in political debate thirty years before.[1] The reaction was common. Bagehot, on hearing of the death of Lord Brougham two years later, saw the race as suddenly grown 'smaller and weaker, if finer, like the second race of Greek deities as compared with the first'.[2] It was the conscious moral dilemma of the Victorians that the analytic spirit might lead to spiritual faddiness and indecision as much as to advancement and reform. To act intelligently, first discriminate: but what if one has to act at once, and what if discrimination only leads to an impotent awareness of ever higher levels of moral complexity? Henry James, the archpriest of such discriminations, allows one of his characters in *The Bostonians* (1886) a bitter diatribe against the tendency of the time:

> 'It's a feminine, a nervous, hysterical, chattering, canting age, an age of hollow phrases and false delicacy and exaggerated solicitudes and coddled sensibilities which, if we don't soon look out, will usher in the reign of mediocrity. . . . The masculine character, the ability to dare and endure, to know and yet not fear reality, to look the world in the face and take it for what it is – a very queer and partly very base mixture – that is what I want to preserve, or rather, . . . to recover' (ch. 34).

But the masculine character is not for the asking. James was as emphatic as anyone that complexity is of the nature of modern human experience; and 'experience is never limited, and it is never complete', as he put it in *The Art of Fiction*. A love of moral puzzles increasingly dominates the high fiction of the age: all a natural outcome of the conviction that morality is cognitive, all tending to confuse as well as subtilize. Since morality is a form of knowledge, and to be studied like another, it comes by a natural process to be investigated by advanced students who concentrate their attention on the difficult cases.

1. *The George Eliot Letters* (1954–56) iv. 248, from a letter of 27 April 1866.
2. Bagehot, *Economist* (16 May 1868); reprinted in his *Collected Works* (1968) iii. 198.

Did Hetty Sorel in *Adam Bede* murder her infant, or Gwendolen in *Daniel Deronda* her husband, or did they innocently allow them to die? Issues like these become the characteristic preoccupations of the Victorian moral intelligence: 'Our interest's on the dangerous edge of things', as Browning's Bishop Blougram observed warningly; a preoccupation with fine marginal cases is more likely to enfeeble than stiffen the will. The process might be a matter for pride, as men naturally take pride in intellectual advance, but it was a pride mixed with reserve and a sense of loss. More and more is known, more understood, but as a reward the age grows sceptical, less given to firm judgements and less joyous in its hopes of change. Henry Sidgwick, writing on Clough in 1869, summed up the new world of rarefied moral judgement:

> We are growing also more sceptical in the proper sense of the word: we suspend our judgment much more than our predecessors, and much more contentedly: we see that there are many sides to many questions: the opinions that we do hold we hold if not more loosely, at least more at arm's length: we can imagine how they appear to others, and can conceive ourselves not holding them. We are losing in faith and confidence: if we are not failing in hope, our hopes at least are becoming more indefinite; and we are gaining in impartiality and comprehensiveness of sympathy.[1]

Truth, as Clough himself had warned a dozen years before, in *Amours de Voyage*, is now 'Flexible, changeable, vague, and multiform, and doubtful'; and that is to be expected and to be feared (one might reply to them both) in any inquiry that sets no limits to its own sophistication.

Such doubts could be profound, even crippling. But doubt is still short of despair. Seeing the truth, and telling it – these are never inconceivables in the Victorian conscience. The new knowledge of the moral order creates a sense of the knowledge still to be found. Cognition is a process, not an end. When Thackeray declined to publish a poem of Elizabeth Barrett Browning on the grounds that its reference to prostitution

1. Henry Sidgwick, 'The poems and prose remains of Arthur Hugh Clough', *Westminster Review* (October 1869); reprinted in his *Miscellaneous Essays and Addresses* (London, 1904) p. 60.

might raise an outcry among his readers, Mrs Browning replied that a state of moral corruption properly required some frank speaking: 'not shut doors and windows, but light and air – and . . . it is exactly because pure and prosperous women choose to *ignore* vice that miserable women suffer wrong by it everywhere.'[1]

The example of French fiction did not invite: many an Englishman believed that the frank sexual reference of the French novel was linked with the moral sink they saw in Parisian life. But between the rival claims of delicacy and truth, truth is slowly the victor. Much of the indignation excited against Hardy by *Tess of the D'Urbervilles* (1891) and *Jude the Obscure* (1895), for example, was directed against Hardy's uncertain grasp of morality, as the reviewers saw it, rather than against his range of reference. 'To accept the love of her husband', writes R. H. Hutton angrily of Tess in the *Spectator* of January 1892, 'without telling him that she had been the more or less innocent victim of a man to whom she had borne a child, was not certainly the act of "a pure woman".' This is sharp moral discrimination rather than prudery, and it is doubtful if the social fiction of the age was seriously inhibited against reporting its abuses by sexual censorship, though such censorship undoubtedly limited the explicitness that could be safely employed. *Oliver Twist* appeared in the first year of the Queen's reign, and in the figure of Nancy it shows how suggestion can inform as efficiently as statement; and the character of Esther in Elizabeth Gaskell's *Mary Barton* (1848) is a fully documented account of prostitution in Manchester. The social fiction of the reign can claim, by the end of the century, to be comprehensive as well as critical.

What most alarmed the age, and understandably, was the wondering reflection where the quest for moral knowledge would all end. Men sought to know everything, even the bitterest truths about the world they lived in. Their literature is a continuous testing ground in the dutiful round of looking facts in the face. Man's highest calling and election, as George Eliot once wrote, is 'to do without opium and live through all

1. W. M. Thackeray, *Letters*, edited by G. N. Ray (Cambridge, Mass., 1946) iv. 227–8.

our pain with conscious, clear-eyed endurance'.[1] But what would it be like to know everything? 'If we had a keen vision and feeling of all ordinary human life', she was to write later in *Middlemarch*, 'it would be like hearing the grass grow and the squirrel's heart beat, and we should die of that roar which lies on the other side of silence' (ch. 20). Fortunately, she adds, all of us are at least a little stupid, even the quickest, and well wadded against reality. That is the last rueful consolation of the moral philosopher. Man will never know the whole of his moral condition, any more than the whole of his physical or social condition. But that is not because such realities are unknowable. It is simply that there is too much to know.

1. *The George Eliot Letters* (1954–56) iii. 366, from a letter of 26 December 1860.

[5]

Laissez-faire and the State

Laissez-faire is the nightwatchman doctrine of state. Government, according to this view, should forbid theft and murder and ensure national defence; but it must refrain from interfering in the economic life of the nation, where market forces should be set free to work at will. As Mill defined the doctrine in his attack upon it in the last chapter of his *Principles of Political Economy* (1848), the state should limit its internal functions to the simple business of 'the protection of persons and property against force and fraud'.

The origins of the doctrine are not mysterious. It is a mid-eighteenth-century theory invented by French economists in their attack on the constrictive policies of the *ancien régime*; and no English term, in spite of the efforts of Carlyle and Mill to invent translations, has ever shifted it for long from its original form. It is an alien doctrine, even in its name: all the more remarkable, then, that so unacclimatized a term should ever have been regarded as English. Acton, who described it very accurately at the end of the century in his Cambridge lectures on the French Revolution, seems to assume there that his audience will need to have it explained to them as a theory remote both in time and place.[1] That was surely realistic of him. No political party in nineteenth-century England can be

1. Lord Acton, *Lectures on the French Revolution* (London, 1910), delivered 1895–99: 'The interference of one man with another, of society with its members, of the state with the subject, must be brought down to the lowest dimension. Power intervenes only to restrict intervention, to guard the individual from oppression . . .' (p. 11). D. H. Macgregor has shown that '*laissez-faire*' was never once used as a term in the 1,500 double-column pages of *Hansard* devoted to the Free Trade debate of 1846; see his *Economic Thought and Policy* (Oxford, 1949) p. 56.

shown to have believed in it or to have attempted to practise it; to that extent this chapter is the history of a myth. But the myth is of intrinsic interest; it is still prevalent, after all, and what is more it is Victorian in its origins – all reasons that guarantee its significance here. This is one of the grander misunderstandings of intellectual history.

The Victorian origins of the myth belong to a literature of protest which, like much similar literature, is mainly directed towards striking utterance. Carlyle's essay of 1839 on Chartism, a strident demand for more government, linked the name of Adam Smith with *laissez-faire* and daringly translated it into 'Donothingism'. That shows that he had not read *The Wealth of Nations*, or at least had not accurately remembered it. Smith had awarded three large functions to the state: defence, the protection of the individual from the injustice and oppression of others, and

> the duty of erecting and maintaining certain publick works and certain publick institutions which it can never be for the interest of any individual, or small number of individuals, to erect and maintain; because the profit could never repay the expence . . ., though it may frequently do much more than repay it to a great society (IV. ix).

Smith does not mention *laissez-faire* in the course of his book, and he should not need to be defended from the charge of believing in it. Nor do Malthus, Ricardo, McCulloch, Bentham or Nassau Senior anywhere speak of *laissez-faire* in their published writings. Mill, writing a year after Carlyle in his famous essay on Coleridge, restates a position already familiar in the works of the classical economists. He calls *laissez-faire* 'the let alone doctrine', echoing Bentham in a version of the term that Samuel Smiles was later to adopt, and calls it half true and half false:

> Beyond suppressing force and fraud, governments can seldom, without doing more harm than good, attempt to chain up the free agency of individuals. But does it follow from this that government cannot exercise a free agency of its own? – that it cannot beneficially employ its powers, its means of information, and its pecuniary resources . . . in promoting the public welfare by a thousand means which individuals

would never think of, would have no sufficient motives to attempt, or no sufficient powers to accomplish?

And he instances state help for 'that large proportion of its members who cannot help themselves'.[1] This is a close echo of the substance of Adam Smith: it is good classical economics.

Nearly twenty years later, in his introduction to *On Liberty* (1859), Mill complained that 'the interference of government is, with about equal frequency, improperly invoked and improperly condemned'. That is the balanced view of the matter. It suggests a tolerance of state welfare, though welfare of a selective rather than of a comprehensive kind. Broadly speaking, such is the keynote of much Victorian social legislation, though the comprehensive principle could be admitted, as in the case of public libraries, where selection was open to practical objections. Some viewed the increasing scale of state welfare with concern, but it was possible to feel a degree of concern and yet accept the case as a matter of necessity. George Eliot, writing to a friend in 1874, noted with disapproval that the poor law could only, in the short run, be conducted on 'the principle of communistic provision instead of provision through individual, personal responsibility and activity'. But she did not demand abolition: it cannot be 'got rid of on a sudden', and her advocacy of the selective principle remained an active one, whatever the practical difficulties.[2]

Some were reluctant when they considered the prospects of state power, some eager. But whatever the motives, it cannot be seriously doubted that the level of government activity rose, and rose largely, during the reign of Victoria. The process was cumulative, undesigned as a totality, and beleaguered by a widespread suspicion of paternalism and of centralized power. If the argument about the rival merits of local and central power tended increasingly to be resolved in favour of central government, that was less on doctrinaire grounds than for reasons of administrative convenience. Again and again, it was the state or nothing. Dickens's Mr Podsnap, in *Our Mutual Friend* (1865),

1. J. S. Mill, 'Coleridge', *London and Westminster Review* (March 1840); reprinted in his *Dissertations and Discussions* (1859) i. 454.

2. *The George Eliot Letters* (1954–56) vi. 47.

might be right in insisting that centralization was 'not English'; but government again and again was faced with the alternatives of acting or seeing nothing done, and again and again it acted: in limiting hours of employment, especially for women and children, from the first effective Factory Act of 1833; in the Poor Law reform of 1834; in vaccination against smallpox, provided by the state in 1840, and in 1853 made compulsory on parents for all children within three months of birth – 'the first continuous public health activity provided by the state',[1] as it has been called. Peel remarked in 1846 that he was doubtful if there were even ten Members in the House who believed that the pure principles of non-interference must regulate the health, education and morality of the people.[2] *The Times*, shortly after, observed that Parliament 'is laying aside the policeman, the gaoler and the executioner, in exchange for the more kindly and dignified functions of the father, the schoolmaster and the friend'.[3] The mere hypothesis of *laissez-faire* was fading into history: T. H. Huxley, years later, was to dismiss Hume's essay on the 'Origin of Government' as 'the police theory of government' in its crudest form, based on the groundless assumption that 'it is wrong for society, as a corporate body, to do anything for the improvement of its members'.[4] If anyone had ever believed that, they had no business to believe it now.

Public libraries in the 1850s, the bitterly controversial Contagious Diseases Act of 1864, later repealed, against prostitutes, and the compulsory schooling provided for in the Education Act of 1870 – all these are evidences of the readiness of Victorian parliaments to encourage welfare and to limit individual liberties in what might be represented as matters of humane or national concern. By the 1850s Britain had begun to resemble a modern administrative state by an accumulation of legislation and by the silent encroachment of bureaucratic power in spheres

1. R. J. Lambert, 'A Victorian national health service: state vaccination 1855–1871', *Historical Journal* v (1962).
2. *Hansard* 3rd series lxxxvi col. 1,062.
3. *The Times* (4 May 1847); quoted by William C. Lubenow, *The Politics of Government Growth: early Victorian attitudes towards state intervention* (Newton Abbot, 1971) p. 15.
4. T. H. Huxley, *Hume* (London, 1879) (English Men of Letters) pp. 14–15.

like education and sanitation. The process was piecemeal and far from deliberate: 'Very few in the two decades after 1833 embraced wholeheartedly a centralized, paternalistic state, one that would regulate labour, clean towns, educate the poor, control the Church, commute tithes, supervise asylums, and manage lighthouses. And yet from 1833 to 1854 Parliament created such a state.'[1]

The historian concludes that the explanation lies in a contemporary principle of 'presumptuous empiricism', or meeting every social problem on its merits. That may be so: but empiricism in these terms is fully within the stated terms of the ideology of the age. It is there in the works of Mill and his predecessors as well as in the legislation that Parliament enacted: those writings had already justified state education and public health on grounds other than paternalism or centralization. Few ages, indeed, demonstrate so intimate a correspondence between word and deed.

Much of the increasing administrative machinery of the state, it is true, derives as much from the increasing scale of national activity as from totally new functions of government. Radical hatred of some of the traditional activities of state was perfectly real, and Dickens illustrates it memorably. The armed services, the Court and the colonies were seen by such men as paradises for aristocratic placemen. By such ingenious devices, many a Radical felt, does a decaying patriciate shrewdly contrive to maintain its nephews and younger sons at the taxpayer's expense. The Circumlocution Office in *Little Dorrit* exists to give employment to Barnacles, who know no art but the art of how to stick; and the radical answer is not to reform it but to abolish it. But whether much of this is based on an intimate knowledge of the workings of Whitehall may be doubted, and Dickens is as capable of demanding state action as anyone on a specific grievance like the protection of authors' rights. He was part of a process which he at times reviled, at times condoned, at times demanded. And around him, in encircling waves, the flood of governmental activity was rising higher

1. David Roberts, *Victorian Origins of the British Welfare State* (New Haven, 1960) p. 100; see also J. Bartlett Brebner, '*Laissez-faire* and state intervention in nineteenth-century Britain', *Journal of Economic History* (supplement) viii (1948).

and higher. The very dynamism of the Victorian economy, private though it essentially was, required increasing activity on the part of the state to regulate and complement it. As Bagehot remarked in 1836,

> The freedom of growth allows the possibility of growth; and though liberal governments take so much less in proportion upon them, yet the scale of operations is so much enlarged by the continual exercise of civil liberty, that the real work is ultimately perhaps as immense. While a despotic government is regulating ten per cent of ten men's actions, a free government has to regulate one per cent of a hundred men's actions.[1]

But the myth of *laissez-faire* went on. Mill believed there were Englishmen who advocated it, and he may have been right, though he does not say who they were. Clough wanted to make himself 'the Apostle of Anti-*laissez-faire*', and thought it important to contest the doctrine of 'the devil take the hindmost'.[2] T. H. Huxley, in a notable article called 'Administrative nihilism' in the *Fortnightly Review* (1 October 1871), speaks of the principled objectors to Forster's Education Act of 1870 as 'a minority, not inconsiderable in numbers, nor deficient in supporters of weight and authority' – and some of this opposition, he claims, comes from those who believe in the 'assumed axiom' that the state should only 'protect its subjects from aggression'. But it is still not clear who, among the notable spokesmen of the age, these victims of an axiom were. The evidence is almost all on one side, and the battle seems forever to be fought against an invisible adversary. Herbert Spencer denied as an intolerable accusation, and with great heat, the charge of being a believer: 'Not only do I contend that the restraining power of the state over individuals, and bodies or classes of individuals, is requisite, but I have contended that it should be exercised much more effectually, and carried out much further, than at present,' and he refers his readers to the chapter on 'The duty of the state' in his *Social*

1. W. Bagehot, 'The character of Sir Robert Peel', *National Review* (July 1856); reprinted in his *Collected Works* (1968) iii. 254.

2. A. H. Clough, *Correspondence*, edited by F. L. Mulhauser (Oxford, 1957) i. 130; Clough uses the last phrase as a refrain to his poem 'In the Great Metropolis'.

Statics (1851). A dozen years later, his indignation undiminished, he wrote *The Man versus the State* (1884) in an impatient mood to clear his name and to define the proper role of government: 'Nowadays,' he wrote, 'the worst punishment to be looked for by one who questions its omnipotence, is that he will be reviled as a reactionary who talks *laissez-faire*. That any facts he may bring forward will appreciably decrease the established faith is not to be expected.'[1] The modern historian of ideas may feel inclined to echo that note of asperity. No matter how often the absence of *laissez-faire* is noted, both in word and in action, in the Victorian age, the label obstinately continues to stick. A. V. Dicey, in his *Law & Public Opinion* (1905) endorsed the view that it had once been a characteristic mid-Victorian doctrine, and the weight of his authority has given long life to the myth; though he has a possible excuse in his brother Edward, who twenty years before had written an article bemoaning the fact that the Liberal Party, which he could no longer support, had abandoned the doctrine in Ireland, in education and in the housing of the poor.[2] Dicey made the view respectable, and it is an almost universal assumption of early twentieth-century political debate that the Victorians had believed in *laissez-faire* and that subsequent generations had abandoned it. Maynard Keynes wrote a monograph in 1926 entitled *The End of Laissez-faire* which took the myth for granted, though perhaps he meant to imply no more by his title than that the functions of the state in western democracies had recently grown and would continue to grow. Scepticism was rare, and the entrenched prejudices of anti-Victorianism have so far proved much too strong for the stony-faced image of nineteenth-century liberalism.

A few have tried to dispose of the myth. Alfred Marshall, in an appendix to his *Industry and Trade* (1919) on 'The

1. H. Spencer, *The Man versus the State*, edited by Donald Macrae (Penguin Books, 1969) pp. 288, 125. These plain assertions have not saved Spencer from being hailed on the cover of this new Pelican edition as 'an uncompromising apostle of *laissez-faire*'.

2. Edward Dicey, 'The plea of a malcontent Liberal', *Fortnightly Review* (1 October 1885): '*Laissez-faire* was our motto, and to that motto I for one adhere still.' There is no evidence, however, that the term was ever a motto of any British party.

English mercantilists and Adam Smith', noted the rejection of *laissez-faire* by the classical economists, but the point went largely unheeded between the world wars. Lord Robbins demonstrated it with full and conclusive documentation in his *Theory of Economic Policy in English Classical Political Economy* (1952); but as if to demonstrate how deep was the prejudice against which he argued, a biography of the previous year had already called Frederic Harrison's *Order and Progress* (1875) 'the one political treatise of the period (other than the works of the English pre-Marxists) which challenges *laissez-faire* economics and argues that the duty of the state is to promote a moral society even if this leads to state interference'.[1] This represents the illusion in all its tenacity. In fact *laissez-faire* economics, one can only insist again, had no status in the Victorian age: no economist or political theorist of stature in England advocated it, no party or group espoused it as a general view, and the duty of the state to promote a moral society is part of the common change of Victorian political debate. The allusion to Marxism is the more puzzling when one reflects that Marx believed in an eventual withering away of the state, a form of let-alone utopianism no liberal in the period can be shown to have considered a serious possibility. Liberals always accepted a role for government in the national economy. They debated not whether it should exist, but what it should be.

How has the myth survived? Partly, it can now be said, through sheer misinformation based on misleading contemporary sources. Some of these, like Carlyle's assertions in *Chartism*, are manifestly unsupported by evidence, and the impertinence of publishing an essay accusing government of 'self-cancelling Donothingism and *Laissez-faire*' six years after the Factory Act of 1833 and five after the new Poor Law was justly remarked at the time. Arnold's allegation in *Culture and Anarchy* (1869) that *The Times* greeted depression and destitution in the East End of London with the heartless comment: 'There is no one to blame for this; it is the result of Nature's simplest laws' (VI. iv) has never been substantiated; either the quotation remains to be found, or Arnold invented it. If the

1. Noel Annan, *Leslie Stephen* (London, 1951) p. 204n.

case for Victorian *laissez-faire* depends on the witness of Carlyle and Arnold, then it is plainly a bad case.

But honest misapprehension has done as much damage as misinformation. It has not always been understood that the works of the classical economists are technical treatises based on assumptions which, though explicit, are not repeated at every point of the argument. These are in their essence hypothetical works; they propose 'models' based on a sophisticated set of qualifications. If certain conditions apply then, on certain assumptions, certain economic consequences will follow. 'Political economy', as Nassau Senior once remarked aphoristically, 'is not greedy for facts: it is independent of facts.' Market forces, for example, work better than state planning within given limits. Many assertions about freedom of bargaining, it has not always been sufficiently emphasized, explicitly apply only to able-bodied male adults, and to limit or forbid the employment of women or children does not infringe any known principle of the school. Even some Victorians sometimes failed to understand the logical status of political economy, and imagined that 'Manchesterism' was somehow hostile to state supervision and welfare. And certainly it was not unknown for those hostile to specific proposals to claim that political economy was on their side. Charles Wood, for example, later Lord Halifax, speaking in the Commons in 1844 against the Ten Hours Bill, objected that whereas the Factory Act of 1833 had been based on the just principle of 'protecting those who could not protect themselves', the logic of that argument was to limit the hours of work of children absolutely, and not just in certain conditions. But male adults could only be injured by a statutory limit on hours of work: 'He for one objected to the course of the Government altogether; he adhered to the principle of Adam Smith, believing it to be most unjust and most injurious to the workman to interfere with his discretion as to the management of his own labour', and he was 'not of opinion that legislation ought to do for him what, if he liked, he could do for himself'.[1] Qualified as it is, Wood's argument might indeed have been acceptable to Adam Smith; but it is not an

1. *Hansard* 3rd series lxxiv col. 680f. (3 May 1844).

argument against factory legislation in general, and its force depends plainly on an interpretation of a matter of fact. Is the able-bodied male operative willing and able to protect his own interests in limiting hours of work, or is he not? The House decided against Wood, who was voted down. It has never been shown that the principles of Adam Smith required them to behave otherwise.

But that truth was to be lost sight of before the reign was ended, and the conscientious abstraction of Manchesterian argument was to be turned against it as a complaint or an accusation. The very strength of the school came to be seen as a weakness. Did the world of the economists really exist? That may be to miss the point, but it is to find another that many were to swallow as persuasive. Toynbee found Ricardo culpably remote from the real concerns of men:

> His powerful mind, concentrated upon the argument, never stopped to consider the world which the argument implied – that world of gold-seeking animals, stripped of every human affection, for ever digging, spinning, watching with keen undeceived eyes each other's movements, passing incessantly and easily from place to place in search of gain, all alert, crafty, mobile – that world less real than the island of Lilliput, which never has had and never can have any existence. A logical artifice became the accepted picture of the real world,[1]

and he assured his late Victorian audience of Oxford undergraduates that the common error of the previous generation had been 'to confuse the abstract science of Economics with the real science of human life' (p. 11).

This is all misunderstanding. Ricardo and his successors never supposed that any given society could, as a matter of fact, be composed of able-bodied male adults who behaved like 'gold-seeking animals'; his *Principles* (1817) are cast in a conditional and hypothetical mould, and most of the argument takes the form 'If this, then this follows'. The accusation of frigidity is equally ill-founded. An economist is under no special requirement to possess deep human sympathies, but Ricardo's letters make it clear that he did, and Maria Edgeworth, who knew him well, speaks warmly of his 'continual life of mind' in

1. Arnold Toynbee, *Lectures on the Industrial Revolution in England* (London, 1884) p. 7.

conversation: 'I never argued or discussed a question with any person who argues more fairly or less for victory and more for truth.'[1] Mill was a dedicated exponent of the sovereign place of the affective in human life, though his *Autobiography* rather than his *Principles of Political Economy*, naturally enough, is the better authority for this aspect of his mind. Economics is a dry subject, at least to those who are not economists; but to turn this necessary circumstance into a charge against the character of the men who invented it is to commit a manifest injustice against their humanity.

The matter may be defended on more general grounds. It is no objection to a hypothesis to show that reality does not wholly conform to its premisses. The economist is entitled to argue that certain consequences follow from certain policies to the extent that certain assumptions are justified. 'Though many of its conclusions are only locally true,' as Mill once wrote, 'its method of investigation is applicable universally.'[2] Much of this method is peculiar to itself. For some reason, the status of such arguments began to be misunderstood in the 1870s and 1880s, when it became fashionable to attribute a blind excess of abstraction to the pioneers of the new science. Alfred Milner, in his memoir *Arnold Toynbee: a reminiscence* (1895), remarked that when he went up to Oxford as a freshman in 1872, 'the *laissez-faire* theory still held the field. All the authorities were "orthodox" economists of the old school. But within ten years the few men who still held the old doctrine in their extreme rigidity had come to be regarded as curiosities' (p. 49). This may reflect, though hardly in accurate terms, a real change in emphasis in academic economics in the 1870s, when the conjunction of 'orthodox' with '*laissez-faire*' became a familiar element in political argument. But it remains misleading in a highly representative way. No evidence is produced that such an orthodoxy ever existed in British economics: no names, no texts, no witnesses.

The defenders of political economy, what is more, were on firm ground when they complained that the explicit limits of

1. David Ricardo, *Works and Correspondence*, edited by Piero Sraffa (Cambridge, 1951–57) x. 168–9, from a letter of 9 November 1821.
2. J. S. Mill, *Monthly Repository* (May 1834).

their inquiry were not always appreciated by their critics. *Hard Times*, when it appeared in 1853, excited some understandable professional resentment. William Ballantyne Hodgson (1815–80), later professor of political economy at Edinburgh, lecturing to the Royal Institution in June 1854 on 'The importance of the study of economic science as a branch of education for all classes', regretted Dickens's attempt to discredit the new science, and denounced him as an ignoramus in economics, especially instancing the passage in the novel (II. i) where Bitzer has his mother shut up in the workhouse on half a pound of tea a year:

> Here Economic Science, which so strongly enforces parental duty, is given out as discouraging its moral if not economic correlative – filial duty. But where do economists represent this maxim as the whole duty of man? Their business is to treat of man in his industrial capacity and relations; they do not presume to deal with his other capacities and relations, except by showing what must be done in their sphere to enable any duties whatever to be discharged.[1]

Economists do not presume to know anything about man other than in his economic role. And were they to do so, one might add, they would presume indeed. Much of the force of the complaint against nineteenth-century political economy is annulled if the science is considered within its proper limits.

There is no doubt, however, that the classical economists claimed to have discovered 'laws' which, their reservations being duly considered, were universally true. This claim has often been derided by their successors; but it is doubtful whether, as a claim of economic science, it is inherently absurd. This is not the place to debate whether the specific laws of classical economy were true or false: all that is in question here is to suggest that they are properly susceptible to judgements of this sort. If their arguments in favour of free trade, for instance, within and between nations and in certain stated circumstances, were true, then the claim to have discovered law was not absurd. It is not implausible to suggest that some

1. *Lectures on Education Delivered at the Royal Institution* (London, 1855) pp. 300–1. See Robin Gilmour, 'The Gradgrind school: political economy in the classroom', *Victorian Studies* xi (1967).

economic realities are what they are independently of whether they are seen to be so or not, willed to be so or not. Macaulay remarked contemptuously to a friend in 1848 that the revolutionaries in Paris were 'refuting the doctrines of political economy in a way a man would refute the doctrine of gravitation by jumping off the Monument'.[1] Such arguments as Macaulay's readily excite hostility, and it is easy to allege that those who use them are disingenuous conservatives offering pseudo-scientific justifications for the *status quo*. That is undoubtedly the dark suspicion that underlies the growing dislike of political economy in the works of late Victorian critics like Toynbee and Dicey. But, justified as their criticisms sometimes are in individual instances, they do not dispose of the view that economic realities are what they are. It was the object of the classical economists to describe those realities; and modern economics, while overturning some of their results and qualifying others, have not demonstrated the undertaking itself to have been an absurdity.

There can be no doubt, in any case, that a conservative interpretation of classical economics is a perversion. The economists themselves saw their proposals as a means not only of increasing the wealth of a whole society but of lessening the differences of wealth between individuals as well. The imminent prospect of democracy, in any case, made the cause of general improvement prudent as well as enlightened; but Adam Smith and his successors defend it on grounds of simple justice. Since workmen are always in a majority, Smith argues in *The Wealth of Nations*:

> what improves the circumstances of the greater part can never be regarded as an inconveniency to the whole. No society can surely be flourishing and happy of which the far greater part of the members are poor and miserable. It is but equity, besides, that they who feed, cloath and lodge the whole body of the people should have such a share of the produce of their own labour as to be themselves tolerably well fed, cloathed and lodged (I. viii).

The prosperity of the workers is no mere practical consideration: it is a matter of equity too. Ricardo develops the theme

1. G. O. Trevelyan, *The Life and Letters of Macaulay* (1876) ii. 193.

forty years later in his *Principles*: 'The friends of humanity cannot but wish that in all countries the labouring classes should have a taste for comforts and enjoyments, and that they should be stimulated by all legal means in their exertions to procure them',[1] adding that the consideration is not only humane, but may also help to prevent overpopulation. Shortly afterwards McCulloch, in his *Principles of Political Economy* (1825), argued in favour of high wages on social and human grounds as well as economic:

> The example of such individuals, or bodies of individuals, as submit quietly to have their wages reduced, and who are content if they get only the mere necessaries of life, ought never to be held up for public imitation. On the contrary, every thing should be done to make such apathy esteemed disgraceful. The best interests of society require that the rate of wages should be elevated as high as possible,

and he goes on to advocate a popular taste for comfort, enjoyment and even luxury. These positions were altogether a familiar aspect of political economy before the reign of Victoria began. It may have been a dry science, but it was not a gloomy one. Years later, Acton saw the long-term political effects of Adam Smith's insistence on freedom of contract in the most radical light:

> We are forced, in equity, to share the government with the working class by considerations which were made supreme by the awakening of political economy. Adam Smith set up two propositions – that contracts ought to be free between capital and labour, and that labour is the source, he sometimes says the only source, of wealth. If the last sentence, in its exclusive form, was true, it was difficult to resist the conclusion that the class on which national prosperity depends ought to control the wealth it supplies, that is, ought to govern instead of the useless unproductive class, and that the class which earns the increment ought to enjoy it.

Abroad, Acton goes on, Adam Smith's doctrine has found its effects in the French Revolution and in socialism, creeds equally

1. Ricardo, *Works and Correspondence* (1951–57) i. 100, from ch. 5 of the *Principles*. See Lionel Robbins, *The Theory of Economic Policy in English Classical Political Economy* (London, 1952), lecture III, 'The condition of the people.'

alien to Englishmen. But the logic of political economy is plainly democratic:

> If there is a free contract, in open market, between capital and labour, it cannot be right that one of the two contracting parties should have the making of the laws. . . . Before this argument, the ancient dogma that power attends on property broke down. Justice required that property should – not abdicate, but – share its political supremacy.[1]

This letter to a prime minister's daughter was written fourteen years after the second Reform Act of 1867 had shared political supremacy, and Acton is concerned to demonstrate a causal relation. The suffrage is in justice a natural consequence of *The Wealth of Nations.* So no doubt it was, given the high-minded premiss that statesmen who can see the justice of a cause will act accordingly. But some of the premisses of the argument are practical as well as highminded. Even the most ignorant, it was possible to believe, would eventually come to see the force of economic argument. Since popular education is improving, and plainly bent on improving further, the assumption is a natural one. Men may try to defeat the facts of economics by devices like trade unions, which force up the cost of labour by strikes and the threat of strikes; and given that employers cannot in practice be prevented from uniting, more and more voices were in favour of making 'combinations' legal. They may even be useful, as Francis Jeffrey argued in an anonymous review of McCulloch's *Principles* in 1825, 'upon any variation of circumstance, to bring things sooner to their proper level – like shakes given to a clogged engine, or the jerks of a machine not working sweetly', though they can never, Jeffrey adds, affect 'the grand result', or at least not for the better. But then in the end the intelligent workman will see the force of such arguments: he will read books like McCulloch's, Jeffrey concludes, and come to understand enough political economy not to kill his golden goose.[2]

1. Lord Acton, *Letters to Mary Gladstone* (London, 1904) pp. 91–2, from a letter of 24 April 1881.

2. *Edinburgh Review* xliii (1825). The article is attributed to Jeffrey in *The Wellesley Index to Victorian Periodicals,* edited by W. E. Houghton (Toronto, 1966) no. 1120.

What, then, was the Victorian political consensus concerning the role and function of the state? The myth of *laissez-faire* can be exploded, but its disappearance leaves behind a host of problems and unanswered questions in the modern mind. These questions, however, unlike the remote speculations of the French eighteenth-century economists, are genuinely the stuff of ideological debate in the age. How far is the individual autonomous, and how far a subject to social forces? What is the proper activity of government in a parliamentary and industrial state? Much of the political literature of the age exists to answer questions such as these; and with Donothingism dismissed as mere hostile rhetoric in a literature of protest, it may at last be possible to consider the positive aspects of the Victorian case.

Mill once told George Grote that he was considering an essay on what society could and should forbid to the individual, and what not. In the event he never wrote that essay, though there is a sense in which his life work is about nothing less, with the essay *On Liberty* its centrepiece. His solution there is based upon the principle of self-protection, 'the sole end for which mankind are warranted, individually or collectively, in interfering with the liberty of action of any of their number'; and the ensuing essay refines and qualifies a principle that bristles with abstract difficulties. Here, at the heart of the English ideology, the careful distinctions between the immoral and the criminal, the nature of free discussion, and the large exceptions in favour of children and backward nations, are meticulously elucidated. These exceptions to individual freedom in Mill's argument are of massive extent: it is not usually noticed that they embrace a large majority of the human race, and arguably a majority of the population of the United Kingdom as it was in 1859. What is more, every member of Mill's perfect society would be subject to limitations upon his personal freedom justly inflicted upon them by government in the interest of maintaining the freedoms of others. That this is, in its broader outline, a widely accepted summary of liberal opinion seems certain. It is exceptional in the degree of abstraction, but not in its conclusions.

Macaulay had argued in similar terms in his speech to the

House of Commons on the Ten Hours Bill in May 1846: 'Where health is concerned, and where morality is concerned, the state is justified in interfering with the contracts of individuals'; and he had no difficulty in demonstrating to the House that Parliament had already so interfered, both in health legislation and in the suppression of pornography; and that, in supporting the further limitation of hours of work in factories, Parliament would have the shade of Adam Smith on its side. In the third chapter of his *History of England*, composed at the same period of his life, Macaulay favourably compared his own age with the state of England in 1685 on the grounds that it had, as the first age in the history of mankind, banned the employment of small children:

> The practice of setting children prematurely to work, a practice which the state, the legitimate protector of those who cannot protect themselves, has, in our time, wisely and humanely interdicted, prevailed in the seventeenth century to an extent which, when compared with the extent of the manufacturing system, seems almost incredible,

and he instances the employment of six-year-olds in the Norwich clothing trade two hundred years before. The industrial revolution, far from creating child-labour, was abolishing it for the first time in human history:

> The more carefully we examine the history of the past, the more reason shall we find to dissent from those who imagine that our age has been fruitful of new social evils. The truth is that the evils are, with scarcely an exception, old. That which is new is the intelligence which discerns and the humanity which remedies them.[1]

This is Whig pride in the achievements of Parliament in regulating an economy. It was no contradiction to have emphasized, at the beginning of the same chapter, that human progress is essentially the work of individuals, that misgovernment rather than social improvement has been the natural and ordinary function of the state through history. Most ages of men have not been governed by a Parliament like Westminster

1. Macaulay, *The History of England* (1849–61) i. 417.

in the 1830s and 1840s. In history as a whole, progress is the work of individuals rather than of institutions: 'No ordinary misfortune, no ordinary misgovernment, will do so much to make a nation wretched, as the constant progress of physical knowledge and the constant effort of every man to better himself will do to make a nation prosperous.' The state is a physician: it prescribes remedies and fits artificial limbs when society is sickly or maimed. But no artificial limb is as good as a leg. The function of the state is to create the conditions in which individual advancement can occur. Both extremes are odious, whether the paternal or the inactive, whether 'a prying, meddlesome government', as he told the Commons in May 1846, or 'a careless, lounging government'. But there is a just mean between them, and it is the business of Parliament to find it.

What is uniformly foreign to all these views is the notion that state action as such, or individual action as such, is intrinsically good. The issue was hardly argued in these terms, as between parties, before the present century. The individual is creative, the state regulative: this is the common Victorian antithesis, but the two parts of that antithesis are widely recognized as complementary. A good society needs both. The collective functions of the nation may multiply, as the young Winston Churchill told a Glasgow audience in October 1906, but many human activities must forever remain individual: 'We do not make love collectively.'[1] Legislation will grow, and it is no disgrace that it should; in an advancing society, indeed, it is a mark of progress. Cornewall Lewis, in his *Remarks on the Use and Abuse of Some Political Terms* (1832), disapprovingly quotes Tacitus's remark that 'the most degenerate states have most laws'. On the contrary, 'the progress of civilization is to multiply enactments in order to suit the extended relations and the more refined and diversified forms of property introduced by the improvement of society' (ch. 15). Men were aware of the advancing role of government; and many saw it, if wisely delimited, as a mark of sophistication. A rising population and a rising complexity of culture bring more and more spheres of conduct within the regulation of the state. 'The higher the

1. Winston S. Churchill, 'Liberalism and Socialism', in his *Liberalism and the Social Problem* (London, 1909) p. 80.

state of civilization,' wrote T. H. Huxley in his article 'Administrative nihilism', 'the more completely do the actions of one member of the social body influence all the rest'.

But not all of this regulation is statist; some is by private agreement. Henry Maine perceived a tendency from status defined by law towards contracts freely made between individuals: 'The movement of the progressive societies', he wrote in his *Ancient Law* (1861), 'has hitherto been a movement from status to contract' (p. 170). It is not only governments that make rules, and not all of the growing regulation of life is legislative. Since rules can make as well as unmake liberty, much of it is acceptable, even welcome. But the state is only one agent among many in the regulative process, if the largest. Men are learning to exchange liberties one with another, to exist peaceably in association, combinations and unions, to make and observe contracts only ultimately sanctioned by the state, and to discipline themselves in the observance of the moral law.

It is this last reflection that gave rise to the gravest puzzles and the most agonizing debates. Are men morally free, or are they mere victims of social forces? Are mind and opinion free, or do men believe what they do only because they have been trained to believe it? Only extremists doubted that the truth must be an intermediate one, somewhere between the inconceivable extremes of man in total autonomy and man as a mere puppet. The cosmic evolutionary process may be irresistible and irreversible, as Tennyson concluded in *In Memoriam*, but it still allows for freedom of intellectual action with the tiny span of a human life. Necessitarian views are not really common in the age; even Hardy, in his novels, did not doubt that men make choices, even if those choices are limited by a tragic fate; and James Thomson, when he wrote in *The City of Dreadful Night* (1880) that he could find

> no hint throughout the Universe
> Of good or ill, of blessings or of curse;
> I find alone Necessity Supreme,

was speaking of the vast and universal process within which

human lives are led, not of the minute choices that each life allows. The fiction of the age makes little sense unless the reader supposes he is watching men and women make decisions which could be otherwise and exercise the sweet or bitter privileges of free will. But the world still looked formidably superincumbent. Compared with a past that seemed leisurely and secluded, the present was all unreflecting bustle. Trollope's characters, as R. H. Hutton remarked in 1882, are 'always more or less under pressure', and 'everywhere time is short'. In Jane Austen's world, three generations ago, 'everybody is what he is by the natural force of his own nature and tastes. You hardly see the crush of the world on any one.' But in Trollope 'the atmosphere of affairs is permanent. The Church or the world, or the flesh or the devil, seems always at work to keep men going, and prevent them from being themselves alone', so that his characters are themselves only 'so far as the circumstances of the day will allow them to be themselves'.[1] This echoes some of George Eliot's ruminations about degrees of moral responsibility in an age of unprecedented hurry and confusion about ultimate ends. On the last page of *Middlemarch* she defends the behaviour of her heroine in a carefully weighed assessment: some of Dorothea's actions had been 'the mixed result of young and noble impulse struggling amidst the conditions of an imperfect social state'. But then 'there is no creature whose inward being is so strong that it is not greatly determined by what lies outside it'. That antithesis, as Mill had already seen, if pressed too hard, poses the problem in an unanswerable form, since it might then assume an unreal antithesis between an individual like Dorothea and a society like Coventry in 1831. An individual, after all, is himself a social force, as Mill proclaimed in *A System of Logic*; and force of circumstance cannot artificially exclude his moral convictions. Between the polar errors of anarchism and necessitarianism, here is the true and middle way. The character of an individual is influenced by circumstance, indeed, but 'his own desire to mould it in a particular way is one of those circumstances.

1. R. H. Hutton, 'From Jane Austen to Mr Trollope', *Spectator* (16 December 1882); partly reprinted in *Anthony Trollope: the critical heritage*, edited by Donald Smalley (London, 1969) p. 510.

... We are exactly as capable of making our own character, *if we will*, as others are of making it for us' (VI. ii. 3).

In all this Mill claims to be engaged in an imaginary dispute with an Owenite socialist, and in the coming half century the question was to prove a major philosophical issue between liberalism and socialism. Socialists tended to see the individual as the merest product of social forces; liberals insisted that the relation was continuously mutual, and that individuals, while moulded by society, could mould society too. Robert Owen had been absolute on the question – an important witness here, since his writings show that the socialist denial of man's freedom to choose is easily pre-Marxian. All human errors, Owen held, proceed from the mistaken assumption that men 'form their own individual characters, and possess merit or demerit for the peculiar notions impressed on the mind during its early growth'.[1] But a man's character, in Owen's view, is always made for him; it is never made by himself. Moral determinism such as this, with its strong implications of conservative acquiescence, repelled liberal opinion. An individual, as Mill often insists, is himself a social force, and if he is passive it is by choice, not necessity. 'One person with a belief', he wrote in *Representative Government* (1861), 'is a social power equal to ninety-nine who have only interests' (ch. 1). A man may choose to see himself as a victim of social forces; he may acquiesce in class-politics and the degradation of a parliamentary system into a mere clash of opposing economic interests. But if he so chooses, let no man deceive himself that it is anything other than a choice. It is simply untrue to assert that politics can only be about a conflict of interests. Men often, and knowingly, vote and speak against their own interests. And when they do, so Mill argues, they often have more influence upon the course of history than do the millions who merely acquiesce in what they suppose to be a law of Fate.

No man is under any necessity to be a necessitarian. Smiles echoes that argument in numerous passages where he demonstrates that he has understood the statist, even the totalitarian implications of Owenism. Character, as he often insists, is

1. Robert Owen, *A New View of Society* (4th edition, London, 1818) p. 106, from the third essay.

formed by the individual, not for him. If the state were indeed to base itself on Owen's principle that individual character is always and only the product of social circumstance, then it could fully justify a programme of destroying the will of the individual to act, to protest and to oppose. Any repressive policy, including a governmental monopoly of expression, could be justified on the easy grounds that no individual opinion, in the nature of things, can ever be more than the result of circumstance. And that is the self-justifying logic of the criminal as well as of the dictator. Dickens's Rigaud, the murderer and blackmailer in *Little Dorrit*, is a man, so he claims, whom society has 'deeply wronged':

> 'You know that I am sensitive and brave, and that it is my character to govern. How has society respected those qualities in me? I have been shrieked at through the streets . . . Such are the humiliations that society has inflicted upon me, possessing the qualities I have mentioned, and which you know me to possess. But society shall pay for it' (ch. 11).

But society is not in a final sense responsible at all, as Rigaud's creator knew, and the claim that it is always to blame seemed to Dickens no more than shallow self-excusing. Some men, like Mr Dorrit, sink through weakness under the unjust weight that authority and the law lay upon them. But all that is moral weakness; and to show that it is so, Dickens gives the prisoner of the Marshalsea a daughter: 'The prison, which could spoil so many things, had tainted little Dorrit's mind no more than this. . . . It was the first speck Clennam had ever seen, it was the last speck Clennam ever saw, of the prison atmosphere upon her' (ch. 35).

A moral independence of environment asks to be seen, in this system, as the ultimate mark of virtue. Men show their worth largely in relation to others; but, in the end, virtue is a property of the individual alone. And that is the fundamental case against the paternalist state: that it misconceives the nature of morality itself. Only the individual can achieve virtue; only the individual can be good or evil. Paternalism does not offend because it violates the principle of *laissez-faire*: it offends because it misconceives the moral law itself. Morality, as T. H. Green insisted, lies in 'the disinterested performance of self-imposed duties' by responsible adults; and paternalism negates morality 'by narrowing the room for the self-imposition of duties and for the play of disinterested motives'.[1] Government may help to create the conditions under which morality flourishes; but will and impulse – the sheer energy of goodness – belong to the individual mind alone. 'Men cannot be made good by the state', Acton once wrote, 'but they can easily be made bad. Morality depends on liberty.' Man achieves the possibility of virtue in the course of achieving higher and higher degrees of independence from circumstance. Good men and great men, Acton held, by the very force of those terms, are 'aloof from the action of surroundings'. This is a relative, not an absolute matter, since in history 'goodness generally appeared in unison with authority, sustained by environment, and rarely manifested the force and sufficiency of the isolated will and conscience'. But then in practice all such matters are relative, since we achieve only degrees of liberty, never liberty absolutely. Since Christ, at least, 'time and place do not excuse'.[2] No free man can plead circumstance to exculpate himself: he is, and he remains, responsible for what he does as a man. He may still complain, and often justly, that law and society make virtue harder than they need to be – to arrive at virtue, as the young Mill remarked, rejecting the doctrine of the do-nothing state, men need 'help as well as forbearance' from authority, since 'Nature is to the greater number a severer taskmaster even than man is to man'.[3] The ideal state would strive to alleviate the force of circumstance, and men should judge its policies as they help or hinder the individual to discover his own liberty for himself.

1. Green, *Principles of Political Obligation*, in his *Works*, edited by R. L. Nettleship (London, 1886) p. 346.

2. Lord Acton, Cambridge University Library Additional MS 4,939; *Historical Essays & Studies* (1907) p. 506.

3. J. S. Mill, 'The right and wrong of state interference with corporation and Church property', *Jurist* (February 1833); reprinted in his *Dissertations and Discussions* (1859) i. 27.

[6]

The Terms of Party Politics

The terms of Victorian party politics remain in the most formal sense an unexplored subject – unexplored not only by modern scholars but by the Victorians themselves, who were usually content to leave political terms to explain themselves by use and context. The only exception amounts to little: George Cornewall Lewis's *The Use and Abuse of Political Terms* (1832), which appeared when the future Chancellor of the Exchequer was a twenty-year-old logician at Christ Church, Oxford, and before he had entered the House of Commons. It deals with such terms as 'government', 'monarchy', 'democracy' and 'freedom' rather than with the names of political parties, and its logic is exacting, even captious. Mill, in a judicious review of the book in *Tait's Magazine* (1832), sensibly urged against it that 'a certain laxity in the use of language must be borne with, if a writer makes himself understood'. This reminder helps to explain the paucity of Victorian analysis of political terms, even to justify it. Definition can only be ancillary: what matters is how men use words in complex and shifting situations. Bagehot, in his obituary of Lewis in 1863, remembered the book without affection. 'You cannot calm the passions of men by defining their words', he objected, abandoning the work to the status of an eternal oddity: 'A little bit of just though almost pedantic thought cropped suddenly up in our crude and hasty English life.'[1]

Party, in any case, was a more than faintly discreditable concept for much of the age, and a touch of taboo restrained Englishmen from any lingering attention to those shifting

1. Bagehot, 'Sir George Cornewall Lewis', *National Review* (October 1863); reprinted in his *Collected Works* (1968) iii. 392–3.

alliances that smacked too often, in their view, of faction or cabal. Of parliamentary institutions they were proud: for the parties that had dominated both Houses of Parliament since 1689 they often felt a more provisional loyalty. Parties were hardly matters, in any case, for analytical curiosity. The Victorians enjoyed an abundance of political journalism, but they had little taste for psephology or for the professional analysis of party machines; perhaps the most notable exception is Charles R. Dod's *Electoral Facts from 1832 to 1852* (1852), an alphabetical reference book for parliamentary elections over twenty years, the candidates being distinguished by their party labels and their predominating interests. Dod provided bare facts; but the first full-scale analysis of the British party system was written no earlier than the 1890s, by Moses Ostrogorsky (1854–1921), a Russian Jew settled in Paris and writing in French: his *Democracy and the Organisation of Political Parties*, which appeared in English in 1902, held the field without rivals for half a century as an academic analysis. The Victorian statesman neither wrote such books nor read them. To the extent that they reveal the inner workings of the party system, he might have felt them careless of trade secrets; to the extent that they are severely analytic, he would have found them distastefully dry. The atmosphere of British party controversy in that century was too colourful for such treatment and, on the whole, too goodnatured: it has never been summed up better than by Trollope's phrase in *Phineas Finn* (1869) about the 'goodhumoured, affectionate, prize-fighting ferocity' of politics (ch. 9); though that phrase fails to notice that some adversaries, including Gladstone and Disraeli, genuinely and cordially disliked each other. Men abused each other who would not hurt a hair of the head. 'There is nothing like it in any other country – nothing as yet', Trollope adds. When a Victorian speaks and writes of his political system, it is this unique atmosphere that understandably fascinates him, and rarely questions of mere terminology.

But the party system was growing firmer, and it would soon claim attention for its own sake. The period between the first two Reform Acts shows the system still loose, by twentieth-century standards, the enormous power of the Whips still largely in the future. But manifestoes, first from individuals and then from parties, were beginning to grow fashionable. The publication of election addresses became commoner after Peel's Tamworth Manifesto of 1835, but party programmes were hardly the usage before the Newcastle Programme of 1891, which became the stated policy of the Liberal Party in the general election of 1892. Party allegiance, in any case, was general, and without it no prospect of office existed. No House of Commons was possible or conceivable without it, as Bagehot remarked in *The English Constitution* (1867): 'Party is inherent in it, is bone of its bone, and breath of its breath', and the simple penalty for disobedience was impotence (ch. 4). It was an institution bred of necessity, and necessity in the end conferred respectability. 'We are divided into parties in this country,' Gladstone told his Midlothian audience in 1879, 'and the division is a healthy one.'[1] Long before the end of the reign there were highminded as well as practical reasons for accepting it. After all, the party division represented something: a genuine division of opinion in the people itself. Erskine May held that each party stood for a 'cardinal principle of government', with authority on one side and 'popular rights and privileges on the other',[2] and he quotes with approval Burke's dictum that party is 'a body of men united for promoting by their just endeavours the national interest upon some particular principle in which they are all agreed'.

How did Victorians conceive, in the most general terms, of the wide variety of political views within the state? The simplest concept by which to explain such varieties is always the spectrum, by which views are subjected to a linear analysis such as left, right and centre. A spectrum of colours, such as black, white and grey, would in principle do as well, but that is a merely theoretical speculation. Colour, oddly enough, plays no consistent part in national (as opposed to regional) politics; and to this day no British political party represented in Parliament possesses a colour or set of colours which is accepted as its own throughout the United Kingdom.

1. W. E. Gladstone, *Midlothian Speeches 1879*, edited by M. R. D. Foot (Leicester, 1971) p. 30.

2. T. Erskine May, *The Constitutional History of England since the Accession of George III* (London, 1863) ii. 2.

The Victorians scarcely knew left and right as political terms with reference to their own affairs. These were continental, mainly French terms, arising out of the semicircular seating arrangements of the National Assembly in the 1790s. Given that the two legislative chambers at Westminster are rectangular, and suited to two parties confronting each other together with a cross bench, the left-right spectrum has little obvious application to the British parliamentary scene. Mill, writing home to his father from Paris about the events of the July Revolution of 1830, which he witnessed, uses 'left' only in French;[1] Acton, in his 1861 essay on Cavour, uses left and right to describe Italian politics in the Risorgimento, but not to describe the English.[2] Most Englishmen knew of such words to the extent that they knew about recent French history. They could have read of that in Carlyle's *French Revolution* (1837), where he had spoken of 'the Left side' of the National Assembly, or the d'Orléans side (I. vi. ii. 308). The *New English Dictionary*, for which editing began in 1879, specifies for the political sense of 'right' only a foreign application: 'In Continental legislative chambers, the party or parties of conservative principles' (sense 17d), and it quotes an English example no earlier than 1887. Macaulay in 1835 writes as if he had never heard of the spectrum except in the context of French politics. In his essay on Sir James Mackintosh he condemns the Legitimists in France for pretending to support their natural enemies in a mean attempt to embarrass government: 'At this very moment we see the Carlists in France hallooing on the Extreme Left against the Centre Left.' But earlier in the same essay he had used the terms left and right in what would now be considered a reverse sense; speaking of those who were disappointed in their hopes of the French Revolution, he explains that 'the force of the rebound was proportioned to the force of the original impulse. The pendulum swung furiously to the left, because it had been drawn too far to the right'.[3] All this suggests that though

1. J. S. Mill, *Earlier Letters 1812–48*, edited by F. E. Mineka (Toronto, 1963) i. 58.
2. Lord Acton, *Historical Essays & Studies* (1907) p. 179.
3. Lord Macaulay, *Literary and Historical Essays Contributed to the Edinburgh Review* (Oxford, 1913) ii. 317, 285.

Macaulay was conversant with French usage, he did not consider himself bound by it when writing English.

But the terms were slowly being acclimatized, though it is doubtful if they became part of the ordinary currency of British political language before the First World War. Bagehot, in his journalism, uses them occasionally: he refers in 1871 to Bright's tendency 'to diminish the power of the left wing of the Liberal party', and five years later he calls Huskisson and the Canningites, in the old Tory Party of the Duke of Wellington, 'the best of the moderate right'.[1] There is also an isolated use of 'left' in an English context by Mark Pattison in his *Memoirs* (1885), an Oxford autobiography composed just before the author's death in 1884. Attacking John Conington, Professor of Latin, who had turned Tory in the long vacation of 1854 on being made a professor, Pattison writes of his having previously 'belonged to the small section of advanced Liberals' and of having filled a prominent place 'in this left wing of the reforming party' (p. 246). The usage is odd, perhaps learned – but no less odd than Gladstone's use of the word to Queen Victoria in a letter of 10 October 1885, with reference to Joseph Chamberlain: 'Mr Chamberlain is known as the most active and efficient representative at this time of what may be termed the left wing of the Liberal party.'[2] Whether Victoria understood this remark must remain uncertain.

Whatever their use of such terms, there is no doubt that the Victorians had a political spectrum of a sort in mind. It is not described in any standard metaphor or widely accepted analogy, whether spatial or other; but it exists. Cornewall Lewis had already observed in 1832 that

> there are two different ways in which classes of things can be opposed to each other: viz. as *contraries*, and as *extremes*. . . . Things are opposed as *extremes* when they do not together make up, or exhaust, the class or genus to which they belong; but there is between them a middle state, from which they are not precisely divided, and into which they insensibly graduate at both its extremities,

1. Bagehot, *Economist* (25 November 1871), *Fortnightly Review* (November 1876); reprinted in his *Collected Works* (1968) iii. 308, 214.
2. *The Queen and Mr Gladstone*, edited by Philip Guedalla (London, 1933) ii. 382.

and he instances old and young, hot and cold, light and dark and the like.[1] This is Lewis's introduction to his chapter on rich and poor, but it might be said of the parliamentary spectrum as well. Often Victorian language implies a force in favour of change, normally libertarian change, meeting a conservative resistance which yields gradually before it. Terms like 'advanced', 'moderate', 'conservative' and 'unyielding' fit this model well. One of the Barnacles in Dickens's Circumlocution Office puts the matter frankly: the bureaucracy he represents in *Little Dorrit* is 'official and effectual': 'It's like a limited game of cricket. A field of outsiders are always going in to bowl at the Public Service, and we block the balls' (ch. 28). But they do not block all the balls, or even attempt to do so, and some Barnacles stick tighter than others; so that the whole process is less like a stone wall than a strategic retreat under fire.

There are other metaphors, at times illuminating if hardly of general acceptance. De Quincey in 1837 suggested the diagram of a sphere or globe: Whigs and Tories, he believed, complement each other; they are 'able to exist only by means of their coexistence'. 'The true view of their relation is this, that each party forms one hemisphere; jointly they make up the total sphere', the Whigs being popular and democratic, the Tories 'anti-popular and timocratic', or in favour of a 'propertied oligarchy'.[2] The hemispheres may be variously described. Macaulay, in his second essay on Chatham (1844), sees each as embodying a great principle essential to the welfare of a nation: one party 'the guardian of Liberty, and the other of order'. The Whigs are 'the moving power', the Tories 'the steadying'. The diagram, accurate or not, is memorably simple.

The distinction often amounts to one between past and future. Mill, in his article on Vigny, draws a wide distinction between the Tory poet and the Radical: the pervading spirit of the one is 'love of the Past', of the other 'faith in the Future': 'The

1. Sir George Cornewall Lewis, *Remarks on the Use and Abuse of some Political Terms* (1832) ch. 13.

2. Thomas de Quincey, 'On the political parties of modern England', in his *Collected Writings*, edited by David Masson (Edinburgh, 1889–90) ix. 373.

partialities of the one will be towards things established, settled, regulated; of the other, towards human free-will, cramped and fettered in all directions, both for good and ill, by those establishments and regulations.' Both poets will love heroism; but 'the one will respond most readily to the heroism of endurance and self-control, the other to that of action and struggle', and he contrasts the Tory love of 'fixed habits and firmly settled opinions', reverence, humility and duty, with the Radical's love of energy, self-will and individual brilliance. Since Vigny is the type of the conservative poet, the type of the radical begins to sound like Byron, especially when Mill adds that 'there will not be so broad and black a line between his good and bad personages; his characters of principle will be more tolerant of his characters of mere passion'.[1]

This is the spectrum not of space but of time, where the future belongs to radicals, and it has a familiar and confident ring. When Mr Slope, the Bishop's obnoxious young radical chaplain in Trollope's *Barchester Towers* (1857), hectors Mr Harding about 'casting away the useless rubbish of past centuries', this is a suitably vulgar version of the same assumption. Meredith, years later, assumes a similar spectrum: the advanced radical, then the 'slow-stepping Liberal, otherwise your half-Conservative in his convictions', merges gently into the Conservative proper.[2]

These easy assumptions on the part of novelists and their readers are open assertions in the works of theorists like Mill, who could see no better model of political description than the linear. In past ages, he argued in *A System of Logic*, it had been possible to argue a cyclic theory of history, as Vico had done, and to see society as self-repeating, or 'revolving in an orbit'; but this does not fit the nineteenth century: 'Those who have succeeded Vico in this kind of speculations have universally adopted the idea of a trajectory or progress, in lieu of an orbit or cycle'; and if this view takes progress for granted, it may be none the worse for that, since the general tendency of history

1. J. S. Mill, 'Writings of Alfred de Vigny', *London and Westminster Review* (April 1838); reprinted in his *Dissertations and Discussions* (1859) i. 291–2.

2. George Meredith, *The Tragic Comedians* (London, 1880) ch. 16.

is henceforth likely to be one of improvement, 'saving occasional and temporary exceptions' (VI. x. 3).

More than twenty years later, addressing the electors of Westminster at a public meeting as a Liberal parliamentary candidate on the point of election, Mill drew the spectrum out to the length of the road from London to Edinburgh:

> Whatever the shortcomings of a Liberal party or government might be, they did not bear in their very names the profession of wishing to keep things as they were. (Hear, hear.) Their name implied that they wished to improve them; and although between the least liberal of Liberals and the most liberal of Conservatives there might only be a little difference, a short distance, still it should be ever borne in mind, and seriously remembered, that this least liberal of Liberals was surrounded by those who were far better men than himself, politically speaking, while this most liberal of Conservatives was surrounded by men who, politically speaking, were far worse than himself. (Loud applause.)
>
> Suppose York was half-way between Edinburgh and London, and two travellers met there from either place, there would be very little, if any, difference in the respective distances they had to go, but that did not decrease in the least the hundreds of miles which London was distant from Edinburgh.[1]

The moderate wings of the two great parties of state meet and are hard to distinguish, but the parties themselves none the less represent different, even opposing views. This is a clarification to be kept in mind, especially when one considers such hybrid terms as 'Liberal-Conservative'.[2] If the views of certain individual Liberals and Conservatives in Parliament, in the country, and in the political fiction of the age are similar, it does not follow from this that the Victorians saw little difference between the two parties – still less that there was little difference. In any spectrum, when a line is drawn, a point on one side of it is next to a point on the other; but the line is still a line, and the sections it separates may still be as distinct as night and day. The high consistency of voting patterns in the 1840s on all major issues other than factory

1. *Daily Telegraph* (10 July 1865) p. 2, column 1.
2. Dod, *Electoral Facts* (1852), e.g. under Cheshire North or Launceston Cornwall.

legislation has already been demonstrated;[1] and that demonstration, in its turn, has made an ideological interpretation of party differences more imperative.

The opposition of the parties was rarely, if ever, seen in simple terms as between rich and poor, or between those who employ and those who are employed. In the parliamentary scene, at least, there was little that had the clarity of a class war in Victorian England, and at no time could the difference between the two great parties be aptly described in this way. Mill in 1839 saw the coming party struggle as between the Privileged and the Disqualified;[2] but that signified a distinction between those who held power, whether through the suffrage, or family position, or membership of the Church establishment, or privileged entry into the higher professions, and those who did not. Some of Mill's Disqualified were prosperous, some perhaps even rich. Nor was there ever any convincing reason for thinking of the poor as especially radical in their political views; though that, as usual, did not prevent some from making that easy and traditional assumption. An American observer, early in the twentieth century, noted that the evil of 'a division of parties into rich and poor, fighting over the distribution of property, has been predicted, but as yet it has certainly not come'; that is a continental disease, 'contrary to the course of English history' and productive of tyranny, whereas in England the 'lines of political cleavage' have been vertical rather than horizontal.[3] The domestic issues that divided the two parties were more often issues of status and opportunity than of wealth; and the age must be pronounced disappointing to those who regard economic issues as fundamental to the political.

1. W. O. Aydelotte, 'Voting patterns in the British House of Commons in the 1840s', *Comparative Studies in Society and History* v (1963). Norman Gash, quoting these findings in his *Reaction and Reconstruction in English Politics 1832–52* (Oxford, 1965), concludes that 'party attitudes on issues in the 1840s showed a considerable degree of consistency, and that ideological differences were much more closely related to party in this period than has always been acknowledged' (p. 217).

2. J. S. Mill, 'Reorganisation of the Reform Party', *Westminster Review* xxxii (1839) p. 418.

3. A. Lawrence Lowell, *The Government of England* (New York, 1908) ii. 533–4.

Even the distinction between town and country, at first blush a more promising principle of differentiation, breaks down before the strength of custom, patronage and religious denomination. Many saw the Conservatives as a country party: but it was often the party of industrial Lancashire, and rarely the party of much of rural Scotland, of the West Country or of Wales. Nonconformity could give the victory to liberalism where social and economic interest, real or imagined, could not. The national spectrum of opinion, however conceived, is only a grand generalization: it can at the best only furnish a bold summary which fails to account for innumerable variations of regional loyalty.

Was the spectrum, even so qualified by this assumption, ever an accurate model? The question was probably as rare in that age as in this. Hardly anyone bothered to question the aptness of terms like 'radical', 'moderate' and 'conservative', just as hardly anyone in the twentieth century questions the significance of terms like left, right and centre. Mill, in *A System of Logic*, had noticed that the spectrum depends upon an assumption of continuous improvement: if we thought that political change was usually for the worse, after all, the term radical would have quite a different connotation, especially for Radicals. He might have added that the spectrum makes an even larger and even more dubious assumption: that all political policies are ultimately of a single kind and classifiable according to a single system. This assumption is plausible for so long as a single issue like the suffrage dominates the political scene, or for so long as issues can be bundled together with an air of reasonable consistency. No doubt something like this could be said of many general elections between 1832 and the First World War. The dog was not chasing its own tail; the cyclic theory of history seemed to have been dismissed by two vast and unrehearsed events, political democracy and the industrial revolution; and dictatorships of the left had not yet emerged, unless in France, to match those of the right. Those who tried to defy the spectrum, like Disraeli, won for themselves a good deal of derision in the process; Trollope, in *The Way We Live Now* (1875), mocks confidently at the beginning of Disraeli's second premiership at 'that hitherto hazy mixture of Radicalism and old-fogyism, of which we have lately heard from a political master whose eloquence has been employed in teaching us that progress can only be expected from those whose declared purpose is to stand still' (ch. 69). The Prime Minister was a paradox-monger, and Mill's theory of a 'trajectory or progress' punctuated by temporary setbacks seemed to fit the facts of the time. It is unlikely that any Victorian decade can be shown to have been inferior to its predecessor in social terms, as such matters are usually understood: in average standard of living, in the reduction of destitution, in health, leisure and the sharing of power. All this helps to justify the spectrum – for the Victorians. Whether it justifies it for the twentieth century is much more doubtful. In this respect modern political analysis, acquiescing in unexamined assumptions about the scope and variety of political opinion, might easily find itself the willing victim of a doctrine designed for another age.

Some of the common names of parties and groups may now be considered.

TORY AND CONSERVATIVE

Conservative tended to replace Tory as a party name in the 1820s and 1830s, though it remained something of a neologism, in this context, down to the accession of Victoria in 1837. Croker, in the *Quarterly Review* for 1830, refers to 'what is called the Tory, and which might with more propriety be called the Conservative Party'. But three years earlier, in a letter to Lord Londonderry of April 1827, the Duke of Wellington was still using the newer term in its French form; the implication is that the governing party, which had led the struggle against Napoleon, was now placing less emphasis upon its origins in Stuart and Hanoverian times and was conceiving itself anew, in European terms, as the party that had triumphed over revolution: 'The object of the great aristocracy', wrote Wellington, 'and of the *parti conservateur* of this country, is to secure the crown from the mischief with which it is threatened.'[1] For the rest of the century and after, Conservative tends to be the more

1. See Elie Halévy, *Histoire du peuple anglais au XIXe siècle* (Paris, 1912–46), especially iii. 61 n.

neutral and descriptive term, only temporarily dispossessed by Unionist after the Irish Home Rule crisis of the 1880s; Tory the more emotionally charged, whether for or against – what a modern linguist might allow himself to call the 'marked' use.

The partial replacement of 'Tory' in the mid-Victorian period, unlike the parallel and simultaneous placement of 'Whig', was interrupted by a conscious Disraelian revival of the name and nature of the old Tory allegiance. Its authenticity is doubtful; Gladstone, in his first Midlothian speech of 1879, was able on this very point of nomenclature to tease Disraeli's second administration, 'which was not satisfied with the title of Conservative, but has always fallen back upon the title of Tory'.[1] The old seventeenth-century word was felt by Young England to have ideological resonance: it signalled the return of the party to the sources of its vitality before the 'phantasma' of a Whig oligarchy had degraded the British constitution. This is the contention of *Coningsby* and *Sybil*: Conservatism is a mere me-too doctrine that has humiliated itself by conceding everything to Whiggery, even the present impotence of the monarchy and the aristocracy. Toryism, by contrast, is the historic faith of Englishmen before 1689, propounded since by lonely heroes like Bolingbroke in the long interregnum of triumphant Whiggery. In his last novel, *Endymion* (1880), Disraeli echoes a still larger claim – a continuous intellectual lineage for Toryism stretching back to Hobbes:

> a succession of heroic spirits, 'beautiful and swift', ever in the van and foremost of their age? – Hobbes and Bolingbroke, Hume and Adam Smith, Wyndham and Cobham, Pitt and Grenville, Canning and Huskisson? . . . Are not the traditions of the Tory party the noblest pedigree in the world? Are not its illustrations that glorious martyrology that opens with the name of Falkland and closes with the name of Canning?[2]

Disraeli apart, however, the party remained strenuously unideological and, as many would have said, totally immune to general ideas. Only the voice of the prosecutor is clearly

1. W. E. Gladstone, *Midlothian Speeches 1879*, edited by M. R. D. Foot (Leicester, 1971) p. 32.

2. Based on a speech by George Smythe, Viscount Strangford, quoted in his posthumous novel *Angela Pisani* (London, 1875)i. xxiv–xxv; *Endymion* ch. 40.

audible here, but it cannot be altogether wide of the truth. Tories were above all things obedient. Macaulay was fond of repeating the story of what Lord Clarendon had replied when asked how the Duke of Wellington as prime minister would persuade the Tory Peers to accept the Catholic Relief Bill in 1829: 'Oh, it will be easy enough. He'll say, "My lords, attention! Right about face! March!"'[1] Bagehot saw the Conservative parliamentary party as mere lobby-fodder, led by a Jew of doubtful reputation, both in love and money, who had changed his party twice already. 'In our own time', he wrote, 'it is easy to vex Tories. You only have to ask "What is Dizzy's next move?" '[2] Between 1815 and 1830, he believed, they had flourished as a government on a simple creed: 'They would alter nothing and they would let nothing be altered.' By the 1860s they stood for four principles: a social system favourable to the aristocracy; the established Church; land as the safest property, and the most dignified; and 'that Liberals should be defeated whenever possible and snubbed always'.[3] Trollope, a sort of latterday Whig, saw them as delayers, trapped in the undignified but unavoidable processes of compromise. Mr Gresham, the Conservative leader in *The Prime Minister* (1876), understands perfectly well that in Parliament he is 'obliged to promote a great many things which he does not really approve'. But he still feels that it is better that Conservatives should do that unhappy work if it must be done: 'As the glorious institutions of the country are made to perish, it is better that they should receive the *coup de grâce* tenderly from loving hands than be roughly throttled by Radicals' (ch. 34).

The radical view of the Tories was naturally still more cynical: they did not aim at good institutions, so Mill believed in 1836, 'or even at preserving the present ones: their object is to profit by them while they exist'.[4] It is a doctrine of 'being in, and availing yourself of your comfortable position *inside* the vehicle without minding the poor devils who are freezing outside'. But even Mill admits there is also an ideal Toryism

1. G. O. Trevelyan, *The Life and Lteters of Lord Macaulay* (1876) i. 159n.
2. Bagehot, *Collected Works* (1968) iii. 77.
3. *Ibid.* pp. 234, 507–8.
4. J. S. Mill, 'Civilization', *London and Westminster Review* (April 1836); reprinted in his *Dissertations and Discussions* (1859) i. 176.

that venerates King, Lords and Commons – old England, indeed, though 'old England as she might be, not as she is'. But an idealistic Toryism is still a remote possibility, especially in the radical mind. It is something that simply failed to develop. The ageing Wordsworth, Coleridge, Southey and others possessed after all a species of ideology, albeit a secretive and largely unformulated one. It is based, Mill suggests, on 'a reverence for *government* in the abstract': 'It means that they are duly sensible that it is good for a man to be ruled; to submit both his body and mind to the guidance of a higher intelligence and virtue', whereas its direct antithesis, liberalism, believes every man should be 'his own guide and sovereign master'.[1]

This sense of a secret Tory faith lingers on among the haunting suspicions of the liberal mind. On the face of them, Tories look like stupid people: even Disraeli had called them so. Their obedience to the party whips appeared cowlike, their faith mere subservience. What is more, their views were racked by contradiction. They talked as if things were bad, and getting worse – and yet they wanted them to remain as they were. They complained and complained – and yet an outsider would say that they were mostly happy men. Trollope, in *The Eustace Diamonds* (1873), views them with an amused and indulgent eye: that of a moderate and generous liberal who cannot hate his adversary. 'The very salt of the nation', he calls them, disagreeing with Mill's lofty strictures about 'the stupidest party':[2] 'He who said that all Conservatives are stupid did not know them.' In fact they have solved, admittedly by sacrificing intellectual consistency to 'a religious creed which is altogether dark and mysterious to the outer world', the grand psychological difficulty of living tranquilly in a changing world. The Conservative is like a 'Buddhist', Trollope believed, strangely at peace with himself and his world:

> Every step taken has been bad. And yet to them old England is of all countries in the world the best to live in, and is not at all the less comfortable because of the changes that have been made. These people are ready to grumble at every boon conferred upon them, and yet to

1. Mill, *Earlier Letters 1812–48* (1963) i. 84.
2. J. S. Mill, *Representative Government* (London, 1861), ch. 7.

enjoy every boon. They know too their privileges and, after a fashion, understand their position. It is picturesque, and it pleases them. To have been always in the right and yet on the losing side; always being ruined, always under persecution from a wild spirit of republican demagogism – and yet never to lose anything, not even position or public esteem, is pleasant enough.

This is the happy and enviable mood of the Tory: 'a living, daily increasing grievance that does one no palpable harm' (ch. 4).

WHIG, LIBERAL AND RADICAL

Here, in the dominant middle of the alleged spectrum, its richest variety is seen at work: Whig giving place to Liberal, as many thought it natural to suppose that Liberal would give place, by a similar process, to Radical. The party flew on three wings, and flew well: in the half century between 1832 and Gladstone's defeat in the mid 1880s, it was in power for some two-thirds of the time, and it dominated the age in terms of its issues and ideas. The three wings may be discussed in order.

Whig. Still the name of a party in 1832, it lapsed into history after the formation of the first Liberal ministry by Gladstone in December 1868. For the generation between, it represented the antique wing of the dominant party of state. Lord John Russell in 1852 thought it a useful way of saying 'conservative Liberal' in one syllable instead of seven.[1] Trollope, no *avant-gardiste*, whose ideal statesman was more or less Palmerston, writes of it in the Palliser novels almost as of a defunct species; in *Phineas Redux* (1873) he speaks of 'former days when there were Whigs instead of Liberals' and when everybody in politics was related to everybody else (ch. 13). In *The Prime Minister* he makes the old Duke of St Bungay, in a conversation with the Liberal Prime Minister about the honours list, use the term Whig as a thoughtless remark of an old man (ch. 64); the Prime Minister's wife, Lady Glencora, is content to use it ancestrally of her husband's family: ' "We are all Whigs, of

1. Spencer Walpole, *Life of Lord John Russell* (London, 1889) ii. 156n. But Dod, in the same year of 1852, does not use 'Whig' at all in his *Electoral Facts*.

course. A Palliser who was not a Whig would be held to have disgraced himself for ever" ' (ch. 77).

But the word was already becoming a legend: it was to die, as 'Tory' was never to die. By the 1870s it is already the dinosaur of British politics, though it can still be used by an individual statesman to describe the state of his mind as opposed to his party allegiance. Sir William Harcourt in January 1874 claimed to have 'hoisted the good old Whig flag', and Henry Reeve of the *Edinburgh Review* wrote to congratulate him, complaining that their party chief, Gladstone, 'was a Tory and is a Radical: but he never was a Whig at all'.[1] In December Harcourt wrote to Goschen that he had been 'preaching Whig doctrines *pur et simple*', adding: 'They are my principles and I mean to stick to them *coûte que coûte*.'[2] Hardly anyone else did. By the age of Gladstone Whiggism was a relic.

But its death was glorious, in the literary sense. Macaulay had attached himself to it in early manhood, seduced by its claims to an historic lineage and the life style it still exemplified, into the first years of Victoria's reign, at Holland House. Its permanent literary monument is his *History of England* (1849–61), a work of such sun-drenched confidence in the future of Whiggism that it is hard to remember, as one reads, that the cause it glorifies was on the point of being swallowed up forever. Its god is William III, its lineage the Protestant succession he had guaranteed; its dogma a constitutional monarchy in a system of traditional checks, sanctified in Burke's 'triple cord' of King, Lords and Commons and led by a landed aristocracy practised in the skills of compromise. Acton, in his Cambridge inaugural of 1895, calls it 'the theory that authority is legitimate only in proportion to its checks, and that the sovereign is dependent on the subject'.[3] Its last historian was Macaulay, its last leader Palmerston, and its last novelist Trollope, who wrote Palmerston's life as a rueful tribute to a dead age and a group of political novels to anatomize and to praise it.

Its lineage, though confidently proclaimed, is dubious. The

1. A. G. Gardiner, *The Life of Sir William Harcourt* (London, 1923) i. 265.
2. A. D. Elliot, *The Life of Lord Goschen* (London, 1911) i. 152.
3. Lord Acton, *The Study of History* (London, 1895) p. 29.

astonishing aspect of Macaulay's claim to derive from the settlement of 1689 is that it went so easily unchallenged. Rhetoric apart, it was not much of a case. In his essay on Mackintosh (1835), Macaulay had already defined his doctrine: 'power is a trust for the people'; and he claims that throughout the eighteenth century, individual backsliding apart, the Whigs had stood firm to that doctrine. An eighteenth-century Whig statesman would have blinked to read that. If they were not exactly unprincipled men, the appeal to principle was not among the more characteristic of their utterances. 'Most Whig ministries', remarked Bagehot, 'have been like low-church bishops. There is a feeling that the advocates of liberty ought scarcely to coerce: they have ruled, but they seem to deny the succession by which they ruled.'[1] They were tentative men skilled in compromise, and to a democratic age they had nothing to say. But they survive in the memory, which is licensed to romanticize, as a way of life. Macaulay, in his adoring review of Lord Holland's journal (1841), was right at least in predicting that the Whig style could not be forgotten. Men will remember, he wrote,

> that venerable chamber in which all the antique gravity of a college library was so singularly blended with all that female grace and wit could devise to embellish a drawing-room . . .; how the last debate was discussed in one corner, and the last comedy of Scribe in another; while Wilkie gazed with modest admiration on Sir Joshua's Baretti; while Mackintosh turned over Thomas Aquinas to verify a quotation; while Talleyrand related his conversations with Barras at the Luxembourg, or his ride with Lannes over the field of Austerlitz.

Liberal. As a political term, the word is often supposed to be continental in its origins, though Sir Robert Peel, writing to Croker as early as 1820, uses it as if it were already current in English: 'Do not you think that the tone of England – of that great compound of folly, weakness, prejudice, wrong feeling, right feeling, obstinacy, and newspaper paragraphs, which is called public opinion – is more liberal – to use an odious but

1. Bagehot, 'Lord Brougham', *National Review* (July 1857); reprinted in his *Collected Works* (1968) iii. 179.

intelligible phrase – than the policy of the Government?', referring to a growing opinion 'in favour of some undefined change in the mode of governing the country'.[1] If the word was current as early as this, its political use may not be totally dependent, as has been supposed, on the Cadiz declaration after the Spanish rising of 1820, though some continued to spell it in the Spanish way as *Liberales*; Castlereagh, indeed, had already used the English word as a term of abuse in Parliament on 15 February 1816.[2]

In the years after 1830 Liberal quickly replaced Whig as the usual name for the chief party of state, though the use was naturally commoner in the mouths of Radicals, in the first instance, than in the mouths of Whigs. 'What we must have to oppose to the great Conservative party', wrote Mill in 1839, 'is the whole Liberal party.'[3] Macaulay, to his dying day, found it easier to use the word of his party than of himself. 'You call me a Liberal,' he once remarked, 'but I don't know that in these days I deserve the name. I am opposed to the abolition of standing armies. I am opposed to the abrogation of capital punishment. I am opposed to the destruction of the National Church. In short, I am in favour of war, hanging and Church Establishments.'[4]

The party itself was a spectrum. Mill in 1839 sees it as 'a phalanx stretching from the Whig-Radicals at one extremity (if we may so term those among the persons calling themselves Whigs who are real Liberals) to the Ultra-Radicals and the Working Classes on the other'. This was the spectrum that had united in 1831–32 to pass the first Reform Bill. It remained a working alliance throughout the age, apart from the split over Ireland in 1886, but always a shifting one; and its centre-

1. John Wilson Croker, *Correspondence and Diaries*, edited by L. J. Jennings (London, 1885, revised) i. 170, from a letter to Croker of 23 March 1820.

2. See Halévy, *Histoire du peuple anglais* (1912–46) ii. 74–5; Donald Southgate, *The Passing of the Whigs* (London, 1962); J. R. Vincent, *The Formation of the Liberal Party 1857–68* (London, 1966).

3. J. S. Mill, 'Reorganization of the Reform Party', *Westminster Review* xxxii (1839).

4. G. O. Trevelyan, *The Life and Letters of Lord Macaulay* (1876) ii. 201. In a letter of November 1852 he wrote that he could easily compromise on the ballot and the franchise, but never on defence: 'I am fully determined to make them eat their words on that point' (ii. 368).

piece remained irreversibly the doctrine of individual liberty. It is a word that suggested confidence. Liberals were men of the future, brisk, brash and contemptuous of yesterday. 'You were a liberal, you pointed forward.' the historian John Richard Green wrote admiringly in 1863 to his old Oxford teacher A. P. Stanley: 'You believed in a future as other "Liberals" did, but you were not, like them, unjust to the present and the past.'[1] The praise is also a warning.

Radical. The term is common in the late eighteenth century and after in directly political contexts; but it has never been the name of a British party. Radicals entered the Whig party during and after the agitation for the first Reform Bill. In the 1830s some thought they were on the point of taking it over – a hope, or fear, that faded in the course of the decade. But for a long time it remained a matter for speculation which was the tail and which the dog. De Quincey, writing as a Conservative in 1835–36, underrated in the short term the Whig capacity for survival. Only the Tories, he argued then, stand in the way of victory for the Radicals: 'The Whigs are the object of their contempt: the Whigs are in their grasp; that party cannot move a step, neither win nor retain office, nor carry any one great public measure – without the support of the Radicals.'[2] But in the same year Mill and Roebuck, conversing with Tocqueville during his visit to England in 1835, were less confident about their prospects: 'hiding behind the Whigs, letting themselves get forgotten', the Radicals 'risked losing their identity to the profit only of the Tories'. They feared extinction: 'The Whigs could not carry on the campaign by themselves, and the Radicals could not support them effectively unless they succeeded *in creating a great excitement*, and that was something they could not do if they just let themselves be carried in tow by the Whigs.'[3] Roebuck, then an advanced young Radical MP, told Tocqueville plainly that he hoped the

1. J. R. Green, *Letters*, edited by Leslie Stephen (London, 1901) p. 18.
2. De Quincey, 'A Tory's account of Toryism, Whiggism and Radicalism', *Tait's Magazine* (December 1835 – January 1836); reprinted in his *Collected Writings*, edited by David Masson (Edinburgh, 1890) ix. 316–17.
3. Tocqueville, *Journeys to England and Ireland* (New York, 1968) p. 72.

Whigs would join the Tories and confront the Radicals as a single party.

The Radical choice of party cannot have seemed obvious. Apart from joining the Whigs, which they did, the Radicals could have joined the Tory party or formed their own. But a complex of historical memories helped them in their choice. The Whigs, as many recalled, had supported French revolutionary ideas – at least some of them had. 'The Whigs were the traditional friends of liberty', wrote George Jacob Holyoake towards the end of the century, looking back over a long lifetime of Chartist and liberal causes. 'The Tories were always against it.' The Tories, he believed, 'would rob you of £1 and give you twopence back'. The Whigs would not give you twopence, but 'neither did they rob you of the pound, and they were in favour of that legislation which would enable you to earn a shilling for yourself and keep the pound in your pocket'.[1] This helps to explain some of the attractions of the Whig party to men whose style of life bore no resemblance to that of the great country house or the London drawing room of Lady Holland. The Whigs had put liberty before patriotism during the French wars, and they might be ready to give individual energy its reward now.

But to some young intellectuals the appeal may have been an interesting compound of the romantic and the practical. The great Whig magnates, by and large, were richer than the Tories; they held grander levées and house-parties, they disposed after 1830 of more patronage, and they were more inclined to engage a bright young man as an assistant, to give him his head and let him work. The Whigs were permeated by such new men in the years that followed reform. Matthew Arnold's engagement as private secretary to the Marquis of Lansdowne in 1847, which should have led to higher things than an inspectorship of schools, is a representative event in the life of a young Victorian of ambition just down from the university. Some of this essential spirit of courtly patronage faded in the course of the reign, with the growth of competitive entrance through the examination system; and Bagehot in the 1870s noted and partly lamented how the two Reform Acts, while

1. G. J. Holyoake, *Sixty Years of an Agitator's Life* (London, 1892) ch. 17.

making for justice, had rendered political life less exciting in temperament and less aristocratic in tone. Both Gibbon and Macaulay had received invitations from noble admirers to accept a seat in Parliament; there was in those days 'a sort of romantic element in the lives of clever young men which is wholly wanting now'.[1] But the Radicals did not regret all that; by the 1870s, after long delays, they had got much of what they had wanted. No wonder they never bothered with a party of their own. The system lay invitingly open to them in 1830, history looked to be on their side, reform was about to happen, and might if they pressed happen again and again. They were never, in the event, to give their name to a party, or to need to do so.

1. Bagehot, *Fortnightly Review* (November 1876); reprinted in his *Collected Works* (1968) iii. 228.

[7]

Political Oratory

The oratory of Parliament and of its new rival, the public platform, has good claim to be considered the most representative literary activity of the Victorians after their social fiction. Its neglect by historians of literature is none the less easy to understand. In their sheer bulk the materials overpower – even if one is to confine attention to volumes of published speeches and the massive quotations that appear in contemporary biographies. If newspaper reports and records like *Hansard* are added, it is plain that no historian can claim to have read as much as one-tenth of what survives. And what he has read is not easily subjected to literary analysis. A speech is an occasion, after all, as well as a document, and the occasion survives as tenuously as the performance of a great actor or the exchanges of a conversationalist of genius.

Oratory is a kind of literature – 'the lyrical function of Parliament', as Bagehot called it in *The English Constitution* – although literary historians entertain some natural reservations which derive both from the general nature of the material and from the vexed problem of transmission. The material itself, as it survives, is a strange and usually unspecified blend of the deliberate and the impromptu. Macaulay loved to compare eloquence to fresco painting: 'the result of long study and meditation, but at the moment of execution thrown off with the greatest rapidity: what has apparently been the work of a few hours being destined to last for ages'.[1] He might have added that, in the curious conditions of Victorian publishing, a statesman could behave more reflectively than any fresco painter

1. G. O. Trevelyan, *The Life and Letters of Lord Macaulay* (1876) i. 185, quoted in the journal of his sister Margaret for September 1831.

working on damp plaster – he could add, subtract and alter the work for publication after it had been delivered in Parliament or in a public meeting. This complicates the issue enormously for the historian, who can rarely be certain that the printed text was uttered in just that form on a given occasion. But what is a defect to the historian is a merit from the standpoint of the literary critic. Revision confirms the status of oratory as literature, since it reinforces the element of deliberation in the texts that survive. And revision, even rewriting, could be extensive. The substance of a speech, as Disraeli put it in an ironical footnote to his early tale *Popanilla* (1828), 'in parliamentary language means a printed edition of an harangue which contains all that was uttered in the House, and about as much again' (ch. 4).

The eighteenth-century luminaries of parliamentary eloquence, such as Burke and Sheridan, had published their speeches on occasion, or allowed them to be published, or seen them published without consent. Unofficial reports were sometimes made; though the Commons, before its destruction by fire in 1834, had no gallery reserved for reporters, and the taking of notes was officially forbidden till the 1780s. But unofficial reports were sometimes made: Sir Henry Cavendish, for instance, took verbatim shorthand notes in the Commons from 1768 to 1774, and his reports of speeches by Burke, Fox and others were partly published from manuscript by the early Victorians.[1] In addition, the age provided itself with texts of what it often regarded as the Golden Age of British oratory in the mid and late eighteenth century, volumes such as *The Modern Orator* (1847), a bulky anthology that fed a taste for viewing the monuments of national eloquence. From the 1820s the fashion for publishing speeches grew; but a probable disparity between the spoken word and the printed text was well known to apply both to reports and to the efforts of book

1. The notes are in 48 manuscript volumes in the British Museum (Egerton 215–62), and were partly published in 1839 and 1841–43. See A. Aspinall, 'The reporting and publishing of the House of Commons Debates 1771–1834', *Essays Presented to Sir Lewis Namier* (London, 1956); Peter D. G. Thomas, 'The beginning of parliamentary reporting in newspapers 1768–74', *English Historical Review* lxxiv (1959).

publishers. Macaulay's bitterness over the unauthorized edition of his speeches by Vizetelly in 1853 led him to bring out from the house of Longmans his own authorized collection of twenty-nine speeches in the following year, drawn from his entire career since 1831, the year after he entered the Commons. *Speeches of the Right Honourable T. B. Macaulay MP, Corrected by Himself* (1854) was a work of self-defence, as Macaulay's bitter preface explains; for though his Commons speeches were substantially accurate in Vizetelly's edition, being 'reprinted from reports which I had corrected for the Mirror of Parliament or the Parliamentary Debates', the rest he claimed to have been grossly misrepresented; and he damned Vizetelly for not consulting *The Times*, where 'my meaning had been correctly reported, though often in words different from those which I had used'. This compliment to the press does not argue reassuringly in favour of the verbal accuracy of *The Times* reporter. Nor does Macaulay make more than the mildest claims for his own accuracy, since the 1854 volume is avowedly a corrected text, his delivery having proved too rapid for the ablest of shorthand writers: 'As I am unable to recall the precise words which I used, I have done my best to put my meaning into words which I might have used.'

Reports of parliamentary proceedings are unlikely to be any more reliable than books, considered as verbatim records. The *Hansard* series, begun by Hansard, Cobbett and others in 1803, was unofficial and had many rivals; during its brief life from 1828 till 1841, the *Mirror of Parliament*, which employed the young Charles Dickens in the early 1830s, was probably its superior in accuracy. All such reports were largely compilations throughout the century; Hansard collected his materials from daily papers and sent proofs to the speakers for correction, so that for much of the period *The Times* is a more original and authentic source for what a speaker actually said in Parliament, as opposed to what he meant to say or what he afterwards wished he had said. Only as late as 1878 did Hansard agree to put a reporter in the gallery for certain special matters not provided by newspapers, including proceedings after midnight; the Commons had no official reports till 1909, though the Lords achieved something like an official system from 1889, having hitherto been content with little.[1] All this diminishes the status of surviving texts as history, though it does not diminish their literary interest.

The tendency of Victorian oratory, from the formation of the great political leagues in the 1830s and after, is a tendency to move from the classic world of parliamentary eloquence, rooted in eighteenth-century antecedents, towards the 'platform', that sudden discovery that belongs to an age advancing in the direction of democracy; and from the platform back into Parliament, now massively influenced by the new world of the public speaker and the crowd. The platform, as its Victorian historian insists, was felt to possess the force of a strange and unheralded element in national life.[2] A readiness in parliamentary debate, an ability to impress and control the House – these had always been useful political virtues. The Pitts, Sir Robert Peel and Palmerston had in varying measures possessed them. But parliamentary eloquence is something more than this, and something that Peel and Palmerston hardly attempted; and popular eloquence is something else again, something they had no need for and which, in any case, they were by temperament too austere to covet. The age was growing brisker, broader and freer in its political debate. Bagehot in 1856 mourned the passing of 'the old delicate Parliament' and 'the gladiatorship which it loved',[3] but he made the mistake of supposing that the reformed parliaments would bear with nothing but exposition and arithmetic. In fact the platform, with its public meetings up and down the country devoted to causes like the repeal of the Corn Laws, in the end revivified parliamentary oratory; Disraeli and Gladstone, even as Bagehot wrote, were building their future careers as party leaders upon it, and the gladiatorial strain in British politics, by the 1860s, was back, to run a bright course through Joseph Chamberlain and Lloyd George to Birkenhead and Churchill. And there, at least on the front benches, it drew to an end, and history since the 1950s has

1. See H. Donaldson Jordan, 'The reports of parliamentary debates 1803–1908', *Economica* (November 1931).

2. Henry Jephson, *The Platform: its rise and progress*, 2 vols (London, 1892).

3. Bagehot, 'The Character of Sir Robert Peel', *National Review* (July 1856); reprinted in his *Collected Works* (1968) iii. 269.

shown that Bagehot spoke not wrongly but too soon. Since 1945 the British Parliament might indeed be said to have given itself up to exposition and arithmetic, and the new mass media have come near to destroying the platform with their fatal doses of intimacy. No Victorian would recognize the demure respectability of the British political scene in the later twentieth century. Oratory has barely survived, and only as the vestige of a few gifted oddities. 'The roar of the crowd', as Baroness Asquith told a meeting at the National Liberal Club in February 1965, 'has been the background music of my life.' The admission is affecting, but party leadership is now played to a music very different from this, and no British party leader since Churchill has based his eminence on the uttered word and the roar of thousands.

The Victorians were less demure. 'Eloquence, in this empire, is power', as G. H. Francis, an early Victorian reporter, put it boldly.[1] Earlier ages had seen men rise to power through that best favoured merit of the working statesman, an ability to control the House; that bent may, but need not, include memorable utterance. The new taste was for the extravagant and the theatrical, and after 1832 the House, of necessity, slowly followed the taste of the nation. No doubt many members, and especially country members, remained lethargic and little better than articulate, if as much. 'Grave files of speechless men have always represented the land of England,' as Bagehot said;[2] and Macaulay, after long experience, spoke almost despairingly of the exacting task of the statesman who took up the challenge of the word at a late hour and strove to 'excite the minds of five hundred gentlemen at midnight'. Lethargy apart, some resented eloquence on traditional grounds: it offended a national respect for sober and unassuming worth. Even Macaulay shrank from the prospect of achieving a merely theatrical reputation – had not his hero Burke been coughed

1. George Henry Francis, *Orators of the Age* (London, 1847) p. 2. The book collects twenty-eight sketches of Peel, Wellington, Macaulay, Palmerston and others, largely revised from a series of articles in *Fraser's Magazine* by a journalist and parliamentary reporter.

2. Bagehot, 'Bolingbroke as a Statesman', *National Review* (April 1863); reprinted in his *Collected Works* (1968) iii. 49.

down in the House? Rhetoric might easily be un-English. Frederic Harrison, with a natural asperity sharpened by Positivism, released his native indignation at a meeting of the London Trades Council in 1868: 'What makes a man minister? Debating power. And what makes a man Premier? Debating power. And what good is debating power to you? what has it ever done for you or for England?' And the answer was deflating: 'It bears the same relation to governing that tournaments did to fighting.'[1] That speaks up for the cause of honest dullness, but it also makes that cause sound lost. By 1870 Bagehot, who had written slightingly of the power of eloquence in the 1850s and after, had to admit that it had become a power 'more penetrative at the moment than any literature'.[2] Like it or not, the word had won.

Several sources contributed. Pulpit eloquence had educated generations to listen to long sermons; and some, like Robert Peel as a boy, had been required to render them back by heart to a parent on returning home from church. The law courts trained many an aspiring entrant to the Commons. And the Golden Age was remembered, even studied. Macaulay, in his second essay on Chatham (1844), invoked an oratorical past in stirring terms in describing the Commons debate of 1766, when the elder Pitt spoke in that House for the last time and Burke for the first: 'a splendid sunset and a splendid dawn'. To some men, at least, oratory seemed supremely English. Such were the native sources: whether the great classical precedents like Demosthenes and Cicero really counted for much is more in doubt. Certainly the influence of Greek and Latin on nineteenth-century oratory is easily overstated. Boys might be trained to make Ciceronian speeches at Eton and Rugby; Macaulay could enthuse, in his essay on Mackintosh, on the orations of Demosthenes and Charles James Fox, where reason seemed 'penetrated' and 'made red hot by passion'; and Henry Brougham, the very type of the rising orator, could steep himself in Demosthenes to prepare a peroration. But the British Parliament created its own tradition, and it is doubtful if its

1. Frederic Harrison, *Order and Progress* (1875) p. 217.

2. Bagehot, 'Mr Bright's retirement', *Economist* (24 December 1870); reprinted in his *Collected Works* (1968) iii. 303.

special atmosphere owed much, or could owe much, to any ancient assembly. Writing privately in his journal in his last years, Macaulay mused amazedly on Cicero's intolerable egotism in his speeches: 'The man's self-importance amounted to a monomania. To me the speeches, tried by the standard of English forensic eloquence, seem very bad',[1] though he conceded that, if more were known of the temper of Roman tribunals, it might be possible to excuse that infinite long-windedness. But the avowal is private, and Macaulay would hardly have expressed himself with so much freedom in public on the honoured name of Cicero. The classics were always to be acknowledged, even if not imitated; their prestige did not sink. But what Victorian speech is radically based on a classical model?

Classical allusions and quotations are something else; and the distinction is worth some emphasis, since the wide range of reference to a few texts, notably from Virgil and Horace, has sometimes been mistaken for a pervasive classical influence on British eloquence. Everyone knows the story of the Member who, at a loss to complete his Latin quotation, heard it shouted back at him by the whole chamber. But that was a characteristic of pre-Victorian parliamentary oratory, and certainly a fading fashion after 1832. Disraeli tells in *Endymion* (1880) of a young Member of the 1820s who made his maiden speech on foreign affairs, 'which permit rhetoric, and in those days demanded at least one Virgilian quotation' (ch. 2). Those days were passing before the mid century. 'In the last parliament', remarks the Father of the House of Commons in the same novel, referring to the Parliament of 1832, 'we often had Latin quotations, but never from a Member with a new constituency.' Charles James Fox, he went on, had been against Greek and French quotations, and against any from an English poet less than a hundred years old; but he had favoured 'as much Latin as you like' (ch. 76). The Duke of Wellington, whose own Latin was notoriously shaky, advised even against that. 'Say what you have to say', he advised one nervous MP, 'don't quote Latin, and sit down.'[2] Curzon, who did not enter the Commons till 1886, thought

1. G. O. Trevelyan, *The Life and Letters of Lord Macaulay* (1876) ii. 456.
2. *Ibid* ii. 197.

classical quotation a mark of the Golden Age down to the death of Canning in 1827, and nothing to do with his own times – a part of the old aristocratic Parliament of wigs, breeches and silk stockings, untroubled by the importunities of constituents; and he doubted if more than a few Members in his own day had ever read a speech of Demosthenes or could translate one of Cicero: 'In my own time I can recall only two Greek quotations in the House of Commons' – both of them from Balliol men. Disraeli, on the one occasion he could be remembered to have quoted Greek, at Glasgow University in 1872, had acquired the quotation from an academic friend just before the meeting, and it is a question whether he knew enough Greek to understand it without an explanation – though this did not prevent him from assuring his academic audience that the remark from Sophocles had been a solace to him throughout his life.[1] Gladstone, who had entered Parliament in 1833, maintained the tradition of quoting Latin, but the habit was seen as an anachronism: one observer praises him for his 'felicity in quotations, an ornament of debate now practically obsolete'.[2] Bright tried it only once, and late, in 1869, but got it wrong; though English quotation was dear to his heart, and he loved to quote Byron. But Bagehot declared that even in the 1830s and 1840s, in Peel's heyday, Members had 'no great real knowledge of the classics', though they might have 'many lines of Virgil and Horace lingering in fading memories'.[3] The classics are a dying decoration to Victorian oratory.

The truth is that ancient eloquence was a source of allusion, and a diminishing source at that, rather than a guide or a model. Macaulay thought Cicero longwinded: Bagehot found Demosthenes a ranter. 'Counsellor Broom was all in a fume', he used to quote, warning parliamentarians against an excess of fervour, adding that Greek oratory is 'scarcely a model to be imitated precisely'.[4] It is even doubtful if it was imitated at all.

1. Earl Curzon, *Modern Parliamentary Eloquence: the Rede lecture* (London, 1913) p. 11 and n.

2. T. H. S. Escott, *Politics and Letters* (London, 1886) p. 57.

3. Bagehot, 'The Character of Sir Robert Peel', *National Review* (July 1856); reprinted in his *Collected Works* (1968) iii. 268.

4. Bagehot, 'Lord Brougham', *National Review* (July 1857); reprinted *ibid.* p. 189.

The British statesman may not harangue. Eloquence is persuasion, and persuasion in that world means a reasonable air. But in other senses a classical training might count for much: a fineness in language born of childish exercises in translation out of and into Greek and Latin, in verse as well as prose. The younger Pitt used to attribute his parliamentary eloquence to his father's insistence on his seeking, as a boy, till he found just the right English word when he translated from the classics. If the orations of the Ancients were not much followed, a Victorian statesman could still be indelibly marked by the totality of a classical education. It taught him that language is not a master, but an instrument to be used.

The general intellectual influence of the classics, as opposed to the oratorical, was enormous and increasing. Here lies the deepest paradox in the whole question of the debt of British oratory to the ancient world. The renown of Arnold's Rugby and Jowett's Balliol guaranteed that the substantive influence of the classics over the minds of English statesmen should soar in the very age in which the fashion for classical quotation was sinking. Mill, a little earlier, had condemned Oxford and Cambridge (neither of which he had himself attended) as places of education: 'The youth of England are not educated', he had complained in his essay on 'Civilization' (1836). But even in 1836 he had excepted in a generous footnote the teaching of Aristotle's *Ethics*, *Politics* and *Rhetoric* at Oxford, adding that they are among the most 'useful' parts of ancient literature.[1] Useful is an interesting term for a young Utilitarian to employ, though it is not easy to be certain why Mill thought Aristotle a useful author in an industrializing state. But it is still possible to watch such intellectual influences at work, and they are impressive to see. They are not to be judged by allusion and quotation, which at times can be little better than a smoke-screen: they relate to an analytical caste of thought, both moral and stylistic, which is highly characteristic of the increasing refinement of British political debate after 1832: a debate less declamatory than that of its preceding age, denser in its reasoning, more deeply concerned with righteousness and more

1. J. S. Mill, 'Civilization', *London and Westminster Review* (April 1836); reprinted in his *Dissertations and Discussions* (1859) i. 199.

minutely attentive to detail. But to judge that refining influence, the orators themselves must be considered.

The new oratory is a creation of advancing democracy: it differs from the Golden Age in its sense of the crowd. That crowd may be literally present, as at a public meeting; or it may be more remotely felt through a system of reported speeches and the ultimate sanction of the suffrage. But the tendency of the age is towards a consciousness of popular opinion and an eagerness to impress. The old style of statesmanship lingered on, at times successfully: Palmerston, to the end a parliamentary debater of the old school rather than an orator of the new, survived as prime minister till his death in 1865, a living example of triumphant anachronism, manipulating the House as he had learned to manipulate it for half a century. His touch was deft, and more cunning than it looked; he lacked, and appeared not to seek, the arts of elaboration; and his admirer Trollope, in his memoir, emphasizes that in all his forty-nine years of ministerial office he never, in either House, spoke 'for the mere sake of effect', and that though he carefully prepared his speeches, at least when young, as a disagreeable necessity, 'he never seems to have regarded the art as the source of his power or the bulwark of his fame'.[1] But the shift of power from Lords to Commons was helping to make oratory useful, even necessary. In 1784 eight out of nine Cabinet ministers had been peers; and Pitt, the only member of the Commons there, sat for Cambridge University, where parliamentary candidates were not allowed to make speeches. The Duke of Wellington notoriously owed nothing to his mastery of language before the Lords. When Tocqueville attended a debate there in 1833, he shuddered with excitement as he saw the conqueror of Napoleon rise to speak, but only to record his profoundest disappointment:

> The Duke began his speech with difficulty and hesitation, and was never completely at ease. It was the strangest sight to see the man, who had won so many battles and defeated Bonaparte, as embarrassed

1. Trollope, *Palmerston* (London, 1882) pp. 14–15. Kingsley Martin, *The Triumph of Lord Palmerston* (London, 1924) shows that he was in no way indifferent to public opinion, however, and that he was skilled in winning favour with the press (p. 58).

as a child reciting its lesson before a pitiless pedagogue. The hero of Waterloo did not know where to put his arms or legs, nor how to balance his long body. He picked up and put down his hat, turned to the left and right, ceaselessly buttoned and unbuttoned the pocket of his breeches as if he wanted to seek his words there – words, to be sure, that did not flow easily from his mind.[1]

Peel, though he could dominate the House, could not excite it: his speeches are those of an earnest, statesmanlike logician. A debater rather than an orator, he belonged to Parliament, not to the platform. As a boy he had been trained by his father to make speeches and to repeat the Sunday sermon; some of these sermons, Bagehot observed waspishly, got into his addresses to the House;[2] and Disraeli, in his life of Bentinck (1852), recording how he had broken with his leader over his repeal of the Corn Laws in 1846, recalls that though Peel was 'the most available talent' as an orator that the Commons had seen, combining prudence with promptness, eloquence always escaped him: 'in the higher efforts of oratory he was not successful', and his vocabulary, though ample and never mean, was 'neither rich nor rare':

He embalmed no great political truth in immortal words. His flights were ponderous; he soared with the wing of the vulture rather than the plume of the eagle; and his perorations when most elaborate were most unwieldy. In pathos he was quite deficient; when he attempted to touch the tender passions, it was painful. His face became distorted, like that of a woman who wants to cry but cannot succeed. Orators certainly should not shed tears; but there are moments when, as the Italians say, the voice should weep (pp. 315–16).

The process towards eloquence was slow, and stolidity lingered. Emerson, in a visit to England in 1847, found the English taciturn and almost wilfully unoratorical: 'A kind of pride in bad public speaking is noted in the House of Commons', he remarked in *English Traits* (1856), 'as if they were willing to show that they did not live by their tongues, or spoke well

1. Tocqueville, *Journeys to England and Ireland* (1968) p. 25.
2. Bagehot, 'The Character of Sir Robert Peel' (1856); reprinted in his *Collected Works* (1968) iii. 262.

enough if they have the tone of gentlemen' (ch. 8). There must have been plenty of ordinary incompetence. Trollope may not have been exaggerating much when he makes Lord Silverbridge in *The Duke's Children* (1880), though already an MP, make his first public speech before a crowded election meeting in terms like these:

> 'My friend Frank Tregear,' he began, rushing at once at his subject, 'is a very good fellow, and I hope you'll elect him.' Then he paused, not remembering what was to come next; but the sentiment which he had uttered appeared to his auditors to be so good in itself and so well delivered, that they filled up a long pause with continued clappings and exclamations. 'Yes,' continued the young Member of Parliament, encouraged by the kindness of the crowd, 'I have known Frank Tregear ever so long, and I don't think you could find a better member of Parliament anywhere' (ch. 55).

Trollope had lost an election of his own a dozen years before, and may be reflecting bitterly here on the talents that lose elections and the buffoons that win them. In many a constituency, and especially in many a country constituency, and on many a back bench, the inarticulate continued to survive. But the leadership was changing.

Henry Brougham, who entered Parliament in 1810 and rose to be Lord Chancellor, was seen by many as a new portent, exploiting language as a popular instrument. G. H. Francis calls him frankly 'the type of the talking power'. Lord John Russell, who emerges from Francis's *Orators of the Age* as an ideal, is said to have compensated for a puny body and presence, and a monotonous voice, by a subtle wit and power of leadership. Macaulay floated upwards on the word, an exponent of literature in parliamentary life; but his success was still that of the old school, less influenced than some by the platform and the flattery of the crowd. His triumph was purely literary: so purely, that it may be asked whether he spoke primarily to impress the House or to impress the readers he hoped eventually to enthrall. Even his nephew admits in an admiring biography that Macaulay had nothing of 'the outward graces of the orator', and quotes the reports of journalists that his actions were ungainly and his voice rapid, loud and monotonous; he 'had not learned the art of speaking from the platform, the pulpit, the forum, or any of the usual modes of obtaining a fluent diction'.[1] He was vehement, dazzling in his memory for facts, names and dates, and the House was spellbound by it all. But his place is as the last survivor of the Golden Age, of that long era where his imagination throve between the Revolution of 1689 and the Reform of 1832; he was not an orator in the new popular tradition. His effects were artistic rather than practical; and though he often spoke in practical causes, his mode was to decorate and dilate rather than to seek to alter the course of events. Between spoken and printed word the proximity here is exceptionally close: 'His speeches read like essays,' Francis noted, 'as his essays read like speeches.' But the same reporter, like many others, found his momentum wonderful: 'You think of an express train that does not stop even at the chief stations.'

The shift to the platform had already begun before Macaulay, who found it uncongenial, had temporarily retired from Parliament with his defeat at Edinburgh in 1847. He was to return to the Commons in 1852, but it is doubtful if he would have relished the age of Gladstone's leadership that was soon to come. Popular oratory was in the ascendant, not only among parliamentary beginners: Gladstone had already sat in the House for thirty years when, on a visit to Newcastle in 1862, he began to discover his power over the crowd. Oratory was entering its theatrical phase: party leaders, by the 1860s, were beginning to perform as star actors, the prospect of the suffrage invited to supreme office, and the Reform Act of 1867 could itself be regarded as a triumph for the platform.[2] What Emerson in the 1840s had noted as a lethargy was passing: other travellers report another atmosphere, as if the nation itself had changed. Speeches can now be dramatic performances in a dramatic atmosphere. Even before the reign began, an American visitor had spoken of 'the morbid excitability of the British public, amounting almost to a mental disease'.[3] What Tocqueville had noticed at the Guildhall in 1833 as a conversation

1. G. O. Trevelyan, *The Life and Letters of Lord Macaulay* (1876) ii. 139–40.
2. Jephson, *The Platform* (1892) ii. 464.
3. Wilbur Fisk, *Travels* (New York, 1838) p. 529, reporting on a visit of 1835.

between orator and audience was moving towards its most intense phase, a dialogue between the one and the many played out between the party leader and what Gladstone at Midlothian exultingly called 'this great ocean of human life'. An observer of Joseph Chamberlain at a public meeting in Birmingham saw him watch the responsive faces of his radical audience with all the marks of a man in passion: 'It might have been a woman listening to the words of her lover.'[1] Those who were hostile to democracy were contemptuous or alarmed; the fastidious remained sceptical; and some, like Trollope, could even doubt that oratory won votes. But after 1867 it was very hard to deny that public speeches were an element in electoral victory. By then two stars stood high in the heavens as rival leaders.

Gladstone and Disraeli faced each other as leaders in the Commons for only eight years; but they were rival orators in the public mind before Gladstone's first ministry and after Disraeli's departure for the Lords in 1876. That most dramatic of confrontations lasted in all for fully twenty years, down to Disraeli's death in opposition in 1881. It was no shadow fight, being spiced with a deep and genuine dislike on both sides, a total contrast in temperament, and deep disagreements on policy at home and abroad. If it was not the most important aspect of British politics in the 1860s and 1870s, it was easily the most arresting.

Gladstone had been recognized as the master of parliamentary eloquence years before he became leader of the Liberal Party. Bagehot in 1860 had called him 'the greatest orator in the House of Commons'.[2] But his consciousness of that talent had grown slowly. When he entered the Commons in 1833 as a Conservative, he lacked all essential attainments as a speaker, and distinguished himself rather for probity and a severe mastery of evidence. Three years later he began a short treatise entitled 'Public Speaking', a highly elementary account which suggests that the young statesman had only just discovered a disturbing truth: 'The manner is not only a thing of moment,

1. Beatrice Webb, *My Apprenticeship* (London, 1926) p. 109.
2. Bagehot, *National Review* (July 1860); reprinted in his *Collected Works* (1968) iii. 415.

but of greater moment than the matter.'[1] That was a realization he had to learn to live with, and he did.

It is doubtful if Gladstone discovered himself as an orator before his early fifties; but before old age he was widely accepted as supreme. This supremacy was of the spoken word: nobody except himself, then or since, imagined that his speeches would read as well as they had sounded. Acton, writing to Gladstone's daughter in 1880 at the start of his second premiership, put the emphasis judiciously: 'I do think that, of the three greatest Liberals, Burke is equally good in speaking and writing; Macaulay better in writing, and Mr Gladstone better in speaking', adding with candour: 'I doubt whether he feels it.'[2] Everyone else seems to have felt it. A few who were not under the spell claimed for themselves an indifference to his spoken word, and even his admirers usually admitted he was humourless and lacking in proportion. A colleague once remarked: 'When I speak, I strike across from headland to headland. But Mr Gladstone coasts along, and whenever he comes to a navigable river he cannot resist the temptation to explore it to its source.'[3] But the general view, even of his opponents, was that his performances in Parliament and in the country were so wonderful to anyone who had seen and heard them that no printed word would ever be able to convey their mastery. 'Posterity must take it from us,' said Balfour in a generous tribute in May 1898 in the Commons, on his death: 'If you go and take down a volume of his speeches and read them, you will not believe what I tell you.'

That is because posterity cannot see the man. His physical dynamism in the House and on the platform gave audiences something to watch as well as something to hear: in the Commons, it is said, he would bang a fist on an open hand, turn suddenly to appeal to his supporters, and allow to gesture and expression the fullest play. Disraeli, by contrast, was

1. British Museum Additional MS 46,681; first published by Loren Reid, 'Gladstone's essay on Public Speaking', *Quarterly Journal of Speech* xxxix (1953). The 16-page manuscript appears to have been written in 1836–38. For a guide to Gladstone's speeches see Arthur Tilney Bassett, *Gladstone's Speeches: Descriptive index and bibliography* (London, 1916).

2. Lord Acton, *Letters to Mary Gladstone* (1904) p. 57.

3. T. H. S. Escott, *Politics and Letters* (1886) p. 56.

immobile: Curzon compares him to a sphinx. Even Gladstone's enemies concede the fascination of the spectacle: one satirist speaks of 'the white-hot face, stern as a Covenanter's, yet mobile as a comedian'.[1] He combined all the gifts of eloquence: his rivals, wrote Acton to Mary Gladstone in the same letter, divided his gifts among them like the generals of Alexander. 'One may equal him in beauty of composition, another in the art of statement, and a third, perhaps, comes near him in fluency and fire. But he alone possesses all the qualities of an orator.' Acton was an intimate; but Trollope, who belonged to an older and soberer tradition, saw his leader as a phenomenon of nature: he 'bursts into speech, that the brightness and splendour and marvel of the moment may be his. . . . Words run riot with glorious fecundity as to leave an impression that some oil might have been expended in pruning their abundance.'[2] That fecundity, which looks perilously like prolixity on the printed page, was often felt to smack of auto-intoxication; but it was an intoxication mixed (so his enemies believed) with calculation, and no one doubted that the excitement was always blended with intellectual control, even a deep ulterior purpose. 'Glozing tongue whom none can trust', an Oxford contemporary wrote of him, hinting at 'mere delusive eloquence'.[3]

Disraeli often made the same charge. A year before Gladstone's return to politics in the Midlothian campaign, Disraeli in a speech of July 1878 attacked his arch-enemy in language that artfully parodied Gladstone's own rotundity of style: 'A sophistical rhetorician, inebriated with the exuberance of his own verbosity, and gifted with an egotistical imagination that can at times command an interminable and inconsistent series of arguments to malign an opponent and to glorify himself.' But rotundity and syntactical elaboration are only a part of the repertory. Gladstone can vary the elaborate with the simple and repetitive, in a style that resembles the great nineteenth-century preachers, and notably those of an evangelical stamp. Parts of the first Midlothian speech of 25 November 1879 must

1. H. D. Traill, *The New Lucian* (London, 1884) p. 198. The book is an attack on Gladstone in the form of an imaginary dialogue between Burke and Horsman.
2. Trollope, *Palmerston* (1882) p. 211.
3. Martin Tupper, *My Life as an Author* (London, 1886) p. 54.

have sounded in familiar style to an audience trained in the traditions of Protestant preaching:

And why, gentlemen, are they not anxious to obtain the judgment of the country? It is surely plain that they are not anxious. If they were anxious, they would follow the rule, and dissolve the Parliament. It is plain, therefore, that they are not anxious. Why are they not anxious? Have they not told us all along that they possess the confidence of the people? Have they not boasted right and left that vast majorities of the nation are in the same sense with themselves? Oh, gentlemen, these are idle pretexts!

An unfriendly observer might note, in this hebraic parallelism of utterance and belabouring of what is not in doubt, an unbecoming reminder of Dickens's Reverend Mr Chadband in *Bleak House*: ' "My friends, why do I wish for peace? What is peace? Is it war? No. Is it strife? No. Is it lovely, and gentle, and beautiful, and pleasant, and serene, and joyful? O yes! Therefore, my friends, I wish for peace, upon you and upon yours" ' (ch. 19).

The device was common, it must be remembered, in Victorian prose: Disraeli was capable of using it too, and without irony; and Gladstone could use the same trick of successive rhetorical questions not only before an audience, but even in print. His review of Trevelyan's biography of Macaulay includes this: 'Was he envious? Never. Was he servile? No. Was he insolent? No. Was he prodigal? No. Was he avaricious? No. Was he selfish? No. Was he idle? The question is ridiculous. Was he false? No; but true as steel, and transparent as crystal. Was he vain? We hold that he was not.'[1] This was a political genius that, unlike Disraeli's, lived in essence far beyond the reach of the comic, at least in public. It made a direct moral demand on the audience. The triumphal procession that Gladstone made from Liverpool to Edinburgh to open his by-election campaign, on a bleak November day in 1879, lit the countryside with beacons, and men and women came from the far Hebrides to hear him speak. This was the supreme triumph of the word in British politics, though not of that alone. Behind words lay

1. W. E. Gladstone, 'Macaulay', *Quarterly Review* (July 1876); reprinted in his *Gleanings of Past Years 1845–76* (London, 1879) ii. 273.

a shrewd sense of the possible, a vigilant consciousness of virtue based on undeviating observance, and faith in a political constitution strangely allied to a faith in a personal God. The draughts of strength he took from vast audiences were no mere drama, but the impulse of an ageing life. In the roar of those thousands lay the destiny to which democracy had come.

The contrast with Disraeli is not in politics alone. Disraeli's career was based, good fortune apart, on language: first the published word, and then the spoken. Unlike Gladstone he was not well connected, and entered the House nearly five years after his future rival after an unseemly struggle for a nomination and a seat. His ability as an administrator, unlike Gladstone's, could be doubted; his respectability, both financial and sexual, was doubted from the start. With all this, his parliamentary rise over thirty years to the leadership of Conservative Party and the premiership, helped as it was by the Tory split of 1846 and the loss of talented rivals to the Liberals, can best be seen as an act of levitation. Disraeli floated upwards on oratory: that was his life's undertaking. Even before he achieved success as a speaker he had glorified the word. Sidonia, the mysterious stranger on an Arab steed whom Coningsby meets and is inspired by, is a master of nothing but language, so far as the novel allows him to be seen: he is a magician with words, and Coningsby, nursing his young ambitions, is understandably bewitched: 'There are men whose phrases are oracles; who condense in a sentence the secrets of life; who blurt out an aphorism that forms a character or illustrates an existence' (iii. 2). Speech is the gift beyond all others, and the novels are written as aids to the aspiring statesman. 'A great thing is a great book; but greater than all is the talk of a great man!'

Disraeli's great man talks of visions, and those visions are remote, grandiose and global. It is fantastic to credit, as one reads *Coningsby* and *Sybil*, written less than ten years after Disraeli's first entry into Parliament, that the visions of Sidonia or Sybil could be the foundations of a successful political career. Disraeli lived to fill all the space, and more, that his words had hollowed out for him in early life. And the visions never ceased. In his last completed novel, *Endymion* (1880), published after he had been twice Prime Minister, he vicariously lived the life of a young hero of the English landed aristocracy whose sister married a fictional equivalent of Napoleon III. These words do not reflect, as Gladstone's did, the images of any known political faith or the hopes and fears of millions. They are the aspirations of megalomania in search of a career. Tory radicalism is more like a ragbag than an ideology, a wild mixture of royalism and populism with a late admixture of imperial fervour. But then it is not its consistency or plausibility that counts. What counts is rather the infinite glitter of language, good-humoured even when ridiculing an enemy, parodistic, epigrammatic and momentarily penetrating. He had a phrase where Gladstone had a flood. That it was all a show, and little more, was suspected from the start: but it was a show to watch. Mendacity amounted here to a habit of mind, and a taste for unacknowledged borrowing was exposed early, when the *Globe* convicted him of plagiarizing Thiers's funeral oration over a French marshal for his eulogy of the Duke of Wellington (16 November 1852). But this is a rhetoric which neither commanded nor expected belief. The great rival could do that. It is a rhetoric to deflate the pomposity of others, to enrapture rather than to convince.

How was the Victorian art of oratory practised and rehearsed? An actor learns his lines, and theatre is ordinarily an effect of training and calculation. It is certain that Victorian orators did not usually proceed in that way. In some sense they awaited the impulse of the moment: 'There is always inspiration in a great crowd', Bright once remarked to Joseph Chamberlain, urging him not to worry about a speech he was to make to a mass meeting.[1] But there was preparation, of a kind, and notes were often made, though not always used. Macaulay's exceptional memory enabled him to speak without notes, even without notes in his pocket; but his speeches were carefully prepared, and only the trick of memory gave an air of the impromptu. With Gladstone and Disraeli notes might be made, and some

1. Austen Chamberlain, 'How great speakers prepare their speeches', in his autobiography *Down the Years* (London, 1935) p. 255. This essay in the form of an appendix appears to be the only extensive account of how British statesmen prepare their speeches, and it reproduces facsimiles of manuscript notes for speeches by Bright, Asquith and Balfour.

have survived; but it is doubtful if, at the height of their careers, they were much held in the hand. Gladstone's secretary once remarked that no one liked to interrupt him on the day before he made a speech; and that though he might not literally be writing his speech, he was mentally engaged upon it: 'He lies on a sofa and *wombles* it on his inside.'[1] Disraeli came to dispense with notes, for fear of growing dependent on them, and claimed to be a master of the impromptu; though such impromptus might be carefully prepared in advance, like the epigrams of a practised conversationalist. One report suggests that he sometimes rehearsed a speech, in whole or in part, to a *Times* reporter 'in whom he placed especial trust'.[2]

The Victorian orator was an actor with a licence to extemporize. If he could think of a better line, or if a movement or a word from the crowd suggested it, he would use it. But he already had his lines, in a sense: they may have been written out, or written as notes, and perhaps in varying degrees memorized: they were not, for the most part, simply invented on the spot.

For the greatest speeches the written source might be very small. The biographer of the younger Pitt, Lord Stanhope, gives a mere ninety words for Pitt's speech on the renewal of war on 23 May 1803, a speech he describes as one that Demosthenes 'must have admired and might have envied'. Bright used to prepare a key sentence in advance, calling it an 'island', for each compartment of an intended speech: 'Then he would swim from island to island, until he landed on the best island of all, which was, of course, the peroration.'[3] Gladstone, at least in his later years, seems to have done with still less. The surviving notes for his first Midlothian speech, for example, consist of about one hundred words for a speech which in its printed form amounts to over ten thousand.[4] Whereas Pitt's notes consist austerely of mere heads of argument signalized by names like 'Portugal', 'Naples', and the like, Gladstone's are

1. *Ibid.* p. 254.
2. *Ibid.* p. 255.
3. Earl Curzon, *Modern Parliamentary Eloquence* (1913) p. 31n.
4. British Museum Additional MS 44,666 f. 69. Cf Gladstone, *Midlothian Speeches 1879*, edited by M. R. D. Foot (Leicester, 1971) pp. 26–58.

more often phrases to set the tone of a paragraph or more: 'Come as a stranger', 'with no doubtful prospects', 'add a new character to the contest', 'early dissolution?' If it were all well and truly wombled, this might easily suffice, though it presupposes a vast confidence based on a long experience in public speaking. The result could be, if not humorous, at least touched with irony: 'Now that will not be disputed; or if it is disputed, and in order that it may not be disputed, for it is very difficult to say what won't be disputed – in order that it may not be disputed I will read from two conclusive authorities.'[1] One can hear a murmur of amused assent flutter upwards at the first phrase, to be cultivated by the speaker appreciatively until the murmur becomes a roar. This is the actor's art, drawing tight the invisible thread between player and public. But here it is also an art of government, and it uses an acquired skill in language to consult a people who have recently entered upon the power to rule.

1. *Ibid.* p. 51.

8

The Parliamentary Novel

The British political novel between Disraeli's *Coningsby* (1844) and H. G. Wells's *New Machiavelli* (1911) is a corpus of fiction unique in the world, and its uniqueness lies in the simple prominence it confers on the parliamentary idea. If I coin the term 'parliamentary novel' to describe it here, it is to give this prominence the notice it deserves. This is a political fiction, but political in a highly specific sense: no nation other than Victorian–Edwardian Britain has ever explored its elective institutions so extensively in fiction.

This uniqueness may seem surprising. It will seem less surprising, however, though not less impressive, when it is considered how difficult history would find it to supply the Victorians with a rival. To begin with, a fiction like this requires a nation, and not only nationhood but a full national consciousness in literature. A federation like the United States is too large and too loose for this purpose, and American fiction down to the mid twentieth century was too regional to allow for it, though it may some day emerge: classic American fiction is about a measurable area like New England, or New York, or the South, or the Mississippi Valley. France did not have enduring parliamentary institutions until after 1871; Germany was not a nation till then, and not a parliamentary nation till much later; and Russia is not a parliamentary state at all. The great rivals in fiction reveal themselves under scrutiny as simply incapable of rivalry in this respect.

The essence of the parliamentary idea, which this body of fiction exemplifies and explores, is a system of institutionalized persuasion in which decision is achieved by deliberation.[1] The system has its sceptics, and it is sometimes suggested that parliamentary institutions are a façade, in the sense that the real decisions are taken outside the two chambers. But this mistake, which is too elementary to be committed by the novelists themselves, is based on an excessively literal view of what a parliamentary constitution is. Parliament is Queen, Lords and Commons; the deliberations by which it makes its decisions are various in place as well as in style, and it is a mere beginner's mistake to suppose that the only arena that is supposed to matter is the floor of the House of Commons. What matters is that the decisions are made by parliamentarians: sometimes in public places, like parliamentary debates or public meetings and assemblies, sometimes in committee, sometimes in private conversations such as the exchanges that regularly occur between sovereign and Prime Minister. The Cabinet, which is the principal decision-making body in the land in matters of national policy, is wholly composed of members of the Houses of Parliament, is itself deliberative (though its deliberations are private) and is in any case subject to the will of Parliament. At every point in these many complexities, persuasion rather than intimidation or force is the characteristic proceeding. When sceptics complain that the system is only spuriously deliberative in that Members rarely if ever change their minds and their votes during parliamentary debates, they fail to notice the numerous other possibilities by which persuasive forces work. Governments do, after all, change their minds, even more often than they admit to having done so, and what is said in Lords and Commons is often among the reasons why they do so. It is an unusual Act of any significance that emerges as law in just the form in which it first appeared as a Bill.

A second objection must be more rapidly dismissed here, since it is the subject of a later discussion. It is sometimes

1. This adapts a phrase of Acton's, who complained in a review of Erskine May's *Democracy in Europe* in the *Quarterly Review* (January 1878) that the new centralizing Swiss constitution of 1874, with its provision for plebiscites, was 'separating decision from deliberation'; Lord Acton, *The History of Freedom and Other Essays* (London, 1907) p. 91.

objected on a variety of grounds that parliamentary institutions, then and now, are undemocratic, or that they fail to represent the popular will. This may be true, but it misconceives the question at issue. A parliamentary constitution need not be democratic, just as a democratic constitution need not be parliamentary – it might be presidential, for example. Most of the novels considered here are about a parliamentary state, namely the United Kingdom between the first and third Reform Acts of 1832 and 1884; down to the second Reform Act of 1867, perhaps one-sixth of male adults had the right to vote, in principle at least and to the limited extent that seats were contested at all. Such a state is neither democratic, at the one extreme, nor oligarchic at the other, since the electorate is too small to merit the first title and too large for the other. Democracy is among the issues raised by these novels, and its prospect is widely accepted even by those who dislike it most. But it is not itself the background of assumption, and this fiction concerns itself rather with an elective and deliberative process for which 'parliamentary' seems the only name.

The parliamentary novel, lightened as it often is with the familiar seductions of English fiction – romantic plots, comedy-of-manners and the like – is conscious of being something momentous. The English novel has sometimes been thought too minutely social to excel at the portrayal of great ideas or the clash of historical forces. Its detail is its strength, admittedly; but the details provided by Disraeli, George Eliot, Trollope, Meredith and others are none the less representative of great institutions and events. This is not always easy to recall as one reads; indeed it would be extravagant to recall it at every point, since the statesman is shown in undress on occasion, humiliated at his family breakfast-table or losing an argument with his wife. It is the paradox of power that the magnate is also a man, and much of the fascination of this fiction arises from the contrast between his public life and his domestic. The Victorians loved to learn of their great men from those who knew them: some of this fiction, especially Disraeli's *romans à clef*, offers among its other interests the spice of gossip. But the simple fact remains that the British Parliament described by these novelists was the most powerful political institution on earth, and both novelist and reader knew it to be so. To be prime minister of England, as Trollope's Lady Glencora remarks to a friend, 'is to be the greatest man in the greatest country in the world'.[1] Any Englishman, the reader is often assured, would wish to be a Member of Parliament. Describing his humiliating defeat as a Liberal candidate for Beverley in 1868, Trollope justifies his decision to stand, in his *Autobiography*, on these momentous grounds:

> I have always thought that to sit in the British Parliament should be the highest object of ambition to every educated Englishman . . . The man in Parliament has reached a higher position than the man out. . . . To serve one's country without pay is the grandest work that a man can do. . . . The study of politics is the one in which a man may make himself most useful to his fellow-creatures (ch. 16).

Having lost at Beverley, he came to see this defeat, by hindsight, as a literary opportunity, and turned a bitter memory into fiction, most specifically in *Ralph the Heir* (1871): 'as I was debarred from expressing my opinions in the House of Commons, I took this method of declaring myself', as he put it in the *Autobiography*. Here was his gratification, since he was 'enabled from time to time to have in this way that fling at the political doings of the day which every man likes to take, if not in one fashion, then in another'.[2]

Trollope's chronology of events cannot be strictly accurate, since the first of the six Palliser novels (1864–80) appeared four years before his Yorkshire candidature; but there is plenty in the Palliser novels and in *Ralph* to confirm that Trollope's later fiction is a commentary on the parliamentary scene by some one who regretted his failure to get in. These books are the summit of English political fiction: they are written from the wings by some one who was never himself an actor, and by one who still feels bound to accept that the best of life is there.

A few Victorians, at least, were conscious of the unique quality of their politics as a stimulant to literature. The parliamentary system is built on persuasion, and persuasion is

1. Trollope, *The Prime Minister* (London, 1876) ch. 72.
2. Trollope, *Autobiography*, edited by F. Page (Oxford, 1950) pp. 317, 184.

achieved by language. There was much to wonder at and admire in a nation where despotism was banished, political discussion free and the possibility of persuasion a continuous spur, and where the fruits of office were yet incalculably great. A young man could hope to change things; he could even hope to change them by talking and writing about them. It is doubtful if this seemed possible to any but a lucky few in any previous age of British political history. And here the novel was supreme. An anonymous critic of Defoe, writing in 1856, calls the novel 'the characteristic literature of modern times' – characteristic because the 'increase of personal liberty has given increased scope and a greater common importance to individual life and character'. All this coincides with 'diminishing political and social restraint' and 'a less formal and exigent code of manners in society'. Freedom brings reflection, leisure makes for introspection, and 'an increased interest in our own characters has naturally given us an increased interest in the individual characters of others' – whereas a hundred years ago and more, in the age of Defoe, the times were ill adapted to the 'quiet contemplation of character', being 'filled with restless petty action'.[1]

The direct link between an open political system and the new political fiction was remarked at the time. The 1830s was the natural breaking-point, and men who entered Parliament then or later were lucky to be alive. 'Throughout the last two centuries of our history,' wrote George Otto Trevelyan of Macaulay's entry into the Commons in 1830, viewing the matter from the high pedestal of Disraeli's England and Gladstone's, 'there never was a period when a man conscious of power, impatient of public wrongs, and still young enough to love a fight for its own sake, could have entered Parliament with a fairer prospect of leading a life worth living and doing work that would requite the pains than at the commencement of the year 1830.' In the preceding age, by contrast, 'argument and oratory were alike unavailing under a constitution which was indeed a despotism of privilege'.[2] But argument and oratory

1. *National Review* (October 1856).

2. G. O. Trevelyan, *The Life and Letters of Lord Macaulay* (1876) i. 155, 156–7.

were a highly possible ladder to success after 1830. Macaulay was offered a seat by a peer who admired his prose; Disraeli rose on words. By the sixties and seventies the union of politics and literature is in many minds a two-way affair: not only is some literature political, like Trollope's Palliser novels, but some politics is highly literary, and men of letters can become prime minister. Influences are reciprocal, by then, and political life is beginning to copy art.

Literature is notoriously an open form – more open than politics in a settled society could ever be. Anyone who can write may write: the profession requires talent but little capital, and even an unknown can thrive at it. This is equally the curiosity of the new political system, that it laid open the avenues of power to the new man. Connections, as always and everywhere, remained useful, but they were no longer literally necessary. Such openness, too, helped to create the new political fiction, which was not merely possible in such an age but almost required by it. Society was no longer swayed only by 'the exclusive machinations of select aristocratic coteries'.[1] Anyone who thinks he can write can try, like the absurd Lady Carbury in Trollope's *The Way We Live Now*. Authorship is a way not only to fame and wealth, but even to power. This curiosity of the Victorian system sets it apart from its successors, in a marked degree, though broadcasting has since partly replaced fiction as a way by which the unconnected can rise. No twentieth-century prime minister apart from Winston Churchill has ever published a novel; and *Savrola* (1900), a very Disraelian romance in the Tory-Radical manner, was written while Victoria was still Queen. But then the complex of conditions that made British politics so literary in themselves, and so amenable to fictional treatment, was hardly to survive the First World War.

The range of the parliamentary novel may be quickly indicated by its major examples. It begins with the Disraelian trilogy, *Coningsby*, *Sybil* and *Tancred* (1844–47), though Disraeli's novels have their occasional predecessors, like Maria

1. T. H. S. Escott, 'Political novels', *Fraser's Magazine* (April 1874), an early account to recognize this group of novels as a new and significant development in English fiction.

Edgeworth's *Patronage* (1814). But *Patronage* is a severe moral allegory couched in contemporary manners, and preaches against worldliness and political involvement: the virtuous man chooses to remain untainted by the pursuit of office. *Coningsby* is a call to involvement, above all an appeal to the young to enter Parliament and restore the ancient constitution to its glory: it is the natural starting-point of this story. The 1850s are surprisingly bare, though Thackeray includes an election towards the end of *The Newcomes* (1853), where old Colonel Newcome, to the consternation of his family, stands for Parliament as a Liberal, utters a variety of opinions on his platform, including some Tory and Radical ones, and finds himself elected. Disraeli stopped writing novels for about twenty years, having provoked not one new vogue but two: for *Sybil* had started a brief fashion for industrial novels, calling on people and Parliament to pay critical attention to the factory system and the unfamiliar problems of the industrial North: Mrs Gaskell's *Mary Barton: a tale of Manchester life* (1848), written just before the publication of *Sybil*; Charlotte Brontë's *Shirley* (1849) and the early chapters of her first novel *The Professor* (1857), written much earlier, in 1846, and rejected by six publishers; as well as Charles Kingsley's *Alton Locke* (1850) and Dickens's *Hard Times* (1854). But the industrial vogue in fiction, though intense in the decade after 1845, did not last as the parliamentary vogue was to last. That taste continued through Trollope's later fiction after 1864, George Eliot's *Felix Holt* (1866), Meredith's *Beauchamp's Career* (1876) and a subplot of Henry James's *Tragic Muse* (1890) to the young Churchill and the middle-aged Wells. The span is of nearly seventy years.

From most of this story the name of Dickens is awkwardly absent. That Thackeray, for the most part, should also be an omission is less surprising, since about half his novels are historical, and his mind as a novelist dwelt less willingly on the contemporary world of the 1840s and 1850s; though it delighted, in *Pendennis* and elsewhere, to recall his Cambridge undergraduate year (1829–30) and his young man's life in literary London. But Dickens does not have that excuse. Outside *Barnaby Rudge* and *A Tale of Two Cities* he is broadly a contemporary novelist: his world stretches from a remembered boyhood in the 1820s down to the immediate controversies of the 1860s. Parliament had been part of his life: he had worked for his uncle's *Mirror of Parliament* in the early thirties as a reporter, and may have sat through the Reform debate of 1831–32. But it was not a part of his imagination. Neither David Copperfield nor the Pip of *Great Expectations* thinks of trying to enter the Commons, as young men do in Disraeli and Trollope: the first, like his creator, becomes a successful novelist, the second a gentleman. The farcical account of a parliamentary contest between the Bluffs and the Blues in *Pickwick*, his first novel, only confirms a lack of interest. 'Shout with the largest', is Mr Pickwick's advice to his friends caught between rival mobs. It is a pre-Reform election, but none of his comments in later novels are less hostile; and since some of them, such as *Bleak House*, have some claim to be considered the greatest social fiction ever written, the awkwardness of this abstention needs to be considered.

The reasons are not clear, and it remains the supreme paradox of the English political novel that Dickens, writing at the high point of its fashion, showed no sympathetic interest in Parliament as a seat of power. Penetrating as his political sense could be, on occasion, the ultimate political question was one he was content to leave to others. Who have the power? how are they chosen, and how is their power limited and controlled? Issues like these do not arise in *Bleak House*, *Hard Times* or *Little Dorrit*, as they do in *Coningsby*, *Felix Holt* or Trollope's later fiction. Dickens's occasional references to Parliament outside the novels, though not hostile to the parliamentary idea as such, suggest that he wilfully refused to grasp the vital connexion between language and power in his own times – an unusual mistake for a man of letters to make. He had a lasting horror of pretension. 'Mr Pecksniff was a moral man,' he wrote in *Martin Chuzzlewit* (ch. 2). 'Some people likened him to a directing-post, which is always telling the way to a place, and never goes there.' He was obsessed with the disparities between what men say and what they do. Oratory excites his special contempt; in an article in *Household Words* (28 June 1851), 'A few conventionalities', he mocks at the style and musical intonation of Commons oratory, as if recalling with pain his early days as a reporter; and the prejudice survives to the end of his life. 'I have very strong opinions on the subject of speechification,' he wrote in a letter of August 1869, in the last year of his life, 'and hold that there is everywhere a vast amount too much of it.' Mr Luke Honeythunder, a large, noisy philanthropist in the last novel, *Edwin Drood* (1870), sums up crushingly Dickens's final view of the professional public man:

> You were to love your brother as yourself, but after an indefinite interval of maligning him (very much as if you hated him) and calling him all manner of names. Above all things, you were to do nothing in private, or on your own account. You were to go to the offices of the Haven of Philanthropy, and put your name down as a Member and a Professing Philanthropist. Then you were to pay up your subscription, get your card of membership, and your riband and medal, and were evermore to live upon a platform, and evermore to say what Mr Honeythunder said, and what the Treasurer said, and what the Committee said, and what the sub-Committee said, and what the Secretary said, and what the Vice-Secretary said (ch. 6).

The satire is so telling that it takes a conscious effort to remind oneself how much Victorian England owed to organized philanthropy and to the willingness of many such men to hold unpaid office. The portrait is funny; it may even, in some respects, be just; but it does not accurately describe the effects of public service, including speechification, on social advance in the age; and its highly characteristic implication that a loud-mouthed self-importance is the chief or only reason why public life is found attractive is hardly worth considering.

In Dickens's novels virtue is private and familial. The sensible man avoids the meshes of public life. Parliament is mostly rigmarole, the law a complicated racket to ensure a living for lawyers, the civil service a Circumlocution Office designed to provide easy employment for the sons and nephews of gentlemen. Generous as Dickens often is in his indignation, this is an impatient and unreflected view, and its omissions are flagrant. Perhaps it is no bad thing for a free society to talk as if it despised and distrusted authority, provided it does not literally believe what it says. This is the curious contradiction that Dickens and many radicals like him embody. They call

Parliament a talking-shop; and they also demand it should act, which is not something to demand of a talking-shop. But the rhetoric of indignant hyperbole is well and widely understood, and such men would surely be surprised to find themselves taken literally. If Dickens thought much in parliamentary life boring and absurd, there is not the slightest reason to doubt that he also thought he lived under the finest constitution on earth. *A Child's History of England* ends with the Glorious Revolution of 1689, as if Dickens were as certain in his heart as any Whig that England, at that moment, achieved her political destiny.

The history of the parliamentary novel, then, largely omits the fiction of Dickens and Thackeray. It begins with Disraeli, a future prime minister, and ends with Wells, who abandoned a public career for love. The beginning and end are apt, even symbolic; but the causes of the rise and fall of the species are certain to be more complex than that. Its heyday was before 1870; technical shifts in the novel itself, especially towards psychological realism, must have harmed it, since contests for power are too bold to be amenable to techniques as minute and subtle as those of James or Joyce. The secret ballot, adopted by Gladstone's first ministry in 1872, robbed elections of some of their robuster fascination such as bribery and intimidation: the measure, excellent as it was for the purity of politics, was to that extent a doubtful blessing to literature. The old open ballot, and the old patronage system which was its natural accompaniment, must have been more colourful to watch and richer in those intrigues and private deals that mid-Victorian novelists and readers had dwelt on with a mixture of fascination and indignation. An uncorrupt election is less interesting in human terms. Trollope, describing Melmotte's candidature as a Conservative in a Westminster by-election in *The Way We Live Now* (1875), remarks cynically on the suddenly representative character of Tory constituency committees since the recent reforms: 'His committee was made up of peers, bankers and publicans, with all that absence of class prejudice for which the party has become famous since the ballot was introduced among us' (ch. 35). Some of the gusto, along with much of the corruption, had gone out of English political life: there would be no more Eatanswill.

But, in a still more pervasive sense, democracy was weakening the social cohesion of a once aristocratic Parliament, and social cohesion works on the novelist's side. It gives him a world that can be circumscribed: a whole society is too much, and *Bleak House* succeeds as the rarest of exceptions to the rule that a social novelist must select something less than a whole nation if he is to create a credible world. In that respect Disraeli, as a pioneer, had been lucky: the Parliament he entered in 1837 was still essentially aristocratic, and it was the aristocratic virtues that fascinated him as an outsider. The suffrage weakened that world by democratic dilution, though only slowly. All British governments were largely aristocratic in composition before the Liberal victory of 1906, Gladstone's as surely as Disraeli's; and as for the Commons, it remained a gentlemanly institution into the present century. The Duke of Wellington's reported remark, on seeing the first reformed Parliament assemble in 1832, that he had never seen 'so many shocking bad hats' in his life, points to a grandly fastidious social sense, but it was an exceptional British MP before the First World War that did not qualify for the not very exacting title of being a gentleman. For thirty years or more after adult male suffrage was granted in 1884 the Commons remained, with individual exceptions, socially homogeneous, though some members had been born to a humbler estate which through luck or effort they had succeeded in bettering. The Commons tended to confer gentility when it did not merely confirm it: Trollope's Mr Lopez, in *The Prime Minister*, sought membership to live down a foreign ancestry and a reputation for shady financial dealings. This was a world worth winning. Members were unpaid, before 1911, and a poor man had no business there; but the status, many felt, and rightly, was worth more than money. 'I know that as a poor man I ought not to be a Member of Parliament', writes one of Trollope's characters repentantly.[1]

Parliament is the best club, but it is best seen (socially speaking) as one element in a larger complex of places to meet and talk. In these novels it does not stand alone: it is supplemented by the West End clubs, where even a Member of Parliament may find it quicker and more congenial to hear the latest political

1. Trollope, *The Duke's Children* (London, 1880) ch. 56.

news than at Westminster; and by the country houses and Scottish shoots that provide the scene for weekends and recesses. This is the three-cornered world of fiction that Disraeli creates and Trollope exploits, the world that Dickens declined to enter both as a novelist and as a man. It is consciously grand. Its fascination lay in its pecking order, which is forever in flux. To watch it was as intriguing as a tournament; and for some men, more concerned with party management than with legislation, the tournament could count for everything. It was life itself.

> Parliament was a club so eligible in its nature that all Englishmen wished to belong to it. They who succeeded were acknowledged to be the cream of the land. They who dominated in it were the cream of the cream. Those two who were elected to be the chiefs of the two parties had more of cream in their composition than any others.

And the chief of the strongest party, as Trollope's Leader of the Commons, Sir Timothy Beeswax, ardently believed, could make dukes, bestow garters and appoint bishops, and 'would have gained an Elysium of creaminess not to be found in any other position on the earth's surface'.[1]

The hierarchy is dynamic, like the social hierarchy itself; at any moment there are those who are moving up and those who are descending. It is open but not egalitarian, whether in fact or in aspiration. It is a system of how to choose leaders and how to displace them, and the creaminess of the mixture is the novelist's great chance. On technical grounds alone he could not deal with a whole nation. The intruder, like Trollope's Lopez or Melmotte, he can depict at length; but the intrusion is felt as such, and it does not impair – indeed it rather confirms – the essential cohesion of the parliamentary world. From the novelist's point of view Victorian Parliaments presented about the right balance of possibilities: an outsider would always want to get in, and might even hope to get in; but what he entered, as if to challenge and defy the Duke of Wellington's distaste, remained still an enclosure with a style of its own.

The world of the nineteenth-century political novel lies here, in the world of Westminster and its complex of

1. *Ibid.* ch. 21.

promotion, rank and marriage. It is a world dominated by aristocratic manners, though not always aristocratic birth; but it is moral enough, and in any case prestigious enough, to escape the charge of mere worldliness. Life was not all Sir Timothy Beeswax. A man might enter Parliament for the loftiest of reasons, and remain there for such reasons, and the probability of all this rises in the course of the century. The sense of moral taint has largely left political institutions by the mid and late century. The monarchy is pure, the royal family largely above reproach, and though the merely self-seeking instinct survives in politics and commerce, it usually has the decency to pretend to be something else. A Victorian reading *Vanity Fair* soon after it appeared in 1848 must have felt that his country had come an infinitely long way in thirty years, and that the changes were all for the good. *Patronage* (1814) is about the moral dangers of political involvement; *Pickwick* (1836–37) shows politics as a farcical sideshow; but in *Coningsby*, only seven years later, politics is an ideal to dangle before the eyes of highminded youth, in *Sybil* a year later it is a task to raise the condition of the people; and in Trollope and George Eliot, in the 1860s, it is the natural arena for men of imagination who seek a life of achievement. The maturing of the parliamentary novel is gradual but wonderfully swift, and it can best be studied by contrasting its two chief luminaries, Disraeli and Trollope. They demonstrate its strengths in the sharpest and clearest light.

If the Coningsby trilogy and the six Palliser novels had survived alone, to be recovered in some archaeological dig, it is easy to guess what the world would have concluded about them. The Disraeli novels are the works of a fantasist, of an outsider infatuated with an aristocratic world he can neither comprehend nor penetrate, baffled but fascinated by the Englishman's capacity to subsist in contraries – 'a Whig, a democratic aristocrat, I cannot comprehend' – and hamstrung by an ideology that could not, in its nature, appeal to the English mind: a compound of romantic royalism and semitic mysticism, at once racialist and populist, with a taste for charismatic leadership and a cult of youth, and a contempt for the Revolution of 1689 and all its works. All English history since Charles II, as Disraeli put it in the conclusion to *Sybil*, was bunk, 'a mere phantasma' ten reigns long in which nothing had borne its proper name:

> Oligarchy has been called Liberty; an exclusive Priesthood has been christened a National Church; Sovereignty has been the title of something that has had no dominion, while absolute power has been wielded by those who profess themselves the servants of the People. In the selfish strife of factions, two great existences have been blotted out of the history of England – the Monarch and the Multitude.

Against Disraeli's mishmash of fantasy and history, Trollope's novels look like the work of an entirely practical and sensible man. Whereas Disraeli held that 'it is the past alone that can explain the present, and it is youth that alone can mould the remedial future', Trollope cares only for the moment as it comes; and he knows no truth, for much of what he writes, beyond the accumulated wisdom of the man of affairs. In Trollope's version of the battle of the generations, it is the middle-aged who know best, though it may be part of their wisdom to accept defeat gracefully at the hands of their children. A young woman, however intelligent, is the least qualified person to choose her own husband, though it may be best after long persuasion to allow her to make her own mistakes in her own way. This is all the sober view of the experienced man of judgement. Trollope's prose, as befits a lifelong official of the Post Office, reveals the subtle nuances of an experienced framer of committee documents. His knowledge of the system is immense: he knows, as the young Disraeli did not, that conceptual consistency does not matter, and that it is possible to declare oneself, as he did in the *Autobiography*, as 'an advanced conservative liberal' (ch. 16) – as one intent on lessening the distances between the ranks of society, but as one still glad a Conservative Party exists to prevent that progress from turning into a rout of all traditional values.

And yet events belie most, almost all, of this contrast. Disraeli twice became prime minister, and spent nearly half a century in the two Houses of Parliament: Trollope's political career began and ended with a single unsuccessful candidature. In the same chapter of the *Autobiography* he tries to explain why. Practical as he was, 'I knew that in politics I could never become a practical man', content to work slowly up the tall tree of power. What is more, he was not a speaker: 'I had no special gifts that way, and had not studied the art early enough in life to overcome natural difficulties.' Disraeli had both talents: a capacity to work and to wait, politically speaking, and a maturing grasp of oratory after his early failures. The contrast is as plain in history as it is unclear, even inverted, in the novels; but that is partly because Disraeli, even in the last novel *Endymion*, speaks of aspiration rather than of fact, whereas Trollope tells of what he sees. The one exhorts, the other describes. It is not a comparison of equals.

Disraeli's achievement, surprising in technical terms, was to marry the English social novel, and more particularly the fashionable Silver Fork style of high society fiction, with that most un-English of forms, the novel of ideas. A contemporary calls *Coningsby* 'a mixture of the novel of manners and the pamphlet of politics'.[1] That the novel of ideas has never flourished in England is notorious; where the French in the eighteenth century have the *contes philosophiques* of Voltaire and others, English has little to counter with but *Rasselas*. Where the Germans and Russians, in the nineteenth, have Goethe, Tolstoy and Dostoyevsky, the English have Peacock; and there are no easy equivalents to Kafka and Mann in this century. The probable reason for the gap is not philistinism but realism: to incarnate an idea in a character, in the usual English view, is to defy the complexity of the human condition. But Disraeli's attempt seems less original if his debt to Scott is considered. As a young journalist Disraeli had visited the old master twice at Abbotsford in 1825, and his first novel, *Vivian Grey* (1826–27), written when all other hopes of a career had come to nothing, exploits a fashion for society novels with strong doses of gossip. Scott's success in *Waverley* (1814) in building a novel on a contrast of two societies, the Whig world south of the Highland line and the feudal Jacobite survival to the north of it, is given a contemporary turn thirty years later in *Coningsby* and *Sybil*, where the action moves from the capital to the industrial north to compare the 'Two Nations' of rich and poor. 'Rightly understood,' the reader is assured in *Coningsby*, 'Manchester is as

1. T. H. S. Escott, 'Political novels', *Fraser's Magazine* (April 1874) p. 525.

great a human exploit as Athens' (IV. i). A technique devised for historical fiction is rapidly adapted to the present. But then the English are now living history: it is the distinguishing insight of the Victorians to see themselves, as no previous generation of men had done, as subject to historical forces and ripe, even at the moment when those forces were at work, for the analysis of the historian and of the social novelist.

Scott's heritage is even more strongly active in Disraeli's faculty for seeing character as historical essence. The figure of the Chevalier in *Waverley* is a shining example: he is a historical personage, Prince Charles Stuart of the Forty-Five; he is also a prince of the old French tradition, his charm of an antique stamp, bearing the mark of a great neighbouring civilization and of another age. Disraeli, with less of steady attention to historical realities than Scott, can perform the same trick from moment to moment. The face of the novelist seems as if pressed against a pane of glass, eager to apprehend the manners and morals of a dying aristocracy with an artistically compelling mixture of puzzlement and fascination. How can such men, the most powerful on earth, bear the weight of ordinary humanity so lightly, and how persist through life with so little blood in their veins? They walk the stage as actors, and yet they feel nothing – at least no ordinary human affections, only the desire for money, title and power. They belong to another age, almost as surely as Scott's personages, except that Disraeli through an acceleration of history has seen and even met them. Here is how in *Coningsby* he wonderingly describes the old Tory leader in his triumph:

> Lord Monmouth, whose contempt for mankind was absolute; not a fluctuating sentiment, not a mournful conviction ebbing and flowing with circumstances, but a fixed, profound, unalterable instinct; who never loved anyone, and never hated anyone except his own children; was diverted by his popularity, but he was also gratified by it. At this moment it was a great element of power; he was proud that with a vicious character, after having treated these people with unprecedented neglect and contumely, he should have won back their golden opinions in a moment by the magic of manner and the splendour of wealth. His experience proved the soundness of his philosophy (iii. 5).

'The magic of manner' is a vulgar but accurate phrase, and Disraeli is more surely under its spell than most of his readers: he would have given something, one feels, to have that manner for himself. Because he cannot, he must seek another path to power: heroic leadership magnified by oratory, a new ideology of Toryism to counter the enemy's, and a new alliance between the failing Conservatives and the industrial masses who, whether one likes it or not, must one day have the suffrage. They won it in 1867, in the event, and by the neatest of reversals it was Disraeli who gave it to them. What he also saw, before more ruthless men were to see it, was that there is no reason to assume that the masses are democratic in sentiment. In some moods, and perhaps soon, the people will want not a committee but a leader; and neither old Tories like Lord Monmouth nor the new Liberals will forever satisfy them. Politics is about fervour, not mere interest. Man is not economic man: he has passions and prejudices, and a political system must learn to flatter them. 'There is no error so vulgar,' Sidonia tells Coningsby, 'as to believe that revolutions are occasioned by economical causes.' Religion had counted for more than anything in the English Civil War: 'the cause then was not physical. The imagination of England rose against the government. It proves then that when that faculty is astir in a nation, it will sacrifice even physical comfort to follow its impulses' (iv. 13). That is a deeper political perception than Trollope was capable of, and it casts a long shadow into the future. 'Even Mormon counts more votaries than Bentham.' Men act out of inclination and passion, not just design. Like so many of his perceptions, it is unsustained, except by the events of his life; but it remains a formidable case to answer.

Trollope's answer was goodhumouredly contemptuous. It is well known what he thought of Conservatives in general. As for Disraeli, he loved to parody him, and pronounced him in his *Autobiography* an epitome of falsity, his novels all 'paint and unreality', misleading young men into fantasies of 'a world more glorious, more rich, more witty, more enterprising than their own'.

The glory has ever been the glory of pasteboard, and the wealth has been the wealth of tinsel. The wit has been the wit of hairdressers, and the enterprise has been the enterprise of mountebanks. An audacious conjuror has generally been his hero. . . . Through it all there is a feeling of stage properties, a smell of hair-oil (ch. 13).

The contempt is English and gentlemanly: no nonsense, no excess, no lies. And this is no pretension in Trollope, who is the master of revealing the art of administration as it is in fact conducted, without fancy and without exaggeration. If one wishes to be informed about process, then these are the greatest political novels: he shows how men are chosen or how they fail to be chosen, how marriage influences power, how statesmen behave in private. He is consciously a step in advance of Dickens and Disraeli. 'In former times,' he explains in *The Warden* (1855), his first successful novel, 'great objects were attained by great work. When evils were to be reformed, reformers set about their heavy task with brave decorum and laborious argument.' But that mood has passed, and the new fashion is not for heavy tomes: 'We get on now with a lighter step, and quicker: ridicule is found to be more convincing than argument, imaginary agonies touch more than true sorrows, and monthly novels convince, when learned quartos fail to do so.' If Mr Sentiment, as he calls Dickens, can right the world's wrongs, let him. Exaggeration is Dickens's forte and his weapon: 'The artist who paints for the million must use glaring colours' (ch. 15). But neither radical change nor glaring colours are for Trollope – rather the human cost of the changes that are already happening. Where change is rampant, it is beside the point to demand that things should change. This is the new note of caution that Trollope, like George Eliot, strikes, and it sums up the intelligent mood of the 1860s and 1870s. The world is growing rapidly different, and the urgent need is not to hasten reform but to count its penalties and to ask, before it is too late to ask, what can be saved and what is worth saving.

Trollope's fiction is of rising excellence in the chief creative periods of his life, and the five Barchester novels (1855–67) and the six Palliser novels (1864–80) both show strong evidences of a learning process in the mind of the novelist himself. He wrote by regular hours, as he recounts in the *Autobiography*, and stands as the classic example of the sort of author who discovers what he has to say only in the process of saying it. The learning process is in any case a theme of the novels: his mastery, at its most individual, lies in describing meetings at which the protagonists begin with one solution in mind and end by accepting another, and sometimes a solution that no one had contemplated. The experience is a commonplace of committees, where shifting alliances and the kaleidoscope of debate draw out agreements and compromises undreamt of by any single member. This is the process of persuasion at its most formal; but it was Trollope who slowly noticed, in the course of the Palliser novels, how fertile was the analogy between the persuasions of politics and those of ordinary life. Rejecting the episodic as a device, he was proud of his talent for keeping two plots running at equal weight from beginning to end of a three-volume novel. But the intuition that public and private life can be thematically linked is one that strongly takes possession of his mind only in the course of the Palliser series. Are the arts of persuading a colleague and persuading a woman not somehow linked? How do men agree in committee or in love? Plantagenet Palliser, Duke of Omnium and Liberal prime minister, is the most powerful man in England, and among the richest; but he cannot hold the love of his wife Lady Glencora or govern his children, as he cannot achieve his heart's wish of lessening the distances between the ranks of society, or even his favourite cause of decimalizing the currency. The paradox of power is one that the parliamentary system renders peculiarly visible and acute. Even the most powerful man cannot get what he wants. No man can, alone.

'How would it be,' wonders Omnium's son Lord Silverbridge in the last of these novels, *The Duke's Children*, after having saddened his father by being returned for Parliament as a Conservative, 'if he should consent to go back to the Liberal party on being allowed to marry the girl he loved?' (ch. 53). To forge that connexion in fiction was to reveal something that must have been real enough in the lives of many Victorian statesmen. Trollope needed it as a matter of design, to bind his narratives together. 'I almost doubt', he wrote in the conclusion to the *Autobiography*, 'whether it be not impossible to have two absolutely distinct parts in a novel, and to imbue them both with interest. If they be distinct, the one will seem to be no more than padding to the other.' But the link, once he saw it, proved to be the interest that held sixteen volumes of fiction together. His characters move with a continuous ease, especially in the later novels, between talk of politics and talk of love. In both they persuade or fail to persuade; most perceptively of all, they sometimes persuade themselves. This is nearer to the inner life of the public man than other political novels, including Disraeli's, ever attempt to be.

The vital political question that animates these novels is one still worth asking. Why do ruling classes give up power? The answer that would do for most countries – violence and the threat of violence – will not do for England, and the parliamentary novel is based on the unswerving assumption that existing institutions cannot be overthrown. The anarchists and terrorists that Henry James dealt with in *The Princess Casamassima* (1886) and Conrad in *The Secret Agent* (1907) are temporary lodgers in British political life; they do not affect the total scene. Disraeli had provided the outline of an answer with his phrase about 'pluck and property', and it is an outline that Trollope abundantly fills in. In Disraeli the phrase is treated with acid contempt – the contempt he reserves for the politics of mere place-seeking; but the principle he lampoons is after all of exceptional interest. Property alone cannot be the answer to the stability of the Victorian constitution: it is at least as likely to provoke revolution as to prevent it. Pluck is more to the point. What the English parliamentary novel shows, in figures as widely different as Disraeli's Lord Monmouth and Trollope's Duke of Omnium, are men who do not lose their nerve. They are studies in coolness. And they are cool in situations in which a mistake could be catastrophic.

The problem of yielding power was one of tempo. Decolonization in the mid twentieth century provides an accurate enough parallel. Few, in either case, doubted that the general process was inevitable; it was possible, however, for intelligent men to differ in both cases about the speed at which events should move. The three Reform Acts of 1832, 1867 and 1884, carried respectively by Whig, Conservative and Liberal governments, happened in good Trollopian fashion, with men voting for and against for a variety of public reasons and an admixture of ulterior motives – changing their views, talking defiance and then backing down, surprising themselves as easily as they surprised one another. Pluck meant a confident hope that the people, once enfranchized, would return the same men to power. Both Monmouth and Omnium are compounds of the timorous and the bold. They know when to press hard and when to remain silent. 'The pear is not ripe' is a favourite expression of Monmouth's, waiting without impatience for public opinion to turn his way. Omnium accepts the premiership without exuberance and watches it slip from him without tears. This is a wisdom beyond ideology, though it needs an ideology to fuel it and to drive it on. And that is the ultimate surprise of the parliamentary novel: its insistence that, in the end, it is after all ideas that count. Its heroes are those who think. Skill is necessary for success, but ideas are what that success is for. Disraeli's young men dream of future greatness through an act of political faith: they demand 'a dogma for a guide'.[1] Trollope's Omnium opens his heart to Phineas Finn on a country walk, in *The Prime Minister*, and reveals himself no iceberg, as his friend supposed, but a man of passionate conviction:

> 'You are a Liberal because you know that it is not all as it ought to be, and because you would still march on to some nearer approach to equality; though the thing itself is so great, so glorious, so godlike – nay so absolutely divine – that you have been disgusted by the very promise of it, because its perfection is unattainable . . .'
>
> The Duke in his enthusiasm had thrown off his hat, and was sitting on a wooden seat which they had reached, looking up among the clouds. . . . He had begun in a low voice (ch. 68).

This was the man the Commons had called a dark horse, and Trollope leaves him a mystery to his wife, his children and his friends. But when he lifts the veil, at this moment, the Prime Minister's passion is convincing. Persuasion, after all, is the only skill by which a parliamentary system can work, and its very process obscures the clarity of such convictions. It turns the wheels. Agreements and compromises, alliances and in-

1. Disraeli, *Coningsby* iii. 5.

herited loyalties are all aspects of its life. But in the end, the parliamentary idea is not just a technique of government: it is about something, it is itself a cause. Without a dogma to guide, some glorious and godlike idea, it would cease to excite faith, loyalty, even interest. And that is just what it does not cease to do.

[9]

Democracy and Equality

When Erskine May, already a clerk of the House of Commons and the author of the chief handbook on parliamentary procedure, was composing the first history of democracy, *Democracy in Europe* (1877), he found its progress delayed by the very tendency he was chronicling, and complained in his journal how 'very laborious and harassing' were the early sessions of Gladstone's first ministry in 1869 and 1870.[1] The incident is of some symbolic value. Democracy for the Victorians was first a fact to be faced, only later a doctrine to be analysed, or accepted, or disbelieved. It was the acknowledged tendency of the age throughout western Europe, a 'rising tide', as Tocqueville, its most penetrating critic, had already called it. Acton echoes the phrase in the opening phrase of his magnificent review of May in the *Quarterly* of 1878, comparing May with Canute. But Tocqueville himself had enlarged his classic metaphor: democracy 'only recoils to come back with greater force; . . . it is always gaining ground. The immediate future of European society is completely democratic'.[2] That, in Tocqueville, is no optimistic assessment, and the qualification embodied in the term 'immediate' needs to be weighed. The tendency of one age need not be that of the next; Disraeli, in *Coningsby*, perceived from a distance a monarchical tendency in modern societies (in the strict sense of power exercised by one man) which has since proved itself a momentous prediction. But the immediate tendency that the Victorians knew was the

1. Thomas Erskine May, from the unpublished *Journal 1857–82* in the House of Commons Library, fol. 161.

2. Tocqueville, *Journeys to England and Ireland* (New York, 1968) p. 52, from notes dated September 1833.

rising tide, and that tide appeared to be engulfing France, Italy and Germany as well as England. For many Europeans it was not so much a cause to be advanced as an event to be studied. The equal distribution of political power by universal suffrage, as James Fitzjames Stephen (no friend to the idea) announced in his *Liberty, Equality, Fraternity* (1873), 'has gone forth, and is going forth conquering and to conquer', and 'the fact of its triumph is as clear as the sun at noonday'.[1] Stephen viewed it gloomily, as a future for wirepullers and their friends, but he did not doubt that it must come.

The English task, pre-eminently, was interpretative, and the ideological problem of the rising democratic tide was to predict its probable effects and to consider how best to lessen the more objectionable among them: to 'make timely preparation for it', as Arnold urged his readers in *Democratic Education.*[2] The tone is warning rather than welcoming, and a welcome tinged with warning makes for the usual Victorian mixture. Mere hostility, like Henry Maine's, is another story: he believed that democracy would inevitably lead to élitism on the part of a credulous Demos, which could be brought to believe in anyone or anything. Acton disgustedly called his *Popular Government* (1885) a Manual of Unacknowledged Conservatism, and claimed that Maine had personally asked him not to review it.[3] Maine's is the antidemocratic extreme, in its most reasoned form. More representatively, the tendency might be accepted, in some degree, and obliged by the very fact of that acceptance to adopt a given tempo and a given tone. 'The brief history of most human things', as George Eliot observed in *Felix Holt*, is 'a mixture of pushing forward and being pushed forward' (ch. 33). But if the simple and unqualified welcome is the condition of being called a democrat, then it is doubtful if any prominent intellectual of the age considered here – whether Macaulay, or Mill, or Gladstone, or Dickens, or Acton – is a democrat in that sense. They believed in a parliamentary, not a democratic

1. J. F. Stephen, *Liberty, Equality, Fraternity*, edited by R. J. White (Cambridge, 1967) pp. 201–2.

2. Matthew Arnold, *Complete Prose Works*, edited by R. H. Super (Ann Arbor, 1960–77) ii. 19.

3. Lord Acton, *Letters to Mary Gladstone* (1904) pp. 212–13, from a letter of 11 November 1885.

system: in liberty, not in popular government. The delusion that Victorian liberalism was democratic is second only to the delusion that it stood for *laissez-faire*: a more qualified delusion, however, since liberalism is compatible with an acceptance of democratic constitutionalism in certain confined circumstances, whereas it is doubtful if it is compatible with *laissez-faire* in any circumstances whatever. It is the nature of these confined circumstances in which democracy is acceptable, and the prospects of achieving them, that need to be considered.

May wrote his history of democracy in the bustle of Gladstone's first ministry from the standpoint of 'an ardent admirer of political liberty', as he explained in his preface, equally opposed to the extremes of royal despotism on the one hand and of mere anarchy on the other. The question to be asked of democracy, when it comes, and even before it comes, is whether it will prove compatible with political liberty; and the answer to that question is nothing like as obvious as it sounds. All this assumes that democracy is first and last a form of government, and it was in this light that an Englishman naturally viewed the matter – as a constitutional idea working its way through the ancient parliamentary forms by means of progressive extensions of the suffrage. He might be aware, as May was, that the word had other applications, especially on the Continent: it might denote the power of popular influence within any form of government; some even thought of it as a revolutionary force; and some again as a social term referring to the lower ranks of society, or to its 'humbler citizens'. All these are possible senses, as May admits, even in England. But the real debate is constitutional. It is about the suffrage and, in the widest sense, its political effects. Democracy is government by the many. What will happen, in Bagehot's vivid phrase, when England delivers herself over to 'the jangled mass of men'?[1] Can liberty survive it?

Liberty has a variety of evils to fear from democracy, and in the strict sense they are incompatible one with another. The argument against democracy, however, is none the less cogent for that: the chain of events set in motion by granting adult suffrage might easily, in unhappy circumstances, lead to a

1. Bagehot, 'The character of Sir Robert Peel', *National Review* (July 1856); reprinted in his *Collected Works* (1968) iii. 242.

succession of disasters as different from one another as despotism is from anarchy. The most modest disaster to be feared was mediocrity – what Mill, in his review of Tocqueville in the *Edinburgh Review* (1840), called 'Chinese stationariness'. Government by ordinary men, it was easy to feel, might well prove to be itself ordinary. Tocqueville, in the first volume of his *De la démocratie en Amérique* (1835), had already drawn attention to the lumpish conformity of intellectual life in the United States, where governmental censorship might not press heavily but where popular convention could simply ignore originality out of existence: 'In America the majority draws a formidable circle around thought. Within these limits the writer is free; but woe to anyone who dares to escape it.'[1] Similar social pressures might some day, if allowed, reduce the intellectual worlds of London and Paris to the timid conformity of New England. Some Englishmen matched Tocqueville in recognizing that the results of democracy were all too likely to be undramatic – that tedium was more likely to be the outcome than bloodshed. 'The great obstacle to originality is the English nation', Bagehot wrote bitterly in 1870.[2] Democracy is more likely to prevent things from happening than to make them happen. The people, after all, are in a deep sense conservative, or what Bagehot in the eighth chapter of his *English Constitution* called 'deferential'. Whether that is a motive for welcoming democracy or opposing it is a matter of taste; even Bagehot, in another mood, could feel that the weight of custom and popular common sense were arguments for yielding to the suffrage, if not all at once: 'Popular judgments on popular matters', he wrote in 1863, before the second Reform Act, 'is crude and vague, but it is right.' That is not the view of an out-and-out democrat, but it is a view that makes the suffrage easier to bear. And it merges into the most sophisticated of all views of the suffrage, propounded three years later by George Eliot in *Felix Holt* (1866). Holt addresses the crowd as a radical, indeed, but as one to whom the suffrage is of secondary importance even before it has been granted. It is no more to

1. Tocqueville, *Oeuvres complètes*, edited by J. P. Mayer (Paris, 1961) i. 266.
2. Bagehot, *Economist* (2 July 1870); reprinted in his *Collected Works* (1968) iii. 526.

men, he tells an unbelieving crowd, than water to a steam-engine:

> All the schemes about voting, and districts, and annual Parliaments, and the rest, are engines, and the water or steam – the force that is to work them – must come out of human nature – out of men's passions, feelings, desires. Whether the engines will do good work or bad depends on these feelings; and if we have false expectations about men's characters, we are very much like the idiot who thinks he'll carry milk in a can without a bottom (ch. 30).

But the greatest power there is, or the steam that works the engines of history, is what men think, 'the ruling belief in society about what is right and what is wrong'. That matters more than any constitution. Democracy can do no more than broaden the base of that ruling belief; but it cannot turn a parliamentary system into something as radically different as either the extreme friends or the extreme enemies of the suffrage hope and fear.

The second evil is the opposite and classic fear of anarchy, or at least of acts so arbitrary, like the confiscation of wealth, that they smack of anarchy. Dickens's two novels, *Barnaby Rudge* and *A Tale of Two Cities*, show that this fear was not incompatible with radicalism: indeed it could act as a spur to orderly reform. The looting and burning of the Gordon Riots of 1780, and the bloodlust of the French mob in the Reign of Terror, are equally examples of how brutal oppression can be turned back on the oppressors who have refused all compromise until compromise is too late. This fear, commoner to continentals than to Englishmen, is ambiguous in its message: it urges men either to accept democracy or to repel it. But it is doubtful whether, in either event, it is a principal fear of the Victorians. It is certainly not prominent among those they publicly voice, and it is unlikely that *A Tale of Two Cities* can be seriously viewed as Dickens's warning to his contemporaries in the age of Palmerston. The Victorian taste for historical fiction describing revolutions was inexhaustible, but it was a taste for the emotional satisfaction of contemplating a fate which the English believed they had escaped.

The third fear, that democracy might lead to tyranny, is of

far greater moment than these. Indeed it is so understandable, and in some circumstances so justifiable, as to make the argument look rewarding for any age of history. What is to prevent the people from choosing dictatorship? In a nation like England, where Parliament is sovereign and untrammelled by constitutional checks, the strictly accurate answer is the most depressing answer of all: nothing at all. The people can dictate, if they choose. If most men want a dictatorship, there is no constitutional bar to prevent them from having it. The effective bar, in practice, is what George Eliot called 'the ruling belief in society about what is right and what is wrong'; and once the suffrage is conceded, that ruling belief becomes the property not of thousands but of millions. Tyranny and its prevention are aspects of public opinion, from that day forward – of what Bagehot called 'popular judgment on popular matters'; and the argument turns irresistibly to the ways by which that opinion can be formed and deformed.

The 'despotism of public opinion', or the 'tyranny of the majority', to use the phrases of Mill and Acton,[1] is the fearful prospect of democracy most intelligently analysed by the Victorian mind. The case is put in a diversity of tones and with a diversity of proffered solutions: but the uniformity of the case itself is an impressive one. Bagehot's complaints about the 'tyranny of the commonplace' strike a lively journalistic note: 'You may talk of the tyranny of Nero and Tiberius; but the real tyranny is the tyranny of your next-door neighbour.'[2] Acton calls the oppression of the majority far worse than that of any minority. Mill's writings on democracy, which cover most of his working life, from essays written before the Reform Act of 1832 down to *Representative Government* (1861), form the most comprehensive account of the political dilemma raised by the advance in democracy in the period, and the most fully reflected attempt to solve that dilemma.

It is now plain that Mill's writings on democracy, scattered

1. J. S. Mill, 'Bentham', *London and Westminster Review* (August 1838); Acton, 'Sir Erskine May's *Democracy in Europe*,' *Quarterly Review* (January 1878). Tocqueville is the ultimate origin of both.

2. Bagehot, *National Review* (July 1856); reprinted in his *Collected Works* (1968) iii. 243.

as they are over more than thirty years, form a more consistent pattern than had once been thought; and equally, that the pattern formed is something far other than a democratic one.[1] This conclusion will surprise only those who confuse democracy with parliamentary government. Mill is a parliamentarian *par excellence*; he conceives of no government as excellent except within the framework provided by a deliberative assembly, and in his brief period in the Commons between 1865 and 1868 he surprised even those who knew him best by his willing discipleship to Gladstone and his readiness to take the Whip. And Parliament provides the indispensable bridge between Mill's principal convictions on the subject: it reconciles, though in no easy or tidy way, his distrustful acceptance of the suffrage and his belief in a clerisy of informed opinion that could guide democracy into prudent paths.

Mill's distrust of adult suffrage was an abiding one, and in his early years it coexisted oddly with a declared belief in such standard radical tenets as the supremacy of the people and the triumph of universal suffrage and the secret ballot. Some of these convictions, including the secret ballot, he later abandoned; but the case for the suffrage was always, in his view, a qualified one, and the years only intensified a scepticism that was there from the start. 'What is right in politics', he wrote in 1832, 'is not the *will* of the people, but the *good* of the people', and the object of radical policy should be 'not to compel but persuade the people to impose, for the sake of their own good, some restraints on the immediate and unlimited exercise of their own will'.[2] This is how 'mere mob-government' or anarchy is to be avoided. It is a view severely limited from the start in its enthusiasm for democracy, and those limitations grow. 'We think that democracy *can* govern', he wrote in a review in 1840, 'it can make its legislators its mere delegates to carry into effect its preconceived opinions. We do not say that it *will* do so.'[3] What it needs to thrive, even to survive,

1. See J. H. Burns, 'J. S. Mill and Democracy 1829–61', *Political Studies* v (1957); reprinted in *Mill: a Collection of Critical Essays*, edited by J. B. Schneewind (New York, 1968).

2. *Examiner* (15 July 1832).

3. *Westminster Review* xxxiv (1840).

is a new learned class. It is upon these assumptions that the highly idiosyncratic and ingenious arguments in *Representative Government* are based: an argument for political democracy through maintaining the open ballot in order to ensure that the exercise of the vote is seen as a public duty; by leaving members unpaid; and by an elaborate system of plural voting designed to abate the numerical predominance of the ignorant. Mill held it to be absurd to suppose that one man's political judgement was as good as another's, and insisted that this evident fact must somehow be provided for in the constitution of the future.

What renders democracy acceptable, in such a system, is that it is parliamentary rather than direct – a 'delegated sovereignty', as he put it in 1832, by which the masses are encouraged to perceive that, political choices being as complex as they are, others may understand the common interest better than themselves.

> The true idea of popular representation is not that the people govern in their own persons, but that they choose their governors. In a good government public questions are not referred to the suffrages of the people themselves, but to those of the most judicious persons whom the people can find. The sovereignty of the people is essentially a delegated sovereignty. Government must be performed by the few for the benefit of the many. . . .
>
> If I vote for a person because I think him the wisest man I know, am I afterwards to set myself up as his instructor, as if I were wiser than him?[1]

The total argument, allowing for changes of view over such technical questions as the ballot, forms a wonderfully consistent pattern of conviction in favour of the supremacy of Parliament and the gentle permeation of parliamentary forms by a popular opinion that accepts the leadership of educated opinion. It is a view at once hostile to oligarchy on the one hand, and on the other to direct democracy and referenda. In twentieth-century terms it is opposed equally to populism and to Gaullism, to government by the many and to government by the few or the one. And if, again, one excepts the technicalities of voting, it represents an approximation to the temper of British politics that

1. *Examiner* (4 July 1832).

followed Mill's death in 1873. Neither the open ballot nor plural voting has survived, it is true; but Parliament over a hundred years has allowed itself to be permeated by popular forces while yet contriving to maintain its ceremonial dignity and prestige, its independence of day-to-day movements in popular opinion, and above all its sovereignty. Its membership of professional persons, and the predominance of graduates, would have been congenial to Mill, who might have been surprised to see that result achieved by payment of Members and by single voting. The techniques proposed in *Representative Government* have not survived, or have not been attempted; but its spirit remains a touchstone of the working system. By contrast, the enthusiasm of the Radicals and the hardheaded scepticism of Bagehot have both worn less well. Bagehot, in *The English Constitution*, published six years after Mill's treatise and as a reply to it, proclaimed that democracy could not work without elements of corruption, intimidation and disorder, and that universal suffrage ought to be delayed for another hundred years, till 1966. But what Mill emphasized, and what Bagehot gravely underestimated, was the educative force of democracy itself. That system, in favourable circumstances, creates some of the sense of maturity which it needs to survive. Both would have agreed that the plunge must be carefully prepared, as a swimmer needs to learn a minimum of skill before he enters the deep end of the pool. But he must enter the water to learn at all, and even when he is proficient his progress goes on and on.

Progress towards the secret ballot, meanwhile, continued independently of Mill's change of heart. A traditional aim of Philosophical Radicalism since the early decades of the century, it had appeared at Lord Durham's insistence in an early draft of the Reform Bill of 1831–32, only to be dropped. George Grote, who entered the Commons at that time, held it to be more important in the short run than the extension of the suffrage, and raised the matter repeatedly in the 1830s; though it was not finally adopted until 1872, when Gladstone introduced it in the teeth of Disraeli's opposition, just a year after Grote's death. In such matters, as Grote had always insisted, his own nation was backward: France had the secret ballot already, he reminded the Commons in his speech of 25 April 1833, and so did twenty of the twenty-four United States. 'By rendering the suffrage secret', he told Parliament, 'you lock this precious prize in a casket, which can neither be stolen by fraud, nor ravished by tyranny.' In fact the extension of the suffrage in 1867 was achieved before its secrecy, so that the tempo of radicalism was less faithfully observed than its substance. A host of picturesque and even riotous ceremonies were lost by Gladstone's measure, and a new purity gained; but it is doubtful if the science of psephology, with all its refinements of statistical analysis of elections, can compensate for the loss of that human world that Dickens described in *Pickwick*, George Eliot in *Felix Holt*, and Trollope in *Ralph the Heir*. But it may be added that those novels and others make a case for the secret ballot even more persuasively that the parliamentary eloquence of Grote.

Behind the argument for and against democracy, from the start, stood a spectre vaster and darker than the suffrage – the issue of equality itself; and indeed the argument about equality, in many ways, is the more fundamental concern of the two. From the beginning of the age equality and democracy are linked in the European debate. Tocqueville, in his *Democracy in America*, uses *démocratie* as a synonym for *égalité* or *égalité des conditions;* equality means equality of political rights, with the strong implication that gross inequality of condition could not long survive an equality of such rights. The French revolutionary slogan, revived by the July Monarchy after 1830, had linked equality with liberty itself. In the history of modern libertarian slogans, then, equality precedes democracy, and democracy as a form of government owes its appeal to the promise it offers to achieve higher and higher degrees of equality itself.

The English debate was not conducted in terms of such slogans, and the political history of nineteenth-century France did not encourage emulation. It was more likely to be used as a warning. 'Here in England,' remarks Trollope's Duke of Omnium to Phineas Finn, who has just dared to murmur the word 'equality' in a suitably incredulous tone, 'we have been taught to hate the word by the evil effects of those absurd attempts which have been made elsewhere to proclaim it as a fact accomplished by the scratch of a pen or by a chisel on a stone.'[1] Words cannot be used so simply. The task is not to carve 'Liberty, Equality, Fraternity' on monuments or to shout at street corners, but to analyse and refine.

Two grand species of equality are united in one word, the political and the social. And they are united rather than confused, since they were widely regarded as being causally linked: political equality, through the suffrage, might confer on the majority the power to impose social equality in wealth and status. The coexistence of the two senses was fully understood by the Victorians, the causal link fearfully apprehended. The liberal task is to achieve political equality while preventing social equality, to ensure that democracy allows to social differences a right to thrive. That objective was highly explicit, and it is mistaken to suppose that the liberal commitment to social inequality was in any way underhand or indirect. It is public and bold. Mill, in the essay *On Liberty* (1859), is outspoken: 'Whatever crushes individuality is despotism, by whatever name it may be called', he declared in his third chapter, 'Of Individuality'. The majority of men, of middling opinions and mediocre talents, form the greatest threat to liberty that the future will know. They have an approved standard, and it is the task of liberalism to oppose it in all its tepid indifferentism: 'That standard, express or tacit, is to desire nothing strongly. Its ideal of character is to be without any marked character; to maim by compression, like a Chinese lady's foot, every part of human nature which stands out prominently.'

Bagehot watched the growth of the suffrage with similarly mixed feelings, and rejoiced, after the second Reform Act of 1867, that equality of voting still allowed for 'a real inequality of influence', though he continued to fear 'the reign of monotony' that might some day come. 1832 had destroyed 'one kind of select constituency without creating an intellectual equivalent'.[2] That was dangerous enough; but worst of all would be the French disease whereby liberty might be sacrificed to equality.

1. Trollope, *The Prime Minister* (1876) ch. 68.

2. Bagehot, *Fortnightly Review* (November 1876); reprinted in his *Collected Works* (1968) iii. 225f.

Under the imperial sway of Napoleon III Frenchmen enjoyed a mere 'equality of impotence'. In France 'the passion for equality is so great that she will sacrifice everything for it. Free government requires privilege, because it requires that more power shall be given to the instructed than to the uninstructed: there is no method by which men can be both free and equal.'[1]

Liberty and equality, so conceived, are alternatives. Others thought so too. Disraeli and Gladstone, by the 1870s, were joined in unusual agreement on the matter: they publicly accepted the need to oppose social equality with all the political strength of the nation. Disraeli's speech to the University of Glasgow in November 1873, shortly before he was returned to office, makes the point in similar terms as an antithesis between France and England: 'Civil equality prevails in Britain, social equality in France. The essence of civil equality is to abolish privilege; the essence of social equality is to destroy class', and he warns his academic audience against the 'moaning wind' now rising in Europe, about to turn perhaps into a raging storm – the demand for 'physical and material equality':

> The leading principle of the new school is that there is no happiness which is not material, and that every living being has a right to share in that physical welfare. The first obstacle which they find to this object is found in the rights of property. Therefore they must be abolished. . . .
>
> The new philosophy strikes further than at the existence of patriotism. It strikes at the home; it strikes at the individuality of man. It would reduce civilized society to human flocks and herds.

That is so far Mill's case, and it is ironic that the leader of the Conservative Party, with his contempt for the excessive abstractions of liberalism, should accept so much of it in all its abstract rigour. Perhaps he thought a university the place for abstractions. And Gladstone, who was proud to call himself an 'inequalitarian', put Mill's case unashamedly, though he oddly substitutes for Mill's admiration of an intellectual aristocracy or clerisy a love of aristocracy itself:

1. Bagehot, *Economist* (5 September 1863); reprinted in his *Collected Works* (1968) iv. 90, 94.

There is no broad political idea which has entered less into the formation of the political system of this country than the love of equality. It is not the love of equality which has carried into every corner of the country the distinct undeniable popular preference, wherever other things are equal, for a man who is a lord over a man who is not. The love of freedom itself is hardly stronger in England than the love of aristocracy.

Matthew Arnold quoted this speech in bitter mood to the Royal Institution in 1878, in an address on Equality, without attempting to disguise the fact that Gladstone had spoken for most Englishmen; and in the opening paragraphs of his address he refers to social equality as 'this Frenchified sense of the term' for which 'almost everybody in England has a hard word'.[1] Acton makes a similar point, but from an anti-French position, in his review of Erskine May: 'The deepest cause which made the French Revolution so disastrous to liberty was its theory of equality'; and he attributes the ideal of liberty to the French middle class, of equality to the lower.[2] This is a remarkable unanimity for the 1870s. Equality, in the French sense of social equality, is widely seen as the enemy of liberty; it is seen (except by Francophiles like Arnold) as the disastrous outcome of the political history of France, where the search for equality has twice led to its apt conclusion in imperial dictatorship. Equality is a motto perverted and misunderstood; and there is an impressive body of English anti-egalitarian theory marshalled to repel it.

The English hatred of equality makes no sense, in the circumstances of a modern state, unless it is rendered consistent with the coming realities of a democratic constitution. How are the majority of men to be made to see that their own interests are best served by accepting the fact of their inferiority to others? Mill believes he knows the answer to that question: the majority of men will perceive their inferiority, intellectually and morally, because it is a fact, and facts in an open society tend to become recognized. It is social equality, after all, that is

1. Arnold, *Mixed Essays* (London, 1879) pp. 49–50.

2. Lord Acton, *Quarterly Review* (January 1878); reprinted in his *History of Freedom and Other Essays* (1907) p. 88.

based on ignorance, on fantasy or on wishful thinking. Men are not born equal in intelligence, neither do they become so; and all the processes of a culture, whether schooling, or the arts, or the conduct of government, serve to remind men of this indubitable truth. To make men free is to make them see their inequality more clearly. The suffrage gives them the power to confiscate and to level; but the educative process that precedes and accompanies it teaches how ineluctable a truth inequality is. All learning, all aesthetic experience, conspire to remind of this great truth. In the contemplation of a masterpiece, in listening to a great teacher or statesman, most men perceive something which for themselves they could not do.

These hopeful arguments, which presuppose an open mind, a readiness to listen and to learn, and a society not ruled by violence, all tend to dispose of equality as a political objective. They do not, however, dispose of all sense of connection between the advance of democracy and an increasingly equal society. Men may see the superiority of others, both intellectually and morally, and accept their leadership; but that leadership may still be exercised to lessen the distances in wealth and status that divide men from men. That prospect needs to be measured against the reasonable certainty that no political settlement, however egalitarian in purpose, will ever in fact achieve even an approximate social equality, still less maintain it; but within these wide limits of probability it is still an intelligent fear. The English dread is less of sudden confiscation than of a gentle erosion; and in that dread, or hope, the seeds of the welfare state may have been sown. A democracy is always inclined to move towards equality, of however limited a sort. This is the moderate warning that men were asked to heed during the long debate over the suffrage. If manhood suffrage comes, the power of governments to preserve the high existing levels of inequality will surely diminish, and it is idle to pretend that inequality of that sort could ever be recovered. 'If you establish a democracy,' Disraeli warned the Commons in March 1859, 'you must in due time reap the fruits of a democracy. You will in due season have great impatience of the public burdens, combined in due season with great increase of the public expenditure.' There will be wars based on popular passion, and ignominious peaces; and 'you will in due season find your property is less valuable, and your freedom less complete'. Mill's boyhood friend, the jurist John Austin, issued *A Plea for the Constitution* in the same year, warning men against the irreversible error that was about to be committed. These are the warnings that, in all their cogency, need to be paired with Mill's. Mill showed that inequality, that essential element of civilization, could be made compatible with democracy; Disraeli and others could still plausibly object that democracy was unlikely to prove compatible with the inequality the realm actually enjoyed.

That extreme inequality, in its economic expression, was based on low taxation and the right of inheritance, and in its most extreme and characteristically English form, on the tradition of entailed estates. That such inequality was enormous is beyond all question; whether it was greater than in previous generations, and especially in generations before the industrial revolution, is among the vexed problems of economic history. It cannot be asserted with certainty either that industrialism increased economic inequality or that it diminished it. It can hardly be doubted, however, that it created the eventual means by which inequality could be diminished, and by which it was diminished – in income, at least, if not in ownership. Pre-industrial societies are not on the whole given to equality, though there are exceptions: a peasant economy free of large landholders, like pre-industrial Switzerland, could in principle produce a relatively egalitarian society in unusual historical circumstances; and the distribution of land during the French Revolution might do much to cash the second clause in the promise of Liberty, Equality, Fraternity. By that date, however, Britain had already begun her industrial revolution, and the enclosures were moving agriculture, on the whole, towards larger units. In these conditions industrialism offered a possibility of greater equality, if not an immediate possibility. Land ceased to be the principal form of wealth; hereditary wealth slowly came to count for less, relatively speaking, in the economy as a whole. Obscure and controversial as these social effects remain, it is still worth noticing that industrialism was rapidly followed by advances towards democracy, and plausible to suggest that it accelerated that advance. The old constitution ceased to be credible when villages, sometimes deserted villages, were represented in the Commons and cities like Manchester were not. The relationship, which is admittedly complex, is likely enough reciprocal: as democracy offered or threatened greater social equality, so did the prospect and even the fact of that equality create situations in which the suffrage had to be conceded.

These arguments have so far concerned the relationship between democracy and social equality, and the degree to which either or both are compatible with individual liberty. If they are complicated as arguments, that can best be justified by emphasizing that three large concepts, none simple in itself – liberty, equality and democracy – are being tested in their connections one with another, and in the shifting circumstances of the greatest industrial society of the nineteenth century. The temper of that debate is understandably complex. Men like Mill, Bagehot, Gladstone and Acton, initiating all political debate from the assumption of liberty as the highest political good, weighed both democracy and equality against that larger objective, and found democracy acceptable with reservations and equality unacceptable. But they were not deaf to the argument that, since democracy had been demanded and conceded, higher and higher degrees of social equality might some day have to be conceded too. Ultimately incompatible with democracy – indeed with any civilized state of any kind – equality might yet contain the seed of some significant moral purpose. This is not the same as confusing equality with justice. That enormous error of judgement they left to others. But the extent to which inequality could be morally acceptable, and the grounds that made it so, remained excusably an unsolved puzzle of the Victorian mind.

Some solutions may be accepted lightly and at once, but they do not solve the deeper issue. Matthew Arnold's address on equality to the Royal Institution in 1878, in its positive aspects, is merely a plea to modify the law of entail and perhaps the right of inheritance. The logical outcome of this argument would be high death duties; but anyone who supposes that these, regarded alone, would make for greater equality is making all sorts of assumptions, some of which may not hold good in the particular case. Death duties limit or forbid inherited wealth; but they do not limit or forbid wealth as such, and their effects – so far as they are not offset by such ingenious solutions of the propertied classes as marrying for money – are more likely to shift wealth to a newer and more energetic order of men than to abolish it. Some liberals would have accepted the force of these arguments; others would point to the social advantages of an independent class with a tradition of public service. In either event, the issue there is not so much equality as the less fundamental difference between old fortunes and new. State ownership, again, whether by confiscation or compensation, hardly touches the question, or at least not in the manner required. If full compensation is paid, then the wealth of the owner is hardly affected; if it is not paid, or only partially, then justice would require some special reason why that owner rather than another should be penalized. In either event, nationalization makes the State, already the richest and most powerful property-owner in the nation, richer and more powerful still: a solution that may have all sorts of attractions to those who believe that wealth and power should be concentrated, but not one that has any business to appeal to an egalitarian.

The puzzle is rather to know what the acceptable limits of inequality are. Trollope's offering on the subject has already been quoted: his Liberal prime minister, the Duke of Omnium, believed that the cardinal distinction between the two chief parties of state is to be found in their answers to this question. The Conservative wishes 'to maintain the differences and the distances which separate the highly placed from their lower brethren':

> 'He thinks that God has divided the world as he finds it divided, and that he may best do his duty by making the inferior man happy and contented in his position, teaching him that the place which he holds is his by God's ordinance. . . . I as a Duke am to be kept as far apart from the man who drives my horses as was my ancestor from the man who drove his, or who rode after him to the wars – and that is to go on for ever.'

But 'the doctrine of Liberalism is, of course, the reverse'. The

Liberal has 'conceived the idea of lessening distances – of bringing the coachman and the Duke nearer together – nearer and nearer, till a millennium shall be reached by –'.

It is at this point in the Prime Minister's flight, as he pauses, that Phineas Finn offers the word 'equality', and is confirmed in his incredulity by hearing Omnium concede that the concept is remotely millennial:

> 'Men's intellects are at present so various that we cannot even realise the idea of equality, and here in England we have been taught to hate the word by the evil effects of those absurd attempts which have been made elsewhere. . . . A good word signifying a grand idea has been driven out of the vocabulary of good men. Equality would be heaven, if we could attain it . . .'

That 'great, glorious and godlike' thing comes oddly from a novelist who publicly claimed to be an 'advanced conservative liberal'. Some of Trollope's effects here are admittedly dramatic: Omnium has to astonish the reader, as a contrast to his slight success as a father and husband, even as party leader, with a moment of deep and passionate conviction. But when he indicates to Finn the poor ploughman in the next field, and asks why he should live so meanly while they live so well, he is very close to the heart of the puzzle that racked the minds of practical men of conscience who cared nothing for the millennium.

The heart of that puzzle lies not in the glory of equality or in the inescapable fact of inequality, but in something far simpler: in the fact of poverty. It is the instinct of most men, when they see deprivation and wonder urgently how to cure it, to suppose that the solution is Robin Hood's. And since taking from the rich to give to the poor can be shown to work, on occasion, the instinct cannot be dismissed as absurd. The welfare state, where it functions effectively, can provide examples. But it is much less obvious than the egalitarian supposes that this is the best way to cure poverty, and certain that it is not the only way. Much of Omnium's conscientious puzzlement, admirable as it is, could have profited from longer reflection. The abolition of that poverty which justly troubled his conscience would neither necessarily nor probably entail equality, and Finn is right to baulk at the word. A society without poverty may still be very unequal. And that lessening of distances by which Omnium distinguishes the Liberal from the Conservative does not involve him in equality either, as he perceives. The Duke and the coachman may be brought closer than they are, in income and in dignity, and yet be distinct and apart. To consider men as different when they are so is to perform the distinctions proper to the critical mind. And such a mind is unlikely to be baffled into supposing equality a good in itself, or itself an aspect of justice. Inequality may be as just as equality, after all, and it is the task of the statesman of conscience to hear the claims of diversity and choice as well as the cry of hunger.

But it is hard to resist the suspicion that Omnium's anguished doubts represents a strain as real in Victorian politics as the confident anti-egalitarianism of Gladstone and Disraeli. Their confidence may have been justified, as an argument. They were right to think the search for equality fatal to personal liberty, and right to suspect that an equal society, if such a thing could be created, would be herdlike and conformist. But that does not dispose of the emotional impulse aroused by the spectacle of rich men and poor living so near one another and failing to share. Whatever the case for inaction, and however argued, the spectacle continues to offend. It is a problem the Victorians analysed with cogency and puzzled over resolutely with a sense of misgiving; but it was not they that solved it.

[10]

Class or Rank

All societies are unequal; but all, it seems nearly as certain, are unequal in different ways and in different degrees; they describe their own inequalities variously, and view them with varying degrees of acceptance. The English, for some reason that has never been explained, have long been inclined to regard themselves, and to allow themselves to be regarded by others, as unequal in some unusual sense, remarkable in their consciousness of inequality. Thackeray, in a *Punch* sketch called 'Waiting at the Station' (9 March 1850) describes a group of women emigrating to Australia, and readily assumes they will find an absence of social difference in the colonies – an absence that will contrast sharply with old England, 'that Gothic society with its ranks and hierarchies, its cumbrous ceremonies, its glittering antique paraphernalia'. Since many Englishmen in that century and in this would assent to that caricature, it cannot be called a truism to emphasize that *all* societies are unequal; the English, in their ambition to describe their own social differences minutely, have often been much too ready to assume that they are describing unique phenomena, and their characteristic tone of muted self-disgust can sometimes interfere with intelligent assessment. This analysis is written on no such premiss: it does not assume that England is or was more class-conscious than other nations, still less that such consciousness is in its nature to be blamed.

Equality is neither a Victorian fact nor yet (unless in the remotest and most utopian sense) a Victorian ideal. Of course, as many knew, in the end humanity is just that: 'All's plain dirt', as Elizabeth Barrett Browning put it in her vigorous way in *Aurora Leigh*. But that need inhibit no one from seeing that social differences exist and matter. Nor does that realization necessarily, or even usually, mean snobbery: it may simply be a matter of seeing things as they are. Since a pecking order is there, it is the business of the social historian and novelist to characterize it: 'The aristocracy of Barchester', as Trollope puts it firmly in the opening paragraph of *The Warden*, 'are the bishop, dean and canons, with their respective wives and daughters.' The Barchester novels are composed to fill in the details of that commanding sentence. Hierarchy is what these novels, and many other English novels, are explicitly about.

Two large questions arise: how best to describe existing social differences, and whether to accept them or to change them. These questions are intimately conjoined, and it will be convenient to consider them together.

The Victorians inherited two opposing systems of social description, one ancient and one modern.[1] In the ancient hierarchical system of rank, differences are numerous, perhaps infinitely numerous, and society is seen as a stepped pyramid of many degrees or ranks, rising from a multitude at the bottom to an aristocracy and monarchy at the top. This model has many advantages. Being traditional, it is widely understood, and any novelist like Trollope who accepts or assumes it can easily anticipate the comprehension of his readers. It is a shared model. That a bishop is more than a dean, a dean than a canon, and the wife of one more than the wife of another – all this is easily accepted by any reader of the Barchester novels before he has passed the first page. It is also a highly supple model. It does not commit those who accept it to any given number of ranks, or to any simple formula as to what constitutes social superiority: whether birth, or property, or income, or style of life, or the intrinsic nature of the occupation, or to any one combination of these. If doctors enjoy a higher social status than dentists, for example, this need not be because they are more highly paid, though as a matter of fact they often are. Simple explanations like that are ruled out by the ease with which counter-examples

1. See Asa Briggs, 'The language of class in early nineteenth-century England', in *Essays in Labour History in Memory of G. D. H. Cole*, edited by A. Briggs and John Saville (London, 1960); and George Watson, 'Sociology', in *The Study of Literature* (London, 1969).

can be produced: a poor duke, for example, counts for more than a rich stockbroker. These complexities of criterion intrigue; they are the source of fascinated interest in much Victorian fiction, and especially in the choice of married partners. When a dean defies a bishop in Trollope, or a mere chaplain a bishop's wife, the drama is played out against an order of nature which is as well understood by the reader as by the novelist. And as in literature, of course, so in life. Hardly anyone treats people as if they were equal, in fact or in fiction; and even when they do, that is still not the same as their supposing that people are in fact equal.

The second or modern system of social description, which the Victorians inherited from a European intellectual tradition of the early and mid nineteenth century, was the system of class. It held that industrialism was abolishing the ancient European rank system in favour of a new and more menacing alignment into two or three vast blocs or classes defined by economic function – an alignment containing within itself at least a possibility of social civil war. This doctrine, which most would now associate with the name of Marx, is certainly pre-Marxian. Beatrice Webb did not have to become a socialist in order to hear it. Born in 1858, she often heard her father, a radical businessman turned Conservative, use abstract terms such as 'labour', which he 'coupled mysteriously with its mate "capital" '; and labour denoted a single social factor, 'an arithmetically calculable mass of human beings, each individual a repetition of the other'.[1] The works of Saint-Simon, which appeared in the France in the years that followed Waterloo, are perhaps the effective starting-point of the doctrine. Disraeli believed in a version of it at least as early as *Coningsby* and *Sybil*, both of which appeared before the Communist Manifesto of 1848; and the young Mill knew of it independently of Disraeli or Marx. On the other hand, it is doubtful if most Englishmen accepted it, though many must have heard of it. It is a foreign doctrine, and an intellectual one. The common reader might pick it up in books that were widely read: *Sybil* (1845) was subtitled 'The Two Nations', and the doctrine of class, or of Rich and Poor, is extensively discussed in the course

1. Beatrice Webb, *My Apprenticeship* (London, 1926) pp. 36–7.

of the novel; but class remains an undigested idea in the English mind, radically different in acceptance from the general acceptance of rank. Hardly any major English novel embodies the idea of class, as opposed to merely expounding it, before Galsworthy's *Man of Property* (1906); and it is not really common to find it embodied in twentieth-century fiction either. Nor, of course, are the terms 'rank' and 'class' employed with any consistency in nineteenth-century English, either in respect of the contrast just described or any other contrast. That contrast is imposed here on a mass of various terminology; but as a contrast it may help to explain how so much popular literature, including the novel, and so much political debate in the nation, succeeded in defying the intellectual fashion for predicting social war as the natural or probable outcome of an industrial revolution.

The traditional doctrine of ranks, profound and widely accepted as it was, has not much profited at the hands of modern analysts of society, perhaps because they have often committed the common mistake of intellectual historians of supposing new ideas better than old ones; though the tendency of sociologists since Max Weber to revive an interest in status as against crudely economic notions of social difference has unwittingly brought social studies closer to the traditional and popular view. That view now needs to be studied in respectful detail. I believe it can be shown that the Victorians and their predecessors possessed instruments of social analysis more sophisticated than the Marxist, and more soundly based on social observation; that they knew what they were describing as observable facts, not as mere abstractions about alleged laws of history; and that in the treatise, the public speech and the social novel they created, notably in the hundred years between Adam Smith and the 1880s, a body of social analysis in which theory and observation are in exceptional harmony.

Since the doctrine of rank is traditional, it possesses (strictly speaking) no natural starting-point; but a convenient point of entry may be found in the works of one of Adam Smith's pupils, John Millar of Glasgow. In his first book, *The Origin of the Distinction of Ranks* (1771), in the opening paragraph, Millar lists the multiple causes of social difference, emphasizing that the economic factor is only one among others. In a later work, *Historical View of the English Government* (1803), he recounts in outline the history of social division, from the three classes of Anglo-Saxon England (the military, the peasantry and the clergy), to the fourth class of artisans added in later feudal England; and he notices a tendency in modern society to reduce the number again to three – landlords, capitalists and labourers; these, he adds, may in turn tend to become two, owners and wage-earners (pp. 331, 334). But this is only the severe outline of his system, not the system itself; and within that outline the number of ranks is infinite: there is 'an endless variety of characters in those who follow different trades and professions. The soldier, the clergyman, the lawyer, the physician, the taylor, the farmer, the smith, the shopkeeper: all . . . are led . . . to contrast something peculiar in their behaviour and turn of thinking' (p. 45). Wealth and poverty, important as they are, are not the sole marks of distinction; they may help to confer rank, but rank remains in the last resort independent of wealth. It is achieved by a complex and habitual system of popular acceptance; it may originate in the possession of property, but it soon takes on a life of its own: 'According to the accidental differences of wealth possessed by individuals, a subordination of ranks is gradually introduced, and different degrees of power and authority are assumed without opposition by particular persons, or bestowed upon them by the general voice of society' (p. 127).

Rank, in fact, is something one is widely supposed to possess; it does not exist independently of consciousness, any more than goodwill, trust and reputation could do. It is ultimately a fact of status. Since there is little that is original in Millar's account at this point, though much that is acute, it is the more remarkable that this highly traditional view of social difference should be regarded as a significant discovery of modern sociology. Marc Bloch's just observation about consciousness is often quoted with approval: 'A social classification exists, in the last analysis, only by virtue of the ideas which men form of it.'[1] This sensible view is already embodied in the traditional theory of the subject in the eighteenth and nineteenth centuries.

1. Marc Bloch, *Feudal Society* (translated London, 1961) p. 268.

Whether it is embodied in the rival doctrine of class is a matter of controversy, and especially of Marxist controversy; but there can be no doubt that consciousness was always an integral part of the doctrine of rank.

One prime difficulty of interpreting that doctrine is already clear. Being held and argued in ignorance of the coming doctrine of class, rank is often debated in terms which easily mislead minds familiar with that doctrine. The very term 'class' is an example. In the traditional view it is simply one term among others to describe a social group; it is not necessarily monolithic, and not necessarily economic in its origins; still less is it involved in predictions of hostility or social civil war. It is simply a general term of differentiation. The traditional use is still familiar in English everyday conversation. If some one were called unusually class-conscious, for example, this would not mean that he was exceptionally conscious of the difference between proletariat and bourgeoisie; it would certainly mean something subtler: that he cared about accent or table-manners, for example. The variety of practical uses of the term 'class' in Victorian England and after needs to be carefully noted. The word can be used in highly relaxed and noncommittal contexts, to describe either minute distinctions or large national groups, and it may commit the author to very little. Macaulay, for example, who plainly cares nothing for the doctrine of class that was becoming fashionable while he was writing his *History* in the 1840s, speaks casually of 'the two classes' of Englishmen as Londoners and countrymen,[1] and goes on to describe their widely contrasting manners in the 1680s. Such quick classifications abound; they are part of the Victorian debate, but they lack all the formality and finality of dogma. It was part of the ordinary business of the historian in that age to offer interpretations of social progress, but that is not the same as proposing laws on the subject. When Thomas Arnold, in an appendix to his edition of Thucydides, instances ancient Rome, late medieval Augsburg and the pre-reform House of Commons as examples of social evolution whereby 'the popular party of an earlier period becomes the anti-popular party of a later', he is drawing attention to a far more tentative and uncertain progression than

1. Macaulay, *The History of England* (1849–61) i. 369, from chapter 3.

a later dogmatist would accept. The movement of history, he argues, is often from aristocracy to wealth, and so to democracy, or 'the ascendancy of numbers'; and in the Commons of 1830 the parties have already ranged themselves as expressions of social forces, 'the advocates of property on one side, and of general intelligence and numbers on the other'.[1] Such arguments can easily mislead an age accustomed to more demanding certainties into supposing that Victorian historians believed in the inevitable laws of history.

Much of the profusion of class terms and class discussion in the mid and late Victorian era becomes more intelligible and informative if it is seen as based on a general assumption of rank and hierarchy. Human beings differ in an infinity of ways in their social characteristics; the theorist, the historian, the statesman, even the novelist, however, may provisionally choose to denominate them as members of vast and shifting groups. Seen in this light, the new doctrine of class is merely an aspect of the doctrine of rank, a manner of grouping according to larger units which socialists and others were later to formalize into something severe and unchanging in its deeper significances. In the English view these are merely a handful of possibilities among others; and less than plausible possibilities, as the century advanced and an awareness grew that the social effects of industrialism were less cataclysmic than they had once seemed in the Hungry Forties.

English interest in social difference is the more tentative and the less fixed in its assumptions for being about phenomena which are there to be seen and felt by everyone. This is self-evidently the strength of the social novel in the period: even when it describes recent and relatively unanalysed conditions, like industrial poverty and unemployment in Elizabeth Gaskell's *Mary Barton*, there is a confident sense on the part of the author of having been present as an observer, if not as an actor. On these very grounds German sociology could be mocked, as George Eliot skilfully mocked at the abstractions of Wilhelm Riehl in the *Westminster Review* of 1856. That magisterial review opens in destructively ironic terms: 'It is an interesting

1. Thomas Arnold, appendix 1 to his edition of Thucydides, *The History of the Peloponnesian War* (Oxford, 1830) iii. 636.

branch of psychological observation to note the images that are habitually associated with abstract or collective terms – what may be called the picture-writing of the mind', and she argues that those who use terms like 'the people', 'the masses', 'the proletariat', 'the peasantry' reveal as much concrete knowledge of any actual social world as a mere passenger might have in the workings of a railway.[1]

But it was not only continental theorists that offended: the English could indulge themselves in abstractions too. Some of these strictures, in a milder form, might apply even to the larger assertions of some English social scientists. Mill, in his 1836 essay on 'Civilization', advances the thesis that power tends to move from individuals to 'masses', and is capable of writing like this:

> At no period could it be said that there was literally no middle class – but that class was extremely feeble, both in numbers and in power: while the labouring people, absorbed in manual toil, with difficulty earned, by the utmost excess of exertion, a more or less scanty and always precarious subsistence . . . We must leave to history to unfold the gradual rise of the trading and manufacturing classes.[2]

This sort of potted social history, if modestly offered, may do no great harm, and much of the Victorian language of class is tentative and unstrenuous in this sense. Bagehot, like Mill, saw the history of his century as the growth of a middle class with distinct characteristics of its own, and believed that industrialism was tending to polarize English society, if only in the sense of intensifying an existing tendency.

> Of course [he wrote in 1856], it cannot be said that mill-makers invented the middle classes. The history of England perhaps shows that it has not for centuries been without an unusual number of persons with comfortable and moderate means. But though this class has ever been found among us, and has ever been more active than in any other similar country, yet to a great extent it was scattered, headless, motionless.

1. George Eliot, *Essays and Leaves from a Note-book* (Edinburgh, 1884) pp. 229–30.

2. J. S. Mill, 'Civilization', *London and Westminster Review* (April 1836); reprinted in his *Dissertations and Discussions* (1859) i. 164.

Nowadays men of the people can become rich, though the difference in status between the new rich and the aristocracy is still there: 'The one speaks the language of years of toil, and the other the years of indolence. A harsh laboriousness characterises the one, a pleasant geniality the other.'[1] This ready mixture of social history with direct human observation is representative of the temper of much of the theoretical discussion of class and rank in the age. In the early century, Bagehot wrote in the following year, 'the refined, discriminating, timorous immobility of the aristocracy was distinct from the coarse, dogmatic keep-downishness of the manufacturer. . . . Lancashire has been a California.'[2] Twenty years later he wrote confidently of class as the natural basis of a just electoral system, but with the same casual freedom in the use of words: by 1832, he argued, a new class had arisen in 'the trading wealth' of cities like Birmingham and Manchester, and 'the best of the middle class felt that they had no adequate power'; but the 'working class' is the new inheritor of power after the second Reform Act of 1867, and the political history of England in his lifetime has been a rapid movement from upper to middle to working-class power: 'The middle classes have as little power as they had before 1832, and the only difference is that before 1832 they were ruled by those richer than themselves, and now they are ruled by those poorer.'[3]

The suffrage, as these passages suggest, was a principal cause of growth in the language of class. If the word refers to large national groups based on major economic distinctions such as capital and labour, then class is the most convenient concept by which to express the social significance of 1832, 1867 and 1884, and it is doubtful if the terms derided by George Eliot could have held the field if the chief obsession of home policy had not made such terms a useful shorthand of debate. She was herself content to take for granted the existence of classes in her article following the Act of 1867, Felix Holt's 'Address to

1. Bagehot, 'The character of Sir Robert Peel', *National Review* (July 1856); reprinted in his *Collected Works* (1968) iii. 249–50.

2. Bagehot, 'Lord Brougham', *National Review* (July 1857); reprinted *ibid.* iii. 162.

3. Bagehot, *Fortnightly Review* (November 1876); reprinted *ibid.* iii. 221–4.

Working Men', a call for moderation that concedes 'it is all pretence to say that there is no such thing as Class Interest'; what is more, the struggle between the classes has been 'part of the history of every great society since history began'.[1] That comes very close to conceding the whole doctrine in all its rigour; but then the political debate over the suffrage required national rather than local terms, and large rather than minute distinctions. In *Essays on Reform* (1867), a symposium in support of the second Reform Act by R. H. Hutton, A. V. Dicey and others, class terms are extensively used, though the variety is wide enough to suggest little consensus in usage. Hutton believes there are essentially three classes in England: an aristocracy set in its ways and 'only in rare cases susceptible to the influence of disinterested political ideas'; a commercial class which stands for peace, except perhaps in the East; and a working class which is sturdily capable of only one idea at a time. The working class favoured the North in the American Civil War, for instance, in spite of the complexity of arguments for and against, because they 'saw but one, and this decided them. Their want of culture stood them in good stead' (pp. 30–1). Hutton regards class allegiance as a fact, and on the whole a desirable one; he praises the 'semi-patriotism' of trade unions or 'trade societies' in their contest with 'the Capitalists', and speaks openly of 'class patriotism' (p. 39) and of 'our middle-class Parliament' (p. 44). This is a very concessive argument to the new fashion for class analysis, and much of it smacks of the simplicities of Marxism; but it lacks curiosity about the alleged laws of history, and is sensibly content to describe things as they are.

Dicey, in the same collection, underlines the connection between the debate on the suffrage and the new doctrine of class. In an essay openly entitled 'The balance of classes', he recognizes a breach between traditional radicalism and the new radical case for the franchise. 'The theory of class representation', he argues, 'is fundamentally opposed to the arguments which, till recently, have been employed by all democratic or radical reformers', such as John Bright. The older

1. George Eliot, *Blackwood's Magazine* (January 1868); reprinted in her *Essays* (1884) pp. 330–1.

Liberal leaders had argued that 'representation should be primarily a representation of persons', and one of classes 'only in so far as it may be so accidentally' (p. 68). That rift, in Dicey's view, is ultimately unbridgeable: it is a strain that liberalism is about to bear. But Dicey is less sympathetic than Hutton to the doctrine of class. Individuals may be described as members of one class or another, it is true; but none the less 'it is as individuals that they either suffer or inflict wrong' (p. 72). In any case, the usual class terms do not apply to England, where classes are 'intermingled': 'the so-called working class is, like all others, notoriously broken into divisions' (p. 74). (This must be one of the earliest surviving instances of the phrase 'the so-called working class'.) An artisan is not the same as a labourer, for instance, and the £10 householders enfranchized in 1832 hold a variety of political and religious views: 'Looked at in one point of view, they may be called a class; looked at in another, they are a disconnected mass of different smaller classes' (p. 82). Even the working class only seems to be that, he continues, when viewed 'from without, and from a distance', when its subdivisions escape notice; though he concedes that there is 'more class feeling among workmen than amongst the rest of the community'. The franchise, in any case, will work against class; in thirty years, or by the end of the century, artisans will be 'as little distinguishable from the rest of the nation as are the men whose fathers in 1832 almost overthrew the Constitution from which they were excluded' (p. 83). This is an optimistic view, and not all its assumptions have been justified. It is unlikely that manhood suffrage worked against class, at least in the long run; and Dicey is so hostile to class that he is uncertain in his grasp of the more traditional concept he defends. The suffrage, he believes, works towards equality, even towards a species of social uniformity. In fact the ranks of society remained and remain distinguishable after the vote had been conceded, though the means of distinguishing them have varied subtly and rapidly from year to year.

Some of the arguments of the political economists, though not arguments for class in the strictest sense, encouraged the class analysis of English society. This was certainly a misunderstanding of their writings, though in some ways a natural one. Adam Smith and Ricardo had described the economic functions of the classes: they were less often concerned with whether these classes differ or resemble one another in respects other than economic. Mill, who is himself capable of using class terminology, noticed in an early article how natural such analysis seemed in the existing tradition of economics: 'English political economists presuppose, in every one of their speculations, that the produce of industry is shared among the three classes, altogether distinct from one another – namely labourers, capitalists and landlords.'[1] But all this is technical analysis that confines itself to highly specific questions of the production and distribution of wealth. Even as a young man Mill had been clear that, in a deeper sense than this, a common interest ultimately unites the employer with the employed. In 1830 he had written home approvingly from Paris, where he was watching the events of the July Revolution, how 'several excellent placards from common workmen' had just appeared on the walls of the city, 'explaining to their fellow-labourers the interest which they had in maintaining the security of property, and the advantage they ultimately derive from all improvements in the productive power of labour'.[2]

This sense of social interdependence and a horror of class ascendancy are among the continuing convictions of Mill's life. They are strongly present in the treatises *On Liberty* and *Representative Government*, where elaborate machinery is proposed to prevent the class preponderance that might arise through universal suffrage; and social unity is a theme of his brief parliamentary career in 1865–68, towards the end of his life. In his address to the electors of Westminster in 1865 he emphasized his fear of class domination, and urged that any extension of the suffrage should take care to 'prevent any class, even though it be the most numerous, from being able to swamp all other classes taken together'. Language like this suggests that class, if not fully accepted as a descriptive tool, is at least found useful to express an intelligent fear: if England is

1. J. S. Mill, *Monthly Repository* (May 1834).
2. J. S. Mill, *Earlier Letters 1812–48*, edited by F. E. Mineka (1963) i. 57, from a letter of 20 August 1830.

not in fact a class society, she is in some danger of becoming one.

It is hard to resist the conclusion that political theorists like Mill were contributing, however unwittingly, to the very divisions which they feared. Class terms, by their sheer convenience, were gaining ascendancy in political debate, and Mill is as capable of using them as any Marxist. That is not to say that he attributes the same significance to them; but a reader unversed in ideology might be forgiven for supposing that he did. The shorthand of economists is turning into the demands of political life; it infects even policy statements like Mill's 1839 article on the 'Reorganization of the Reform Party', where he had called on the Whigs and their allies to encourage cooperation and to legislate in favour of industrial partnership by which workmen could become capitalists:

> Such, then, are some of the duties of the government of the Middle Classes towards the working class: duties which those classes cannot leave unperformed, without drawing upon themselves the retribution which sooner or later awaits all classes or bodies of men who seize the powers of government and emancipate themselves from its obligations.[1]

Can such language be explained unless it is supposed that Mill, and others like him, failed to notice that they were conferring a credibility on such terms as 'middle class' and 'working class' which would run far beyond the convenience of economists – which might even come to represent the main issues of political debate? Mill's own readiness to use such terms trapped him in the end: a member of his audience, at an election meeting in 1865, rose to ask him a challenging question: 'How do you explain your writing that the upper classes are liars, and the lower classes – the working classes – habitual liars?'

Mill admitted he had written something like it; a passage of the sort appears in his *Thoughts on Parliamentary Reform* (1859), where he had claimed that in England 'the higher classes do not lie, and the lower, though mostly habitual liars, are ashamed of

1. J. S. Mill, 'Reorganization of the Reform Party', *Westminster Review* xxxii (1839).

lying'.[1] His defence more than satisfied an audience of supporters, who greeted it with applause; but the ice was thin for skating: 'The passage applied to the natural state of those who were both uneducated and subjected. If they were educated and became free citizens, then he should not be afraid of them. Lying was the vice of slaves, and they would never find slaves who were not liars. It was not a reproach that they were what slavery had made them.' Then he had to answer a question on his opinion that 'the lower classes had not as much right as the upper classes to have as many children as they pleased', and he replied with equal skill that *no* parents should have more children than they could support and educate.[2] Such use of class terms was surely embarrassingly divisive in that context – embarrassing, especially, to some one who had always rejected the notion of class interest in favour of the total claim of humanity.

That was the common liberal claim of the age. Conservatives tacitly represented a privileged class; demagogues of various hues might claim to represent the lowest classes; but liberals, whatever use they made of such terms, were hostile to class as a political weapon. That at least is the declared position. Acton believed that Locke's great political legacy, passed on to Montesquieu, the Enlightenment and the American Revolution, was to rescue political power from the classes: 'By his idea that the powers of government ought to be divided according to their nature, and not according to the division of classes . . . Locke is the originator of the long reign of English institutions in foreign lands.'[3] This is an abiding claim to uniqueness, and the claim continues long. Meredith, in his last years, wrote a letter in support of his local association in terms that Mill and Acton would have approved; the Liberal Party, he declared, is 'the only party that has ever taken a forward step on behalf of

1. *Thoughts on Parliamentary Reform* (1859); the pamphlet is reprinted in his *Dissertations and Discussions* (London, 1867) iii. 44.

2. *Daily Telegraph* (10 July 1865) p. 2, cols 1–2. Mill refers to the question in his account of the incident in the last chapter of his *Autobiography*, but not to his reply. On his view of population see his *Principles of Political Economy* II. xiii.

3. Lord Acton, *The History of Freedom and Other Essays* (1907) p. 54, from his 1877 lecture 'The history of freedom in Christianity'.

the country and in defiance of interested sections'.[1] The whole is greater than the part, and common humanity is more than class. However much men like Mill may use class terms as analytical tools, they reserve the right to withdraw from the partisanship that others were eager to impute.

The liberal rejection of class as a political weapon, then, was maintained with difficulty in the debate that surrounded the suffrage and the diffusion of class terms by the political economists. Other tendencies assisted the defeat of class; and its defeat, in the end, is the most important of all facts to record. That the first industrial nation failed to register the widely predicted effects of industrialism is an astonishing achievement; that its party system failed to organize itself in terms of class is the chief and most public evidence of that achievement. The Liberals were never simply the party of the poor against the rich; though it is possible to argue, with numerous exceptions, that they were the party of the industrial poor. Regional and religious differences always counted for too much to allow class parties to arise in any clear form, and even the distinction between town and country does not fully describe the clash of party. Class did not happen on a national scale in British party politics in the nineteenth century. It was predicted with hope or with fear, it was mocked, analysed and discussed; and some of those who predicted it with the greatest certainty were among those who hated it most. But it cannot, in the end, be called the deciding factor in the party struggle. As a doctrine, class is like an actor who spends most of his life in the wings waiting to go on.

How was class defeated? One answer lies in the fact that industrialism rapidly created hierarchies of its own, including wage differentials, no less complex than those of the old order it had replaced. Another answer may lie in the movement of society itself towards achieved rather than assigned roles: from roles assigned to an individual from birth, as in the hereditary principle, to those earned by personal qualities. Wordsworth had noted the change sourly near the beginning of the century: 'The wealthiest man among us is the best', he had written in a

1. George Meredith, *Collected Letters*, edited by C. L. Cline (Oxford, 1970) iii. 1475.

sonnet of 1802 ('O Friend'), complaining that England was now the victim of new men and a prey to greed and fashion. Much of the fiction of the age – *David Copperfield*, *Pendennis*, *Great Expectations* – might be seen to illustrate and celebrate a social tendency that Wordsworth had disliked. Men found it progressively harder to believe that it was just for a man merely to inherit his status. It must be earned. Dickens's Pip, who does not merit his good fortune by his own labour but by a single act of kindness, has to learn by the end of *Great Expectations* that wealth can only be gained by sweat and suffering. Status may look dignified; but it is not so to those who win it by their own efforts. The ideals of work and self-help are in the end inimical to class. They diminish the sense of separation between rich and poor; they allow some of the poor to become rich, others to believe they could become so; and they cream off the best of the lower into the middle and even high ranks of society, leaving the lowest relatively leaderless. If all this converts a righteous envy of privilege into a sense of personal failure, that sense may be more painful than envy itself; but it is also less likely than envy to turn into revolutionary causes. That men should achieve their own status in life, and know they are at liberty to do so, is one of the stabilizing elements in post-industrial England.

Status, moreover, is infinitely multiple, and here the traditional doctrine of rank achieves not merely a higher degree of descriptive accuracy than class, but a higher potential for social stability as well. Arnold Toynbee, in his Oxford lectures *The Industrial Revolution* (1884), observed that since the movement from status to contract there had been another movement 'from contract to a new kind of status determined by the law' (pp. 30–1), along with a host of new social conventions more complex than any body of law. And complexity distracts from class-hostility. A civil war demands two sides, neither more nor less; and the tensions within English industrial society have always been more complex than that. The doctrine of rank emphasizes this complexity: as the doctor is superior to the dentist, so is the barrister to the solicitor, the butler to the footman, the artisan to the labourer. There is no end to rank, and that is why men are fascinated by it. It is worth watching, as it is worth trying to estimate one's own status within it. 'The English wish to have inferiors', Tocqueville remarked on his visit to England in 1835 – unlike the Frenchman, who wishes not to have superiors:

> The Frenchman constantly raises his eyes above him with anxiety. The Englishman lowers his beneath him with satisfaction. On both sides there is pride, but it is understood in a different way. . . .
>
> Does this effect not arise from the fact that the Englishman was used to the idea that he could advance himself, but the Frenchman could not? The one to be something had to destroy what was above him, the other had to seek to raise himself to this higher rank.[1]

This puts another aspect of the matter with great insight. An Englishman looks down with disdain and up with admiration, having plotted his own place in the hierarchy. These are not the conditions that make for armed revolution.

Technical advance is politically more ambiguous, and might work in either direction. Macaulay, in the third chapter of his *History*, had noticed the enormous increase in speed of transport achieved by his own age in the 1840s; but he did not reflect on its potential for class conflict. A national clash between capital and labour, like the General Strike of 1926, hardly seems conceivable without rapid communications, and the development of railways after 1830 was felt at the time to be destined to far-reaching social effects. But if transport favours class, education favours rank, and to many Victorians it looked as if education was winning and would continue to win. Public libraries, compulsory schooling after 1870, and the spread of universities to the industrial cities all seemed likely to lessen distances, in Trollope's phrase, and to vary and complicate the differences that survived. Tennyson's first published utterance as a peer – he had taken his seat in the Lords in March 1884 – was the poem 'Freedom', which appeared in *Macmillan's Magazine* in the following December; and there he wrote of the 'golden dream'

> Of knowledge fusing class with class,
> Of civic hate no more to be,
> Of love to leaven all the mass
> Till every soul be free.

1. Tocqueville, *Journeys to England and Ireland* (New York, 1968) p. 60.

That dream was beginning to look practical, as a future hope, by the 1880s. Knowledge was an intrinsic good; it was also a path to social unity and a remedy for envy and hate.

Social difference is a matter of consciousness, and there can be no doubt that Victorians were conscious, after the mid century, of having turned a corner. The 1840s are the period of acutest anxiety on this score, and in some ways Disraeli's pronouncements illustrate this awareness more clearly than any others. In the Hungry Forties he had bemoaned the condition of England; and in *Sybil* he had claimed, or allowed his character Gerard to claim, that 'there is more serfdom in England now than at any time since the Conquest' (III. v). That claim may be hysterical, like some of Gerard's ensuing remarks: he believed that the English peasant before the Wars of the Roses was 'better clothed, better lodged and better fed' than those of 1845; that 'he ate flesh every day, he never drank water, was well housed and clothed in stout woollens'. That may be nonsense, though it was nonsense that some men listened to. But a quarter of a century later a changed Disraeli, as Leader of the Opposition, spoke at Manchester in April 1872 of a fear outlived and a prosperity newly attained. 'You have established a society of classes which give vigour and variety to life', he told his audience, with all equal before the law and an open aristocracy; and they may have wondered what had become of the Two Nations as he went on: 'You have not merely a middle class, but a hierarchy of middle classes, in which every degree of wealth, refinement, industry, energy and enterprise is duly represented', while the working classes have been civilized over two generations by higher wages and greater leisure, 'the two civilizers of man'.

This speech shows some awareness of two contrasting systems of social classification ('not merely a middle class, but a hierarchy of middle classes') and of the triumph of the old doctrine over the new. It is a far cry from the open appeals to class loyalty that Parliament and the people had heard forty years before, when Brougham had urged acceptance of the Reform Bill in October 1831 in these terms: 'I speak now of the middle classes – of those hundreds of thousands of respectable persons – the most numerous and by far the most wealthy order in the community: ... the genuine depositories of sober, rational, intelligent and honest English feeling', men who cared as little for an epigram as for a cannon-ball, Brougham added, but who seemed ready in the agitation of the reform campaign to march, by their hundreds of thousands, into the mouth of danger to win a power they thought theirs by right. A few weeks after Brougham's fiery speech a National Union of the Working Classes organized meetings to protest against the hereditary principle; and fourteen years later Disraeli wrote in defence of agricultural labourers that they were no better than serfs. That is the length of the road from division to harmony that England had traversed in only forty years. But the journey was made because many men wanted to make it: it was not an historical necessity. If unhindered, England might well have fallen into what Charles Kingsley called a 'hateful severance' of class and class. 'The real danger to England now', Bryce wrote in *Essays on Reform* (1867), 'is not from the working class, for no working class in any country was ever more peaceably disposed than ours is, but from the isolation of classes' caused by industrialism. This isolation is a fear and not, as in Marx, a hope. 'Government by a class is always government for a class; a Commonwealth therefore knows nothing of classes.'[1] That is the purest Gladstonian sentiment, and it took on an increasingly confident ring in late Victorian times. 'The danger', as Acton was to put it, 'is not that a particular class is unfit to govern. Every class is unfit to govern'; but 'the law of liberty tends to abolish the reign of race over race, of faith over faith, of class over class'.[2]

What words did the Victorians use to describe the orders of their society? They lacked, in a formal sense, a single system of terms, but the lack hardly amounts to a misunderstanding, and consistency would not have been natural in such a matter. Whether a 'class' (working or middle) is singular or plural remains an open question: R. H. Hutton's 'The political

1. *Essays on Reform* (1867) p. 277.

2. Lord Acton, *Letters to Mary Gladstone* (1904) p. 93, from a letter of 24 April 1881. A similar phrase is quoted by Mary Gladstone Drew in her *Acton, Gladstone and Others* (London, 1924) as a favourite of her father's: 'The danger is not that a particular class is unfit to govern – every class is unfit to govern' (p. 16).

character of the working class' is misprinted 'Classes' in the table of contents of *Essays on Reform*, and it is doubtful if anyone noticed or cared. The point is not altogether trivial, since the singular usage allows for, though it does not require, a monolithic interpretation which for the sake of clarity I have emphasized in this chapter; but for the Victorians the word was commonly a general term for any extensive social group. Cornewall Lewis, in his *Remarks on the Use and Abuse of Some Political Terms* (1832) devotes only one chapter to terms of social description; and there he is satisfied with 'rich', 'middle class' and 'poor' and the divisions within them. Disraeli uses the same terms resoundingly in his political trilogy; Elizabeth Gaskell with less emphasis and in familiar tones in *Mary Barton*: 'John Barton's overpowering thought, which was to work out his fate on earth, was rich and poor; why are they so separate, so distinct, when God has made them all?' (ch. 15). A number of overlapping and almost synonymous terms describe the larger divisions: rich, upper, the masters; middle; poor, working, labouring, lower; all in conjunction with 'class' or 'classes'. The sophistication of this terminology lies in its possibilities of combination, notably with such terms as upper, middle and lower, which are all subject to qualification. The sense of hierarchy is very plain in such words. Few before Dicey protested at the loaded and inaccurate implication of 'working' or 'labouring' man or class, with its curious suggestion that others do not work; though Hardy was to protest against it silently in his journal. In January 1888 he declared himself privately to be neither a Tory nor a Radical, but against privilege whether aristocratic or democratic; and by democratic privilege he meant 'the arrogant assumption that the only labour is hand-labour – a worse arrogance than that of the aristocrat'.[1]

Some idiosyncratic usages came and went. Bagehot once wrote facetiously of 'that second order of English society which, from their habits of reading and non-reading, may be called *par excellence* the scriptural classes'.[2] He evidently found 'middle

1. Florence E. Hardy, *The Life of Thomas Hardy* (1962) p. 204.

2. Bagehot, 'Lord Brougham', *National Review* (July 1857); reprinted in his *Collected Works* (1968) iii. 162.

class' too broad a term to be continuously useful: in *The English Constitution* he refers to the despotic power of the new order of 1832, 'the ordinary majority of educated men' (ch. 7). But the invention of class terms is a game anyone can play, and it has few rules or none. Charles Booth, analysing the four million inhabitants of London in his *Life and Labour*, divides them into eight categories, ranging from the unemployed, the casual labourers, and upwards through those with intermittent or small earnings to those on regular and higher earnings, and eventually to the 'lower middle class' and 'upper middle class' (i. 33). That terminology, like many others, was understood by many but adopted by few.

Technical terms of foreign origin, such as 'bourgeoisie' and 'proletariat', are of rare occurrence in the context of contemporary English life. 'Proletariat' and 'proletarian' are terms that would be familiar to any student of ancient Rome, or to a reader of Rousseau, and there are scattered examples of them in seventeenth- and eighteenth-century English: one form, for example, occurs in Butler's *Hudibras* (I. i. 714). And there are occasional references to them in journalism and sociology from the 1850s; Matthew Arnold uses 'proletariate' in a letter of December 1880.[1] But these are affected or scholastic usages, like those of 'bourgeois' and 'bourgeoisie'; though like left and right they could be used in a specifically continental reference. Macaulay, in Paris soon after the July Revolution, writes in his journal how the 'bourgeoisie' of the city conducted themselves after the overthrow of Charles X.[2] George Eliot uses the word facetiously in a letter on the German Empress: 'I suppose a royal toothache is much like a bourgeois toothache.'[3] No weight can be attached to these examples, and it is plain that the Victorian description of society, ample as it is, could flourish without such words. Even Beatrice Webb, writing as a socialist in her autobiography *My Apprenticeship* (1926), uses 'proletarian' in inverted commas, and regards it as part of the 'cut and dried creed of the Marxian socialist' (p. 190). It had a

1. Matthew Arnold, *Letters 1848–88*, edited by G. W. E. Russell (London, 1895) ii. 188.

2. G. O. Trevelyan, *The Life and Letters of Lord Macaulay* (1876) i. 166.

3. George Eliot, *Letters* (1954–56) v. 187.

Marxist ring long before that, though it is of course no more a Marxist invention than the class analysis of society itself.

Through all this, amazingly, the status of gentleman survived, and its survival down to the mid twentieth century remains hard to explain. In an hierarchical society it was an aspect of that hierarchy, but so exceptional an aspect as to defy some of the deeper principles of the system. One of those principles is gradation. Victorian society is not a matter of broad distinctions, though the extremes of upper and lower are broadly placed. The distinctions are more often fine, delicate of interpretation, and complex in their origins. The aristocracy is open, not exclusively based on issues of title, and capable of being penetrated by the outsider. But at some point well above the middle of the social pyramid runs a dividing line: those above it are gentlemen and ladies, and those below it are not. It is no qualification to say that there are doubtful and borderline cases: a borderline case merely emphasizes the existence of a border. Nor is the principle much modified or softened by the reflection that gentility, like the nobility, can be penetrated. Even Sam Weller in *Pickwick* hopes to be a gentleman: ' "Now I'm a gen'lm'n's servant. I shall be a gen'lm'n myself one of these days, perhaps, with a pipe in my mouth and a summer-house in the back-garden" ' (ch. 16). It is an achievable role, without a doubt: Smiles, in the last chapter of *Self-Help* (1859) entitled 'Character: the True Gentleman', calls it 'the crown and glory of life' to be aimed at by every conscientious Englishman, something 'constituting rank in itself' and better than wealth, or high birth, or knowledge. It is not surprising that in the preface of 1866 to a new edition of the book, he regretted his title, 'self-help', which might mislead some into thinking it 'a eulogy of selfishness'.

How gentility was achieved is not a matter that Smiles explains. But the openness of the system was politically significant. Tocqueville, writing his last impressions of England in 1833, concluded that its open aristocracy would save it from revolution, being 'founded on wealth, a thing that may be acquired, and not on birth which cannot', and he remarks on the corresponding difference between the English 'gentleman' and the French 'gentilhomme'.[1] Peel once remarked that it takes three generations to make a gentleman, but that process was much accelerated in the course of the reign, and it is doubtful if it was true in Peel's time, unless in some very exacting sense. It could be done in one. Macaulay, in a letter of 1833, remarked that 'the curse of England is the obstinate determination of the middle classes to make their sons what they call gentlemen'; as a result of which, he adds dejectedly, the country is overrun with unemployed clergymen, lawyers, doctors, authors and clerks, 'who might have thriven, and been above the world, as bakers, watchmakers or innkeepers'.[2] More than thirty years later T. H. Green, speaking on the Reform Bill of 1867, noticed the unfading attraction of the genteel, even aristocratic style of life to thousands of Englishmen born outside it. 'A great capitalist generally ends by buying a great estate,' he remarked. 'The English gentleman, we are sometimes told, is the noblest work of God, but one gentleman makes many snobs.'[3]

That the status of gentleman had an economic base is undoubted. To achieve it, as Sam and Pip know, there must be a private income sufficient to release one from the need to work. If one works at all, the work must be consistent with the status of a gentleman, such as the higher professions. Membership of the House of Commons, which was unpaid, both exemplifies the status and confirms it to perfection. Some thought the concept had a sexual bias, but then it is probable that in all ranks of society the male was more determinant than the female; as one of Trollope's characters, a gentlemanly suitor to a young woman who is his social inferior, remarks to her, a man can 'raise a woman to his own rank, whereas a woman must accept the level of her husband'.[4] But it had long possessed a moral tinge, and that tinge was to grow more pronounced: Dr Johnson in his *Dictionary* (1755), distinguishing five senses of the word, beginning with 'a man of birth', gives as his second sense 'a man raised above the vulgar by his character or port'. Samuel Smiles would have agreed with that.

1. Tocqueville, *Journeys to England and Ireland* (1968) p. 51.
2. G. O. Trevelyan, *The Life and Letters of Lord Macaulay* (1876) i. 331.
3. T. H. Green, *Works* (London, 1888) iii cx–cxi.
4. Trollope, *The American Senator* (London, 1877) ch. 30.

That such a system should survive an industrial revolution at all is one of the great wonders of social history. In fact it survived and flourished. It had far greater staying power than the aristocracy. And it remains throughout the century, though not unchanging, one of the absolutes of the social system. It is never totally moralized – a gentleman can behave in a manner unbefitting in a gentleman – and it somehow outlives both the violent economic changes of the age and the more delicate refinements of social difference. Some held that the intrinsic superiority of the English upper orders explained the paradox. Cobden, appealing as a free-trader for an end to the Corn Laws in the Commons in March 1845, addressed the House in these stirring terms:

> You gentlemen of England, the high aristocracy of England, your forefathers led my forefathers; you may lead us again if you choose; but though – longer than any other aristocracy, you have kept your power, while the battlefield and the hunting-field were the tests of manly vigour, you have not done as the noblesse of France or the hidalgos of Madrid have done; you have been Englishmen, not wanting in courage on any call,

and he called on them to join in the new mercantile age: 'You may yet do well.' Many of them did. But their survival remains a puzzle. It looks as if they supplied an element of certainty in the constant flux of social distinction in the age, and that many welcomed that certainty. Perhaps the army offers a useful analogy: it has many ranks, and ranks may be added or abolished over the years. But it retains one fundamental distinction throughout – the distinction between officers and the rest.

[11]

Race and Empire

The two great divisive ideas of mankind are race and class, but there is a striking difference in the interest that attaches to the attitudes of Victorian intellectuals to one and the other. That difference may be bluntly stated: when an Englishman, then or now, talks of social difference, he talks about something that he directly knows; when of race, of something in which his convictions are much less likely to be based on observation. On the one he is a mine of information; on the other, more probably, of misinformation – of assumptions hastily made or borrowed, of airy theories, of preconceptions in favour of equality or discrimination. Race, as Freeman remarked, is essentially 'a learned doctrine', in the sense of being 'an inference from facts which the mass of mankind could never have found out for themselves'.[1] Since the Victorians, by the end of the era, governed about one-quarter of mankind, and in every continent, the question cannot be overlooked. But as a chapter in intellectual history the emphasis falls, for once, on historical rather than intellectual importance. Victorian views of social difference are profound and subtle in a way that ensures their permanent interest on intrinsic grounds. Their views on race are less often that, though they have something more than the fascination of a museum-piece.

Race has divided the twentieth-century mind even more than the Victorian, and it will be as well to put some recent assumptions into critical perspective. The confusion between justice and equality is a familiar one; only a little less familiar, the

1. Edward A. Freeman, 'Race and language', *Contemporary Review* (February 1877) and *Fortnightly Review* (January 1877); reprinted in his *Historical Essays: third series* (London, 1879) p. 181.

confusion between equality and uniformity. Many believe that to treat men justly means to treat them in the same way; and that to do that means to assume that they are in fact the same. These are not on the whole Victorian mistakes, but they are mistakes which make the Victorians harder to understand. A post-Victorian reaction against 'racialism' (a word the Victorians hardly possessed) has taken the form of a profound disinclination to believe in racial characteristics; and many now believe that if the races could be shown to be different, it would follow that they should be treated differently in the sense of being discriminated against. It is doubtful if many Victorians would have understood that argument, and still more doubtful that it is a good one. To confuse theories of race with 'racialism' is to confound a wide range of doctrines, not all of them foolish, into the simple pattern of a modern nightmare. Victorian theories of race, where they are unconvincing, are usually so because they are based on inadequate knowledge, but it does not follow from this that the whole inquiry into racial differences is absurd or evil. Some modern handbooks announce their dismissal even on their title-pages: Jacques Barzun's *Race: a Study in Superstition* (1937) is a representative of that sort of intellectual facility; another study of the subject, devoted to Matthew Arnold, begins its preface: 'This book deals with some of the maddest of theories and one of the sanest of men.'[1] This is to dismiss the question even before it is posed. Whatever their weaknesses, Victorian race theories deserve more serious treatment than this.

Most Victorian references to race in a political context are not strictly assertions about ethnology. 'Race' commonly means something wider and less precise than that. When people say that a man is a Jew if he thinks he is one, this is much closer to the general Victorian consciousness in such matters than any pure inquiry into historical ancestry; though ancestry is of course among the considerations that apply. Race is more often a matter of cultural affinity and allegiance, and 'cultural' needs to be understood here in the broadest sense – it includes language, religion and ways of thought. This wider concept of race has become less familiar because it has been overshadowed

1. F. E. Faverty, *Matthew Arnold the Ethnologist* (Evanston, 1951).

by doctrines of a scientific caste. Some of those doctrines take their rise in the Victorian age, but they are hardly a part of the general consciousness of the age. Perhaps Winston Churchill was the last British statesman to use the word 'race' in an uninhibited Victorian sense: 'It was the nation and the race dwelling all around the globe that had the lion heart', he told a parliamentary assembly on his eightieth birthday, referring to the events of an earlier premiership in 1940. By 'the nation and the race' he meant something like those English-speaking peoples whose history he was then completing, a history abridged into one volume before his death as *The Island Race* (1964); and by that Churchill meant, more or less, the white Commonwealth and the United States, united in this view by a common language and culture and by a respect for free institutions. A Victorian would have had no difficulty with that usage, though he might also have known that the word 'race' had a more precise and scientific sense as well. 'And we, then, what are we? what is England?' asked Arnold in his lectures *On the Study of Celtic Literature* (1867). It was a question that interested his contemporaries, and one that historians between Macaulay and Churchill tried to answer.

The Victorian interest in race is vastly in excess of that of any previous generation of Englishmen, and it is the culmination of a long-developing interest that owes its beginnings to a fascination with regions and nations. In many ways the novel represents this development in a more convenient form than political prose. The late eighteenth-century novel shows an occasional interest in the regional, both in French and English, in *La Nouvelle Héloïse* (1765) and *Humphry Clinker* (1771); but novels radically concerned with portraying the life of a region probably begin in Europe with Maria Edgeworth's *Castle Rackrent* (1800), a tale written before the Union about the remote world of rural Ireland; and Scott instantly accepted that challenge for Scotland, beginning *Waverley* soon after 'so as in some distant degree to emulate the admirable Irish portraits drawn by Miss Edgeworth'.[1] Ireland and Scotland are regions which are almost nations; and both novelists, being Unionists,

1. Scott, *Waverley* (Edinburgh, 1814) ch. 72, 'A postscript which should have been a Preface'.

are intrigued by evidences of a fading regional sense. ' 'Tis sixty years since' Scott subtitles his first novel, astonished that the last flicker of Scottish nationhood, the Forty-Five, should be so recent an event that a few men could still remember it. These novels analyse dying societies as microcosms: the little worlds of the Irish or Highland estates mirror the larger hierarchies of the whole United Kingdom. The extension of the idea is rapid and perhaps not yet complete: Manchester in Disraeli and Elizabeth Gaskell, Yorkshire in the Brontës, the West Midlands in George Eliot, the West Country in Hardy. But all these later instances, unlike the Irish and Scottish pioneers, are about regions that aspire to be nothing more: curious phenomena of the kingdom, they seek to be no more than themselves, and hardly even aspire to survive forever as distinctive entities. They may die out, or they may absorb the rest. In the case of Manchester, they belong to the future, and the whole nation may one day come to be like it; or, in the case of the Brontës, George Eliot and Hardy, regions are fascinating backwaters, abundant in a sense of landscape and weather and illustrating the vanishing rural virtues. 'Village tradition,' wrote Hardy to Rider Haggard in 1902, 'a vast mass of unwritten folk-lore, local chronicle, local topography, and nomenclature – is absolutely sinking, has nearly sunk, into eternal oblivion.'[1] The novel in this dimension is a public remembrancer: it rescues little worlds from oblivion. These are the books by which the Victorians studied their own diversity, but it is not a diversity which they expected to last. They capture it before it flies.

Irish Catholics apart, regionalism is not a divisive force in literature or in politics. It is a way of studying the nation that arose out of the Union of 1800: how it happened, of what parts it was composed, and what local features might be worth saving or, at the worst, worth remembering. Nation is the immediate successor to region in popular consciousness: by the mid century it is ineradicably planted in Spain, Germany, Italy, some constituent parts of the Austrian empire, even Belgium. But British nationhood, unlike all these, is not embattled; it does not arise, as these others did, out of reactions to French

1. Florence E. Hardy, *The Life of Thomas Hardy* (1962) pp. 312–13.

revolutionary fervour, and it has no need for a demonstrative rhetoric like Fichte's or Mazzini's. Arnold's question 'What is England?' is in a milder key. Perhaps for this reason, the quiet Victorian debate about British nationhood has not won much attention. But it is an essential part of the political debate, and a principal means by which the doctrine of liberty rooted itself in the particular conditions of the British parliamentary state.

It is a highly characteristic fact of eighteenth-century radical ideas to suppose that the most significant political assertions are general, in the sense of being true for all mankind. The 'truths' of the American and French revolutions, as publicly proclaimed, were decidedly of this sort: 'all men', as the Declaration of Independence put it, 'are created equal . . .' The doctrines of Godwin and his disciple Shelley are the English equivalent; Bentham is another. The Victorians were sceptical of these universal assumptions. Mill, from the vantage-point of the new age, held it to be one of the defects of the utilitarian system that it failed to take account of national character, and in his essay on Bentham he protested gravely against the omission:

> That which alone causes any material interests to exist, which alone enables any body of human being to exist as a society, is national character: *that* it is which causes one nation to succeed in what it attempts, another to fail; one nation to understand and aspire to elevated things, another to grovel in mean ones; which makes the greatness of one nation lasting, and dooms another to early and rapid decay. . . . A philosophy of laws and institutions not founded on a philosophy of national character is an absurdity.[1]

That is an interesting assertion in the mouth of a young radical, and it marks off the radicalism of the Victorians from that of their predecessors. But literary developments alone would have made any other conclusion difficult. It would have been hard, in the light of the regional and historical novel, to maintain the view that the tribal differences of man are of accidental and secondary interest, or that they await the millennial day when they will drop away to reveal mankind in his pure humanity.

1. J. S. Mill, 'Bentham', *London and Westminster Review* (August 1833); reprinted in his *Dissertations and Discussions* (1859) i. 365–66.

> The painted veil, by those who were, called life,
> Which mimicked, as with colours idly spread,
> All men believed or hoped, is torn aside;
> The loathsome mask has fallen, the man remains
> Sceptreless, free, uncircumscribed, but man
> Equal, unclassed, tribeless, and nationless . . .

That was Shelley's millennium in *Prometheus Unbound* (III. iv). It is not a Victorian sentiment. Liberty for them is not the abandonment of history but its fulfilment. Man discovers himself more fully by learning to know his tribe or nation; liberty is fully compatible with patriotism, and with an enthusiasm for the patriotisms of others. The liberal mind warms to the national struggles of other peoples: to the Greek struggle against the Turk, to the subject peoples of the Russian and Austrian empires. Nationalism is a concept as likely to be misunderstood by the twentieth century as racialism; but certainly the Victorian radical is a partisan of what Mill calls national character. He does not believe in the possibility of Shelley's 'unclassed, tribeless and nationless' utopia. He does not even want it.

To the extent that a nation, actual or aspiring, must be united by a common culture or race, liberal nationhood was always a racial concept. Bagehot sometimes writes as if nation meant much the same as race. A nation has its characteristic strengths, he wrote in 1852, and they can endure through the generations:

> The Jews of to-day are the Jews in face and form of the Egyptian sculptures; in character they are the Jews of Moses – the negro is the negro of a thousand years. . . . The fact is certain, the cause beyond us. The subtle system of obscure causes, whereby sons and daughters resemble not only their fathers and mothers, but even their great-great-grandfathers and their great-great-grandmothers, may very likely be destined to be very inscrutable. . . . Nations have one character, one set of talents, one list of temptations, and one duty . . .[1]

The jump from facial resemblances to talents and duties will seem abrupt, and it is this jump that turns the theory of race

1. Bagehot, *Inquirer* (24 January 1852); reprinted in his *Collected Works* (1968) iv. 50.

into one of culture and nationhood. Just as the inhabitants of the British Isles have regional characteristics and, ultimately, a national character, so do other nations and aspiring nations around the world. The argument of the novel and of political prose, in the 1840s and 1850s, widens to include the whole of that prospect. It is an enlargement prescribed both by the direction the novel was moving in and by the progress of scientific knowledge. The doctrine of race, as Freeman remarked, is 'the direct offspring of the study of scientific philology' vulgarized in the popular mind.[2] It is not an ignorant view but an educated or semi-educated view. Philology, ethnology, even the doctrine of evolution conspired to make men believe that mankind could not forever be excluded from the analysis that had reduced the rest of the natural universe to an ordered system.

The scale of racial types in nineteenth-century fiction is wide, but not so wide as to include all the principal divisions of man. The Asian hardly appears till near the end of the century, in the early fiction of Conrad and Kipling; the negro hardly appears at all. Maria Edgeworth, with her curious faculty for attempting untried subjects and leaving them to other novelists to develop, had written a novel on race, *Harrington* (1817), in opposition to antisemitism. Disraeli propounds doctrines of race in *Coningsby* and in his later novels; but he confines the range of his fiction to the scenes of British government – Westminster, the country houses and the clubs, with excursions into the industrial north and occasional invasions from without by a cosmopolitan sage. Race is a dogma rather than a fact in Disraeli's novels: it is proposed with insistence, though rarely demonstrated in action, as the great and neglected fact of a future science of humanity. Most political debate, in Disraeli's view, is in comparison with all this mere empty rhetoric: 'progress and reaction', as he put in his life of Bentinck (1852), 'are but words to mystify the millions. They mean nothing, they are nothing, they are phrases and not facts.' Reality lies elsewhere: 'All is race.' In *Endymion*, the last novel, he calls it 'the key of history'. But a Jew as fantastic as Sidonia does not quite justify the assertion that racial types have become a subject

1. Freeman, *Historical Essays: third series* (1879) p. 184.

for fiction as early as the 1840s. And no one who had followed the contemporary debate on race would imagine that Disraeli was an original thinker on the subject. The Edinburgh anatomist Robert Knox, for example, had delivered lectures in the early and mid 1840s, later published as *The Races of Men* (1850), and Knox begins his book with an assertion that 'in human history race is everything'. The book, which Charlotte Brontë knew and which Disraeli might easily have known, concludes that there are 'remarkably organic differences' between the races, in mind as well as body, and looks forward to an Anglo-Saxon republic before the end of the century which would end the legacy of the Norman Conquest and found a European confederacy to exclude both Celt and Cossack. Knox, like many others, crudely confuses race in the physical sense with language and culture, an error Freeman was later to expose. But his medical evidence, limited as it is, gives the political racialism of Disraeli the pretext of a scientific foundation.

By the 1860s and after something more serious and permanent than Disraeli's shallow dogmatism had entered the English novel: a sense of race, in certain fictional characters, allied to the culture and innate properties of a people. George Eliot's honeymoon in Prague in 1854, with George Henry Lewes, marks something of a watershed: they heard a Jew read from the Talmud in the oldest synagogue in Europe, and her interest in the Jewish question, even in Zionism, was henceforth assured. *Daniel Deronda* (1876) represents those interests in too bookish a form to be altogether convincing; but Ladislaw in *Middlemarch*, whose continental origins are delicately implied, is a more compelling portrait of a wandering intellectual who might introduce into English life, to its reluctant advantage, a sense of continuity more ancient than English civilization itself. 'I fairly cried', she wrote in a letter in 1866, on visiting a synagogue in Amsterdam, 'at witnessing this faint symbolism of a religion of sublime far-off memories'; and four years later she interpreted the Franco-Prussian war in terms of a larger significance than of a struggle between nations: 'The war is in some respects the conflict of two differing forms of civilization. But whatever charm we may see in the southern Latin races, this ought not to blind us to the great contributions which the German energies have made in all sorts of ways to the common treasure of mankind.'[1]

Much of this amounts to a sense of inadequacy in English civilization. That sense is stronger still in Carlyle and Matthew Arnold, who proclaim in more strident tones than George Eliot's the claims of Germanic heroism and of the Hellenic spirit. Theories of race, as everyone knows, are often assertions of one's own superiority; but they can also be the exact reverse. They can arise out of a sense of inferiority, or at least of incompleteness, and they can point towards the alleged virtues of other races as if to models and exemplars. Since the dark side of racialism is well known, it may be useful here to emphasize the bright side as well. In Victorian literature that side is a good deal commoner than the dark. Disraeli is perhaps a dubious advantage to the argument: when he divides the human species, in *Coningsby*, into 'five great varieties' (Caucasian, Mongolian, Malayan, American and Ethiopian), and distinguishes within the first a special place, along with the Saxon and the Greek, for the Hebrew – that 'unmixed race' of 'unsullied idiosyncrasy' (I. x) – some elements of self-recommendation are evidently present. But these novels drew the attention of the polite classes of England to the virtues of Jewry and, whatever the private motives that underlie them, they are clearly designed to widen tolerances and to excite a sense of admiration for a race other than the English.

But where Disraeli is an example of 'bright' racialism in a qualified sense, George Eliot is an unqualified example. Matthew Arnold's four lectures on Celtic literature, delivered in 1865–66, are another: the Saxon is a philistine, he told his Oxford audiences, the Celt a possessor of magic and melancholy, 'sociable, hospitable, eloquent, admired, figuring away brilliantly'. This is social criticism of Victorian England lightly veiled as ethnology. Seen in wider perspective, much Victorian literature is based on a series of images of more perfect worlds than the realities of an industrial state allow: or, if not in a general sense more perfect, at least capable of contributing something that England has lost or never possessed. Browning's Renaissance Italy, FitzGerald's antique Persia, Carlyle's

1. *The George Eliot Letters* (1954–56) iv. 298; v. 113.

Germany, Arnold's Greece, Morris's northland, and eventually Kipling's India – the English mind in the nineteenth century suddenly widens into the contemplation of many alien prospects. This is the literary heritage of race, as the Victorians understood race. Some of it may have been excessive and silly, but it is the reverse of complacent and superior.

The dark side of racialism was well known too, though not well respected, and its chief documents in the period are cranky in tone, couched in paradoxical terms and often subject to instant and indignant reply. The Victorian intellect did not openly assert an innate superiority over another race and hope to get away with it. That sort of superiority might be quietly nursed and remotely implied; but it is not a part of the public Victorian debate except in a few controversial figures. The abolition campaign leading down to the American Civil War of 1861–65, and the Jamaican revolt against Governor Eyre which followed that war by a few months, in October 1865, form two grand occasions that excited prejudice and counterprejudice. The first, momentous as it was, was not English, but it involved England in political debate for and against participation and for or against aid for North or South, and it was the last act in the long drama of slavery in English-speaking countries. The Eyre case, in which the governor of a British colony was accused of the brutal suppression of a rising of negro freemen, divided intellectual opinion in astonishing ways, with Mill leading an attack on the governor and Carlyle and Dickens ranged on the other side. In both cases the issue was the racial equality of black and white.

The negro debate was peculiarly lucky to embrace three great names in public controversy: Carlyle, Mill and T. H. Huxley. Essentially conducted within the periodical press, it included fiction only in imports like Harriet Beecher Stowe's *Uncle Tom's Cabin* (1852); but by then the debate had long been active in the British press. Carlyle's article 'Occasional discourse on the nigger question', published in *Fraser's Magazine* in December 1849, sixteen years after the abolition of slavery in the British empire and a dozen years before American emancipation, attacked the abolitionist cause with merciless contempt. 'That unhappy wedlock of philanthropic Liberalism and the Dismal Science' of political economy, Carlyle called it. His argument for racial character is emphatically about inferiority. The negro is 'poor Quashee'; he should be forced to preserve his character and to work, with a touch of the 'beneficent whip'. He is a 'swift, supple fellow; a merry-hearted, grinning, dancing, singing, affectionate kind of creature,' and the proper business of government is to keep him so. Anything else is 'rosepink sentimentality'.

Mill's anonymous reply to Carlyle, in the following number of *Fraser's* (January 1850), is significantly re-entitled 'The negro question'. It indignantly rejects the doctrine of work, and any notion that one race might be 'born wiser' than another, and denies that a negro when freed could only be a servant. In Mill's reply Africans join the ranks of peoples to whom civilization owes much, though only speculatively: it is possible, Mill argues bravely, on the evidence of ancient Egyptian sculpture, that 'the earliest known civilization' was negro and that the Greeks learned civilization from them. This exchange of animosities between former friends is the most lucid documentary example of the two sides of Victorian racialism. It also shows how difficult neutrality was, though Mill believes he is arguing for negro equality, not ascendancy. It is common ground between Carlyle and Mill that the negro has a negro character, and that it is either better or worse than the Anglo-Saxon. He is not just 'a man and a brother'.

The Carlyle–Mill debate is a simple antithesis based on a simple assumption. That Thomas Henry Huxley, biologist, 'agnostic' (a word he coined to describe his own religious position) and evolutionist should also be hostile to the notion of racial equality is more significant, and less easily predicted, than the vehement claims of Mill and Carlyle. With his dispassionate and scientific intelligence, Huxley regarded human equality as nonsense. Years later, from a radical standpoint, he was to write an attack on the ideal of political equality, 'On the natural inequality of men'. The American Civil War provoked him to write a characteristically original analysis which appeared a month after Lincoln's assassination and some months before the Jamaican revolt. The intellectual inferiority of the negro, he argued, is a general fact, and it is no answer to show that the generalization admits of exceptions: 'It may be quite true that some negroes are better than some white men; but no rational man, cognisant of the facts, believes that the average negro is the equal, still less the superior, of the average white man.' Free, the black man will be unable to compete intellectually with his 'bigger-brained and smaller jawed rival'.[1] Huxley is not against emancipation; but he is for it on unusual grounds. The average inferiority of the negro, he argues, like the average inferiority of women, is properly considered an argument for equality in education. The negro will not compete successfully, on the whole. But this is a reason for letting him try: the white man has little to lose. In fact the real justification for abolition, as will soon appear, is to help the white man to wash his hands of responsibility, and the master will benefit from it more than the slave.

In all this debate the racial status of the English themselves was a matter for puzzlement. No one supposed them a pure race. The mixture, however, might be considered agreeable, to the outsider as well as to the native. Emerson in his *English Traits* (1856) spoke admiringly of the English pedigree as derived 'from such a range of nationalities that there needs sea-room and land-room to unfold the varieties of talent and character' (ch. 4). But that variety might still contain the seeds of conflict. An easy identification of race with class, and deriving from the Norman Conquest, was part of the loose change of racial speculation: 'Saxon industry and Norman manners never will agree,' remarks Mr Millbank in *Coningsby*. The English are a bastard breed. Some explanation was needed why they should have gone so far and risen so high, if only a facetious one, and the nature of the mixture might be part of that explanation.

But the sheer dignity of nationhood was bound to raise problems for the world, and problems to which the Victorians could give only scant attention. The deep threat of nationalism was still to come. For the nineteenth century, the successful states were nations in a fully realized sense. England and France were possessors of an ancient unity, political, linguistic and cultural,

1. T. H. Huxley, 'Emancipation – black and white', *Reader* (20 May 1865); reprinted in his *Collected Essays* (London, 1893–94).

and their capitals were the accepted centres of the whole life of the state. Italy and Germany were to imitate these forms after 1860 and 1871, many east European states briefly and belatedly after 1918, and a host of Afro-Asian states after 1945. The rights of small nations is a mark of the new liberal. It is an obsession of the elder Gladstone, of the young Lloyd George, of many late in the century and after who supported the causes of subject peoples in the moribund empires of Turkey, Austria and Russia. But whether nationalism, in the end, is a liberal or a conservative force is an unresolved debate. Some prescient spirits, like Acton, could see that its radical rhetoric masked something traditional and backward-looking. 'Nationality', he wrote to Gladstone in 1888, 'is the great carrier of custom, of unreflecting habit and transmitted ideas that quench individuality.' Its great adversary will prove to be conscience, which 'gives men force to resist and discard all this'. The new spirit of nationalism is politically various, potentially aggressive, and not, as he warned Gladstone, a cause to be indifferently supported. 'Nationality has to be dealt with discriminatingly. It is not always liberal or constructive. It may be as dangerous when its boundary is outside that of the state as salutary when inside.'[1]

The range of liberal views on race, then, shows plenty of 'bright' racialism, or admiration for cultures other than one's own, and little that is superior or hostile, though the negro rarely achieved the interest and dignity of other coloured races of the earth. All this stands in contrast to the socialist record, which is racialist in the dark sense almost from the start. The issue hardly arises in the pioneer of English socialism, Robert Owen; but antisemitism is an early component of continental socialism, and it is sometimes an aspect of late Victorian socialism in England as well. Since Jews are often capitalists, and still more often thought to be so, the link between socialism and antisemitism is not mysterious; and those who suppose that the anti-Jewish policies of Stalinist and post-Stalinist Russia run counter to the traditions of socialism are only revealing their ignorance about those traditions. Proudhon, for example, was an extreme and fanatical antisemite; in his notebooks in

1. Lord Acton, *Selections from the Correspondence* (1917) p. 182, from a letter to Gladstone of February 1888.

1847 he calls the Jews 'this race which poisons everything by meddling everywhere without ever joining itself to another people', and he wanted them expelled from France and their synagogues abolished: 'The Jew is the enemy of the human race. One must send this race back to Asia, or exterminate it.'[1]

Marx, who had been christened a Lutheran and who took no interest in Judaism, was at once a racialist himself and the subject of the racialism of others. His early essay on the Jewish question dismisses the problem; but his enemies, especially among the French socialists, never allowed it to be forgotten that he was a Jew; and he was convinced that the races differed importantly and (to judge from his use of invective) that some are inferior to others. In *Das Kapital* he announced that 'racial peculiarities' would among other factors cause variations and gradations in otherwise similar economic systems (iii. 919). That detail is given no prominence; but in his letters a more vehement spirit emerges. In 1862, writing to Engels about his guest Lassalle, for whose success he felt an envious hatred, he linked antisemitism with a contempt for the black races:

> It is now perfectly clear to me that, as the shape of his head and the growth of his hair indicate, he is descended from the negroes who joined in the flight of Moses from Egypt, unless his mother or grandmother on the father's side were crossed with a nigger. This union of Jew and German on a negro basis was bound to produce an extraordinary hybrid. The importunity of the fellow is also negroid.

Engels was equally hostile, and on similar grounds: Lassalle's 'thirst to push his way into polite society, *de parvenir*, to smear over the dirty Breslau Jew, for appearance's sake, with grease and paint, was always revolting'.[2] In his 1892 preface to the first London edition of his *Condition of the Working Classes in England*, Engels remarked on the decline, for reasons of efficiency in a growing economy, of petty swindling, and drops a reference to 'the pettifogging business tricks of the Polish Jew, the representative in Europe of commerce at its lowe sttage'.

1. See George Lichtheim, 'Socialism and the Jews', *Dissent* (New York) (July–August 1968). The text of Proudhon's *Carnets* has been edited by Pierre Haubtmann, 2 vols (Paris, 1960–61) ii. 337.

2. E. H. Carr, *Marx* (London, 1934) pp. 172, 162; Marx-Engels, *Werke* (East Berlin, 1964) xxx. 259.

The strain continues, and it enters English socialism too. H. G. Wells, writing a few years later in *Anticipations* (1902), the first volume in a trilogy describing a socialist utopia of the future called the New Republic, sees no future at all for the Jew as such. He is 'the mediæval Liberal', will intermarry and abandon usury with the coming of socialism, and 'cease to be a physically distinct element in human affairs in a century or so'. Other inferior races will be less fortunate:

> For the rest, those swarms of black, and brown, and dirty-white, and yellow people, who do not come into the new needs of efficiency? Well, the world is a world, not a charitable institution, and I take it they will have to go. The whole tenor and meaning of the world, as I see it, is that they will have to go. So far as they fail to develop sane, vigorous and distinctive personalities for the great world of the future, it is their portion to die out and disappear (p. 317).

In a sequel, *A Modern Utopia* (1905), Wells pressed the argument further home. In spite of the 'very real nobility' of the English idea, he argued, Darwin had made it hard to believe in: 'Life is a conflict between superior and inferior types' (p. 327); and he argued that if a race could be shown to be inferior, then 'there is only one sane and logical thing to be done' with it, 'and that is to exterminate it', much as one should exterminate defectives (p. 337). The educated Victorian mind would not have thought it a paradox that liberal empires like the British have dissolved themselves willingly, while socialist empires like the Russian and the Chinese have stabilized themselves and even expanded. The intellectual origins of socialism suggest no contradiction here. Some early Fabians, like Sidney Webb, were imperialists; and Oswald Mosley, when he was elected to Parliament in 1918 as a Conservative on a socialist programme, used as his slogan 'socialistic imperialism' before he joined the Labour Party.[1] The statist mind sees empire as an opportunity to govern, to indoctrinate and to plan.

Victorian Britain was beyond all possibility of choice the heart of an empire. It inherited empire, and for the widest variety of

1. Sir Oswald Mosley, *My Life* (London, 1968) p. 91.

reasons found itself, by the end of the century, burdened with more. Many Victorians knew rather than realized the weight of imperial responsibility. To a curious degree they needed to be reminded of the fact, and it is doubtful if imperialism was in any sense a popular political idea before Disraeli's second premiership of 1874–80, and certain that it was rarely a decisive element in general elections or even (certain crises excepted) of parliamentary sessions. The Irish problem easily outweighs the entire imperial theme in British political debate in the later decades of the reign. One or two exceptions may be noted: the death of General Gordon in Khartoum in 1885 contributed to the Liberal defeat of 1886; and the 'khaki' election of 1900, at the height of the Boer War, was inevitably dominated by the issue of war. But foreign policy counts for more than colonial, and home policy for more than foreign, in most of the electoral struggles of the age.

What is more, few convenient political terms existed, until late in the century, to illustrate the idea of empire. 'Imperialism', to an Englishman of the 1850s and 1860s, was more likely to refer to the centralized absolutism of Napoleon III's Second Empire than to any doctrine of overseas expansion. When Acton, lecturing in 1877, speaks of Legitimacy repudiating the Revolution and Imperialism crowning it, he refers of course to the last of the Napoleons,[1] though he is writing at the height of the Eastern Question and of the long debate about guarding against Russia the route to India. Even 'empire' was as likely to refer to a state as to a system of overseas possessions, though Adam Smith had already used the word in the more modern sense in *The Wealth of Nations*, and in the nineteenth century that usage was to grow.[2]

1. Lord Acton, 'The history of freedom in Christianity', reprinted in his *History of Freedom and Other Essays* (1907) p. 58.

2. Adam Smith, *Wealth of Nations* (1776): 'To found a great empire for the sole purpose of raising up a people of customers may at first sight appear a project fit only for a nation of shopkeepers' (vol. ii, IV. 8, 3; Everyman edition vol. ii, p. 110). The last phrase, contrary to legend, is not Napoleon's, and Smith may be quoting it here from an American source. For a use of 'Empire' in the older sense, to refer to a single state or nation, see G. H. Francis, p. 116 above; and for recent studies, A. P. Thornton, *The Imperial Idea and its Enemies* (London, 1959) and Richard Koebner and H. D. Schmidt, *Imperialism: the Story and Significance of a Political Word 1840–1960* (Cambridge, 1964).

The intellectual and imaginative impact of British imperialism in its greatest age surprises by its moderation, and one might almost say by its triviality. Popular pride in empire, so far as it ever existed, belongs rather to the imperial twilight of the early twentieth century. In the fiction of the period, apart from the growing fashion for boys' stories on colonial themes in the 1880s and 1890s, the impact is slight. For Dickens colonies are mere repositories; Emily in *David Copperfield*, a fallen woman, finds sanctuary in Australia; her friend Martha, a prostitute, even finds a farmer-husband there, since wives are scarce; and Mr Micawber, most revealingly of all, becomes a magistrate. Magwitch the convict in *Great Expectations* returns with a hard-earned fortune from the same place, but none of these examples are exactly inviting. Between 1815 and 1890 more than twelve million emigrated from the British Isles to the colonies and the United States; but to most this was a tragic or shameful story rather than a matter for pride. The colonies for Dickens, and many others, are for those who have failed at home. 'That is how families get rid of troublesome sprigs,' remarks a character in *Middlemarch*, regretting that Ladislaw had not been packed off to India. The real impact of empire on adult fiction is not until the 1890s, in the works of Kipling and Conrad; and the greatest of all English imperial novels, E. M. Forster's *Passage to India* (1924) is later still. Both Kipling and Conrad write of distant lands with an air of defying fashion, as if they felt themselves obliged to create the taste by which they hoped to be enjoyed. Conrad, in the preface to his first novel, *Almayer's Folly* (1895), anticipates disapproval of what a lady had fastidiously called 'decivilized' fiction – of 'that literature which preys on strange people and prowls in far-off countries, under the shade of palms'. The classic English novel is metropolitan or regional. For empire, as for race, one needs to turn elsewhere for the evidence.

A mid-nineteenth-century Englishman, surveying the world from the security of a prosperous nation confident in its internal peace, might be forgiven for thinking that human history was bent on betraying whatever arguments could be advanced in favour of despotism. The free peoples of western Europe, and their colonies and former colonies overseas, were everywhere stronger and richer than the tyrannical states of Asia and Africa. China and Russia were despotisms; they were also backward. India, notably among the vast imperial responsibilities of England, owed her trade and internal security to British energies, and whatever hopes she might some day have of achieving, for the first time in her history, a measure of popular government. The world observed the profundity of the British political secret, though they might not understand it. It was not, for the most part, an order imposed, but rather a benefit acknowledged. In the seventeenth century, as Seeley had urged in his last of his lectures on *The Expansion of England* (1883), England had made the greatest of all political discoveries, 'and taught all the world how liberty might be adapted to the conditions of a nation-state' (p. 307). This is the ultimate sanction of empire. It is a training in liberal government. The knowledge of that subtle art is an ancient historical possession of the English, and their duty is to transmit it.

There is no clear evidence that British imperialism and Victorian doctrines of race are linked in any causal way. The continuous history of the British empire begins with settlements in North America in the early seventeenth century; in the seventeenth and eighteenth centuries the Indian subcontinent was slowly permeated by traders, soldiers and officials. Neither event was clearly based on any assumption, favourable or unfavourable, about the native races of either continent. It is a fantasy to suppose that the British conquered one quarter of the land surface of the world out of a doctrine of racial superiority; the abundant assertions of English superiority in the period (and they are very doubtfully racial assertions) refer to such rivals as the French, the Spanish and the Dutch rather than to the coloured races. All these reflections concern the impulse of empire, and what statesmen and others believed and said in England; what prejudices may have developed elsewhere, like the 'settler mentality' of whites in southern Africa, is another story. These reflections assume, what is more, the modern sense of terms like 'race' and 'racial'; a Victorian, who was more likely to see such matters in cultural rather than in strictly ethnological contexts, might easily feel that England could assert a political superiority over India as a fact of recent history. Macaulay, reviewing Gladstone's youthful work *The State in its Relations with the Church* in the *Edinburgh Review* in 1839, shortly after returning from four years in India, remarks that there 'the superiority of the governors to the governed in moral science is unquestionable', adding: 'the conversion of the whole people to the worst form that Christianity ever wore in the dark ages would be a most happy event'. That is neither a religious nor a racial enthusiasm on Macaulay's part: it is an honest declaration of horror against a system of religious observance which he regarded as cruel and pernicious. The technical inferiority of the subject peoples, and their native inability to create free and stable forms of government or to learn of Christianity without help – all these are matters for ordinary comment; but the argument as it is conducted, from Burke and Palmerston to Gladstone and Balfour, is commonly in the mixed terms of moral responsibility and national advantage, especially in terms of commerce and the frustration of European rivals. The English ideology of empire is not racialist.

Two views, at the extreme, governed the Victorian notion of empire, one for and one against. Seeley calls them the bombastic and the pessimistic – the one all 'wonder and ecstasy'; the other viewing empire as an 'excrescence' exposing England to costly wars all over the world.[1] These views correspond only loosely to party allegiances. The radical view of empire remained cool to the end, even hostile. Commerce is good; but commerce that entails sovereignty needs to be looked at with suspicion; and colonies, in the radical view, are little better than the army, the Church and the civil service as convenient dumps for aristocratic placeman. Empire might spread a fuzz of indolent time-servers like Dickens's Barnacles across the face of the world. Cobden, in a letter of 1835, lumped colonies, the armed services, the Church and the corn laws together as 'merely accessories to our aristocratic government'. But he was an enthusiast for trade: 'Not a bale of merchandise leaves our shores, but it bears the seeds of intelligence and fruitful thought to the members of some less enlightened community.' The radical view may be hostile to colonies, but it is not hostile to expansion.

1. Sir John Robert Seeley, *The Expansion of England* (London, 1883) p. 293.

At the other extreme stands Disraeli, whom Seeley may have had in mind when he spoke of the bombastic view of empire. Disraeli was the first political leader to make of the imperial idea, in a dynamic and advancing sense, an instrument of policy and of popular inspiration. Though his early interests in the question had wavered, even approaching at times the radical position, he committed the Conservative Party to imperialism for nearly a hundred years in a speech at the Crystal Palace in June 1872. The depth of that conviction remains forever in doubt. Twenty years before, he had called the colonies 'a millstone round our necks', and it is notable that imperialism is scarcely a theme of his fiction at all. His imperial motives during the second premiership of 1874–80 represent a highly individual mixture of political opportunism and of cosmopolitan romance. The creator of Sidonia cannot have failed to sense an historical irony in an advocate of semitic wisdom leading a government to gain dominion over the Suez Canal.

Between Seeley's two extremes the mind of Gladstone hovered, but his utterances were closer to the radical than to the Disraelian position. Some of his speeches illustrate that curious property of the Victorians that they should need so often to be reminded of the uniqueness of their historical situation. His first Midlothian speech at Edinburgh in November 1879, for instance, suggests that he expected his audience to be more interested in taxation and in European policy than in the affairs of remoter continents: 'There is no precedent in human history for a formation like the British Empire. A small island at one extremity of the globe peoples the whole earth with its colonies. Not satisfied with that, it goes among the ancient races of Asia and subjects two hundred and forty millions of men to its rule . . .' But the strength of that empire, he continues, is within the United Kingdom, a mere thirty-three million – less than the population of France, or Austria, or Germany, or Russia; in spite of which 'we have undertaken to settle the affairs of about a fourth of the entire human race scattered over all the world'.[1] And his entire speech is a demand to curtail those responsibilities, not to enlarge them: are they not enough?

1. W. E. Gladstone, *Midlothian Speeches 1879*, edited by M. R. D. Foot (Leicester, 1971)pp. 46–7.

But arguments about over-extension, the cost of empire and the dangers of aristocratic government fade with the enlargement of the suffrage and the sheer spectacle of the world role into which England had unwittingly fallen. Even radicals like Dilke could not withhold an interest from that spectacle. In 1866–67 he travelled the world and wrote *Greater Britain* (1868), which wonderingly describes what would now be called the English-speaking world. The areas of British settlement, he calculated, including the United States, were perhaps four and a half times as large as the Roman Empire at its greatest extent; and by 1970 the English race, or those whose first language was English, would number some three hundred millions.[1] That estimate has proved broadly accurate, perhaps a slight understatement, and before such a spectacle and such a prospect it was hard to be unimpressed. The imperial urge may have been slight, considered as a popular sentiment at home, and the attitudes of governments to annexation often grudging and reluctant. But once empire was there, it was bound to generate its own warmth and enthusiasm. The history of that enthusiasm, however, is not mainly Victorian.

But then, as the Victorians rightly saw, Greater Britain was not strictly an empire at all. Its principal member, the United States, had ceased to be a colony in the eighteenth century. Some of its most problematical colonies, like the African, are almost afterthoughts of imperial history, acquired in the 1880s and after, and no one supposed that British sovereignty would survive there. And yet language and culture have survived and prospered as few Victorians dared to hope. Even Dilke, in his judicious prophecy of three hundred million speakers of English, did not predict that this fraction of mankind, numbering less than one-tenth of the population of the earth in 1970, would be speaking a language that had by then become the *lingua franca* of the world. That is an achievement that is still to be measured by events themselves, and it is not surprising if the Victorians failed to estimate the consequences of what, in the enormous scattering of English culture across the world, they had helped to create.

1. Sir Charles Dilke, *Greater Britain* (London, 1868) ii. 406.

[12]

Socialism

The great rival of liberalism shares all its pretensions as an ideology. Socialism matches its rival, claim for claim. It has a rival philosophical source: not the Enlightenment, now, but German idealist philosophy culminating in Hegel. It pretends to the characteristic completeness of an ideology or a faith; as Bertrand Russell wrote of German Marxism in the 1890s, it is not just a political programme but also 'a religion and an ethic'.[1] If it is allowed that anarchism, as an idea, has no continuous history, and that conservatism has no ideology – none, at least, on which it is dependent as a political force – then socialism stands as the one considerable ideological rival of liberalism, or individualism (as the antithesis is often put), in the Victorian age. And that rivalry is fascinatingly paradoxical. It is one of like and unlike, of attraction and hostility. It is the story of two jealous brothers such as Cain and Abel. Like brothers, the two ideologies compete for success and for the admiration of others. Neither profits, in the long run, from the existence of the other. And yet no one can know one of them without knowing both.

The word 'socialism' may have been first used in Robert Owen's *Cooperative Magazine* in 1827, in which case it would be among the few terms of international politics to have an English origin; but the matter of origin is veiled in doubt. 'Communism' has a slightly more certain claim, as a word, to English origin: an English Christian Socialist, Goodwyn

1. Bertrand Russell, *German Social Democracy* (London, 1896) p. 1. As Russell explains in the 1965 preface to a new edition of his first book, he wrote it as an orthodox Liberal at a time when German socialists were still 'completely orthodox Marxists'.

Barmby (1820–81), claims to have invented the word on a visit to Paris in 1840; he founded the Communist Propaganda Society in the following year.[1] The distinction between the two terms has never been easy, but it was seen early to rest on the more materialistic sense of Communism which, as J. M. Ludlow put it in 1851, 'starts with the *thing*, and is in essential antagonism to absolute property; Socialism starts from the *person*, and is in essential antagonism to human discord and rivalry'. As a term, socialism is the more humanist in its associations; it was to prove assimilable into the parliamentary system, as communism was not; and it could attract those whose interest in German metaphysics was slight or non-existent.

It is doubtful, however, if socialism has any clear continuum in nineteenth-century England. Owenism, at the beginning of the century, had been a doctrine of cooperation, and it had failed on practical grounds. Christian Socialism, in its brief heyday between 1848 and 1854, was also based on cooperation, but derived less from Owenism than from recent French ideas endowed with a new Anglican emphasis. It faded quickly, partly on practical grounds; partly because England was not ready, if she ever is, to be governed by highminded Anglican clergymen; and partly because the rising industrial prosperity of the years after 1850 was not conducive to its progress. Ludlow, writing on Lassalle in the *Fortnightly Review* in April 1869 in an article Meredith was to use as a source for his novel *The Tragic Comedians* (1880), acknowledged that in England a socialist demagogy like Lassalle's, who had been killed in a duel five years before, would be unlikely to flourish. Lassalle had been an accomplished and unprincipled Messiah-Jew, Ludlow wrote, but his ideas will not prosper here: 'Our sturdy English habits of self-help will probably in the main hinder them from doing much mischief.' That is because the existing system works too humanely and too well; with trade societies and cooperative shops for workpeople, 'it becomes a joke to tell our working men that they can do nothing to help themselves,

1. *Apostle* no. 1 (1848). On the largely continental origins of 'socialism', 'communism' and many related compounds that have failed to survive in English, see Arthur J. Bestor, 'The Evolution of the Socialist Vocabulary', *Journal of the History of Ideas* ix (1948).

and must wait for state aid'. English socialism, by that time, had made two false starts in Owenism and Christian Socialism. Only with the third, in the late 1870s, was it to take root.

By the 1870s socialism was again an active hope or an active fear. Mill, an early voice of warning, decided to write a book on socialism in 1869, provoked by the second Reform Act. William Cunningham, later Archdeacon of Ely and Professor of Economic History at Cambridge, writing as a young man in the *Contemporary Review* (January 1879) in an article called 'The progress of Socialism in England', saw it as an advancing doctrine, though he believed it to be advancing on practical rather than idealistic grounds. Englishmen, he wrote, think of it as a foreign doctrine, arising in France and Germany and spreading into the United States; but it is 'making slow but sure and steady progress in this country'. Not, perhaps, among trade unionists, who know capital to be necessary. But there are many who hate Mammon, and there is fear of depression, especially among the rich. Cunningham makes the pregnant prophecy that, as the case for state control of the economy grows, socialism will flourish not as a poor man's faith but as a solace to the wealthy, both to purse and conscience: it is 'not as a remedy for the miseries of the poor, but rather as an alleviation of the cares of the rich, that socialism is coming upon us' (p. 252). This was written only months before Gladstone's Midlothian campaign and the ensuing Liberal election victory of 1880.

Cunningham's is a predictive voice, though not the only one. The Queen had noticed something similar, and with alarm. Six years later Victoria wrote to her Prime Minister that many, including herself, were 'greatly alarmed by the destructive doctrines which are taught', and that they would 'welcome warmly any words of Mr Gladstone's which affirmed that liberalism is not socialism and that progress does not mean revolution'. Gladstone gave her that assurance, though he agreed that 'a disposition to favour' socialism had already 'made considerable way with the two chief political parties in the state'.[1] This view is confirmed by other observers. Henry

1. *The Queen and Mr Gladstone 1845–98*, edited by Philip Guedalla (London, 1933) ii. 380, 382.

Sidgwick, writing in the same year, agreed that all political observers felt that socialism 'is flowing in upon us with a full tide', and that it will mean 'a great extension of governmental interference' in the affairs of individuals, as well as a hostility to traditional political economy.[1] This is a judgment of the state of intellectual opinion, and it partly confirms Cunningham's view that late Victorian socialism was a doctrine for the ruling classes rather than an incursion from outside the traditional arena of British politics. Socialism does not invade British politics: it is born within it. All these voices, what is more, sound fatalistic. The late Victorian mind has ceased to be confident about its ability to resist socialism forever, or even for long.

It remains striking, however, that the Victorians did successfully hold socialism at bay throughout the reign as an organized political force. In France and Prussia, by the 1870s, it was a party as well as a creed; it could be kept out of office, indeed, but not out of parliamentary assemblies. At Westminster, by contrast, it remained unrepresented until Keir Hardie entered the Commons in 1892, it did not become even an element within a group with parliamentary ambitions until the Labour Representation Committee of 1900, out of which the Labour Party was to grow, or a principal party of state until 1918. John Rae called the England of the early 1880s 'the only great country where socialism has at present neither organ nor organisation that reaches the public eye'.[2] By 1900 it had progressed further in the United States, at least in local government, than in England. For the English it looked like a foreign doctrine, for the most part, and one to be fearfully watched. And there was plenty of intelligent and informed hostility. Erskine May, who did not allow a clerkship of the House of Commons to interfere with his freedom to publish Gladstonian opinions, called socialists and communists, in his introduction to *Democracy in Europe* (1877), 'the most mischievous and dangerous fanatics of European democracy'; and European in

1. Henry Sidgwick, *Contemporary Review* (November 1886). In *The Elements of Politics* (London, 1891), in a section on 'Socialistic Interference', he equated extreme socialism with collectivism.

2. John Rae, *Contemporary Socialism* (London, 1884) p. 59.

this context means continental: 'As their wild schemes for the reconstruction of society are repugnant to all the principles of liberty and to the eternal instincts of mankind, they must not be confounded with the recognised principles of political democracy.' They believe the individual to be 'no more than a mechanical part of the whole community: he has no free will, no independence of thought or action' (pp. lxiv–lxv.) Liberty, if socialism ever comes, will be surrendered to the state and lost forever.

Socialism was not less foreign for the circumstance that Marx resided in London as a political refugee for nearly forty years. But then the progress of English socialism, as an idea if not as a political movement, was essentially independent of Marxism until the 1880s. It is doubtful if Marx achieved the acquaintanceship of any major English author on any terms beyond the merely perfunctory, and *Das Kapital* was not published in English until four years after his death, in 1887, apart from a feeble version serialized in the journal *Today* in 1885–89. Hardly any Englishman noticed its existence earlier than that. Ludlow, the Christian Socialist, was sent a copy of the first volume by Marx, who had just read his *Fortnightly* article on Lassalle and was encouraged to find an Englishman who could read German; but Ludlow, in spite of his knowledge of the language, could make little of it, and found it hard to believe that any Englishman could read it through.[1] Acton had recommended it to Gladstone soon after, in 1873, as 'the Koran of the new socialists',[2] but there is no reason to suppose that Gladstone read any of it. William Morris, who did not become a socialist until the last dozen years of his life, read it in the early 1880s in a French translation, but it cannot be called the chief element of his political faith. *Das Kapital* is a book that had to wait long to be noticed in the land that had given its author sanctuary. Russell, in his *German Social Democracy* of 1895, writes as if Marxism would be of remote anthropological interest to his English readers, though he is aware that the German doctrine reopens a controversy broadly familiar in

1. N. C. Masterman, *John Malcolm Ludlow* (Cambridge, 1963) pp. 306–7.

2. Lord Acton, *Selections from the Correspondence*, edited by J. N. Figgis and R. V. Laurence (London, 1917) p. 169.

England concerning the opposing merits of socialism and individualism. Only the first steps of Marxism are trodden by the Victorians. H. M. Hyndman read *Das Kapital* in French in 1880, and founded the Democratic Federation in the following year on Marxist principles; and he describes in his autobiography how he visited Marx in his London home. In 1884 his group became the Social Democratic Federation, and before the end of the century the Fabian Society was regarding Marx as one of its sources. But Victorian socialism before the 1880s is essentially pre-Marxian. If Englishmen regarded socialism as a foreign doctrine, as many did, it was because of events themselves, such as continental elections and revolutions. In England it was an idea, elsewhere a political fact. But by the 1880s the idea had gained a significant foothold on the intellectual life of the nation.

That the idea could be so skilfully prevented from becoming a fact is a phenomenon of extraordinary complexity. From the earliest years of the reign socialism had signified massive state interference in the economic life of the nation, and notably in the relations between employer and employed, with a view to achieving higher degrees of economic equality. The Victorian viewed such a programme with mixed feelings, and nothing that happened in the course of the reign was calculated to make those feelings simpler. As for economic equality, he did not doubt that what Trollope called a lessening of distances might be desirable, though he was unlikely to believe that absolute equality, either of wealth or of income, was either desirable or possible. As to state interference in the economy, he would regard that as a present fact rather than a future prospect, though he might doubt the case for more and contest any easy assumption that the individual had no economic rights of his own. More than that, he might, like the Queen, regard socialism as a revolutionary rather than as a parliamentary idea, and associate it with violence and confiscation. This was the fear that the title of 'Fabian' was designed to set at rest; it was not in itself an irrational fear, though it was capable of revealing itself in irrational ways. Macaulay's remark that the crowds at the Great Exhibition of 1851 seemed full of socialists, and his even odder remark that Dickens's *Hard Times* was expressive of a 'sullen socialism', both seem touched with paranoia, and show how the events of 1848 on the Continent had stirred up bitter memories of Jacobinism. But Macaulay and the Queen only represent the emotional extremes of the matter. The analytical observer has more interesting things to say.

Mill, in his introduction to *On Liberty*, had noticed the new threat to human freedom that might emerge from democracy itself. Liberalism had flourished in an atmosphere in which most men thought of government as alien and hostile. But what would happen if they were to come to think of it as their own – 'their tenants and delegates, revocable at their pleasure'? The suffrage had already led to the predictable result that 'the limitation of the power itself' was attracting less and less interest. 'The nation did not need to be protected against its own will', Mill runs on ironically, summarizing the arguments of his opponents:

> There was no fear of its tyrannizing over itself. Let the rulers be effectively responsible to it, promptly removable by it, and it could afford to trust them with power of which it could itself dictate the use to be made. Their power was but the nation's own power, concentrated, and in a form convenient for exercise.

These dangerous sentiments already prevail in continental liberalism, where individual liberals who are prepared to admit any limit to governmental powers 'stand out as brilliant exceptions'. The phrase must have been meant to be read and understood by Tocqueville, to whom Mill sent a copy of the essay as soon as it appeared in 1859; though Tocqueville was already dying as the book appeared, and his copy lies unread. But Mill's warning, of which he would utterly have approved, is a plain one. The grim danger of political democracy is that it may sanction, or appear to sanction, the unrestrained exercise of power. It may sacramentalize government. *Vox populi vox dei* is no reassuring slogan for those who can conceive what the future powers of an industrial state will be like.

Mill suggests that the argument is in large measure a national one. English lovers of liberty are hostile to the powers of the state, continentals (with rare exceptions) tolerant or welcoming. The antithesis is profound in its implications, and derives in his view from 'the peculiar circumstances of our political history'. In England 'the yoke of opinion is perhaps heavier, that of the law is lighter, than in most other countries of Europe; and there is considerable jealousy of direct interference, by the legislative or the executive power, with private conduct'. This is because the English think of government as 'representing an opposite interest to the public', and 'the majority have not yet learnt to feel the power of the government their power, or its opinions their opinions. When they do so, individual liberty will probably be as much exposed to invasion from the government, as it already is from public opinion.'

There is an inverse relation, then, between the power of public opinion and the power of the state; and the more power or tyranny is exercised by the one, the less the other is likely to claim or to need. The case for civil liberty has good reason, in fact, to detach itself from mere permissiveness. Popular prudery, for instance, may serve as an effective bar against the tyranny of authority: relax it, and Westminster and Whitehall may one day usurp with far more terrible force the functions of Mrs Grundy. If they do, democracy will be of no use to prevent that greater tyranny: on the contrary, it is among the reasons why a tolerance of state power is already increasing. This is the rational and analytic aspect of the Victorian fear of socialism, at its most sophisticated, and it is doubtful if it has ever been cogently answered. Socialism is 'the infirmity that attends mature democracies', as Acton was to put it years later.[1] When men make government their own, they cease to hate and fear it; and when that fear ceases, the chance for tyranny is there.

But while distrust for state power did not quickly diminish in Victorian England, statute after statute were so altering the realities of the situation as to change the arguments and reshape the rhetoric of debate. Mill could see that hostility to state action had already begun to wane and that, given the spread of the franchise, it might some day disappear as an effective political instinct. Some thought its diminution rendered socialism

1. Lord Acton, 'Sir Erskine May's *Democracy in Europe*', *Quarterly Review* (January 1878); reprinted in his *History of Freedom and Other Essays* (1907) p. 63.

superfluous. England was achieving state supervision of the economy without it: what, then, has socialism to do with England? Cobden, in a letter of March 1844 explaining his abstention from voting on the Twelve Hours Bill, where he had found himself in disagreement with both sides of the House, said he hoped that the attempt to limit working hours by legislation would at least have the excellent effect of making men see 'the necessity of taking anchor upon some sound principles, as a refuge from the socialist doctrines of the fools behind them'. Socialism meant state planning as early as that. The letter is quoted by John Morley in his *Life of Cobden* (1881), and he unsurprisingly agrees with Cobden's use of the word. Such legislation, Morley held, was indeed 'socialistic': 'It was an exertion of the power of the state in its strongest form, definitely limiting in the interest of the labourer the administration of capital.' But all this, in his view, is already past history, and to the extent that such legislation is socialist, much British legislation can already be similarly regarded. In the intervening thirty years and more since Cobden's letter, the nation has acquired 'a complete, minute and voluminous code for the protection of labour' against pollution, accidents, excessive hours of work and bad conditions, and regulations for holidays and schooling. If we add the Poor Law, Morley concludes, then 'we find the rather amazing result that in the country where socialism has been less talked about than any other country in Europe, its principles have been most extensively applied.'[1]

Socialism is not so much mistaken as irrelevant, in this view: its principal demands have already been met. That is Dicey's view, too, in his 1898 lectures at Harvard, where he begins from the curious assumptions that England was governed by Benthamites after 1832, and that Benthamism involved *laissez-faire*. But that period, imaginary as it may have been, came to an end in the mid-sixties, and Dicey calls the years between 1865 and the end of the century the 'period of collectivism'. Collectivism in this view is the same as socialism, 'which favours the intervention of the state, even at some sacrifice of individual freedom, for the purpose of conferring benefit upon the mass of the people', and it represents the accumulating tendency of

1. John Morley, *The Life of Richard Cobden* (London, 1881) i. 302–3.

the last third of the century.[1] Dicey is not a lover of paradox. He is merely a victim of the assumption that early Victorian governments believed and practised, or tried to practise, a doctrine of total withdrawal by the state from the economic life of the nation. It follows from this, in his argument, that labour laws and welfare provision are socialist or collectivist. The argument is not partisan: it is discouraging to socialist and antisocialist alike. The socialist may feel his objects to have been rendered superfluous and his claims to office dismissed; and the antisocialist that what he supposed a dangerous utopianism is already a humdrum fact.

The relation between socialism and the principal parties of state is equally a vexed question. Given the spectrum of politics, as it was supposed to be, stretching from Radical to Conservative, there was no easy solution to the problem of where socialists were to be placed on such a linear system. If they were extreme revolutionaries, as the Queen and others feared, it would seem natural to put them somewhere to the left of the Radicals. To the extent that their doctrine arose out of manhood suffrage, and could be dubbed a disease of democracy, the same conclusion seemed to apply. But revolutionary and confiscatory as socialism might be, it was not necessarily anticonservative, and its entry into the intellectual scene in the 1880s and into the parliamentary after 1906 created difficulties, both conceptual and terminological. A third party may or may not prove a strength to the constitution; but one that exists in a triangular relation to the other two is certain to confuse the clarity of debate. Hyndman in 1885 had two of his parliamentary candidates subsidized by the Conservative Party, and it was not unusual to notice similarities between the state-controlled economy demanded by socialists and the reverence for authority of the conservative mind. An English journal in 1881, commenting on a Prussian election, noted the 'extravagant faith' of the German working classes in the power of the state, which had achieved so much that it might be expected to abolish poverty too; and it quoted from Mommsen's electoral address a passage emphasizing the coincidence of views between Bismarck and the

1. A. V. Dicey, *Lectures on the Relation between Law & Public Opinion in England* (London, 1905) pp. 64–5.

socialists: 'the state as conceived by the Chancellor closely corresponds to the state as conceived by Lassalle' – a fact that explained the reluctance of socialists to campaign openly against Bismarck's government.[1]

But after 1900 political alliances were with the Liberals, who were seen as the magnetic centre for all groups dedicated to social reform. They were a 'huge hospitable caravanserai', as H. G. Wells called them,[2] by their very nature multitudinous, and ready to welcome, because confident of dominating, any group hostile to the existing order. This hospitality was eventually to cost them dearer than they could have supposed in the triumphant General Election of 1905–6, when Liberal candidates were withdrawn to make way for Labour; it seemed to justify itself in the period 1910–14, when there were Liberal gains from Labour at by-elections; but it collapsed, as a party strategy, after the division of Liberalism in December 1916.

The uncertainty about natural allies reflects a profound difference within socialism about its own doctrine. Beatrice Webb is said to have divided socialists into A's and B's, or anarchists and bureaucrats, but this is merely a witty summary of a long existing split. Mill, in his unfinished *Chapters on Socialism*, had noticed the same thing:

> Among those who call themselves socialists, two kinds of persons may be distinguished. There are, in the first place, those whose plans for a new order of society . . . are on the scale of a village community or township. . . . The other class, who are more a product of the Continent than of Great Britain and may be called the revolutionary socialists, propose to themselves a much bolder stroke. Their scheme is the management of the whole productive resources of the country by one central authority, the general government.[3]

Mill thought that the first would be difficult, the second still more so – a prediction that failed to take account of the prospect of totalitarian socialism. That state socialism is both practical

1. *St James's Gazette* (25 October 1881).
2. H. G. Wells, *The New Machiavelli* (London, 1911) iv. 8.
3. J. S. Mill, 'Chapters on Socialism', *Fortnightly Review* (February–April 1879); reprinted in his *Essays on Economics and Society*, edited by J. M. Robson (Toronto, 1967) p. 737.

and durable is a fact which the Fabians, a dozen and more years later, would have known how to argue, and which the twentieth century has amply confirmed. State socialism is the bureaucrat's dream and, after the bureaucrat's fashion, it works. That men of free instincts can have been induced to want it remains one of the wonders of intellectual history. It will forever seem astonishing that those who hate authority should wish to confer total power upon the state, and that those who object to capitalism should demand that the state, that greatest of all capitalists, should become greater still. These contradictions now seem fantastic. But they are well documented in the period, and the arguments can best be marshalled under two heads, the pragmatic and the scientific.

The pragmatic arguments for state socialism were disagreeably strong. Given the premiss that a private and competitive system based on the profit motive should be superseded, only two large possibilities presented themselves, and Mill described them with great accuracy. The first has to do with cooperation, or industrial partnership, or co-ownership: what Mill calls 'the admission of the whole body of labourers to a participation in the profits, by distributing among all who share in the work, in the form of a percentage of their earnings, the whole or a fixed portion of the gains after a certain remuneration has been allowed to the capitalist'.[1] The notion was open to numerous variations: it was a principal element in Owen, in Fourier, in Mill's own later reflections, in Christian Socialism, in L. T. Hobhouse's *The Labour Movement* (1893), in modern liberal programmes for industry, and elsewhere. Its objections are practical, and relate to the education of workers and their ability to conduct industrial enterprises without calamity. If they are not final objections, they seemed very nearly so to most Victorian and Edwardian minds, including socialist minds. Ruskin, in *Unto This Last* (1862), insisted on 'the impossibility of Equality' and held that nothing could alter the simple truth that some are born to lead and some to follow. The superior should be appointed to 'guide, to lead, or on occasion even to compel and subdue, their inferiors according to their own better

1. *Ibid.*, p. 743.

knowledge and wiser will'.[1] He was against the division of property. The failure of cooperative ideas to take possession of English socialism is a familiar fact of later political history. Rupert Brooke, when he entered King's College, Cambridge, in 1906, is said to have remarked to his fellow-student Hugh Dalton, then secretary to the University Fabians: 'I'm not your sort of socialist; I'm a William Morris sort of socialist', but he soon saw the difficulties of his position and turned himself into a Fabian.[2] The paper he delivered there in 1910, *Democracy and the Arts* (1946), is a highminded defence of collectivism. Brooke's example shows that the transition from A to B could be effortless and rapid.

But it is doubtful if socialism was ever a libertarian doctrine in any dedicated sense, and doubtful whether such pre-Fabian theorists as Ruskin and Morris were as anarchistic as some of their admirers supposed. Ruskin, in *Unto This Last*, declares himself in favour of views which, if seriously translated into political programmes, would be a little short of totalitarian, though it is doubtful if he considered their consequences closely. In his preface, for instance, he demands that the state should have the power to take any unemployed person, put him into an institution and set him to work there at a fixed wage; that 'being found objecting to work, they should be set, under compulsion of the strictest nature, to the more painful and degrading forms of necessary toil, especially to that in mines and other places of danger', and that he should not receive payment until he has 'come to sounder mind respecting the laws of employment'. And yet nobody associates the name of Ruskin with labour-camps, and he might himself have been surprised to be told that he was in favour of state direction of labour. The demand that 'all must work' is vital to Morris's programme too: it is the theme, for example, of his pamphlet *Useful Work versus Useless Toil* (1885), which is a diatribe against idleness and unrewarding labour. The use to which modern dictators have put this doctrine is notorious, but there seems no reason to deny

1. John Ruskin, *Works*, edited by E. T. Cook and A. Wedderburn (1903–12) xvii. 74.

2. Sir Edward Marsh, 'Memoir', in Brooke, *Collected Poems* (London, 1918) pp. xxix–xxx.

that forced labour is what the more idealistic of Victorian socialists meant. From the 1860s, at least, there is little or no socialist opposition to proposals for an omnipotent state. 'The Socialism advocated by the Fabian Society is State Socialism exclusively,' announced Fabian Tract No. 70 in 1896. Once it is accepted that man must be changed from a free being at liberty to seek his own profit into a member of a planned society that obliges all to act unselfishly, the power of the state is an inevitable requirement. No power less than total power could achieve a change like that. On practical grounds, all socialism is state socialism.

The scientific reasons for the rise of collectivism are intellectually more intriguing. Behind much late Victorian socialism lies the assumption, and even the assertion, that science has nothing more to conquer on earth than mankind in its social relations. The physical world has been subjected by the natural sciences; it has been transformed out of all sense of mystery and magic, rendered tidy and intelligible, and harnessed to a great industrial revolution. But man's social relations remain untidy. They are a jungle: a mere 'cascade of accidents', as the hero's father laments in Wells's *The New Machiavelli*, leaving his son two images to contrast in his mind: 'one a sense of the extraordinary confusion and waste and planlessness of the human life that went on all about us; and the other of a great ideal of order and economy which he called variously Science and Civilization, and which . . . many people nowadays would identify with socialism – as the Fabians expound it' (ii. 4).

The Victorian era had been 'a gigantic experiment of the most slovenly and wasteful kind', and no one in the present century, Wells believed, will value 'their prevalent art and the clipped and limited literature that satisfied their souls' (ii. 5). What is more, man's social relations are superstition-ridden, as surely as man's comprehension of the natural world once was. For what else can it be but superstition to speak of the 'laws' of political economy? If man can harness the forces of nature, he can harness his own powers too. The early Fabians rest their case on the future of a scientific society governed by experts. *Fabian Essays* (1889) is a symposium by many hands; its authors, in the preface, proclaim 'a common conviction of the necessity of vesting the organization of industry in a state identified with the whole people by complete democracy'. But democracy does not mean the right of the people to choose when they do not choose socialism. Shaw's most corrosive irony is reserved for those who suppose that men should be allowed to administer merely because they are popular enough to be elected: Wells's *Anticipations* (1902), which describes a socialist utopia, confers total powers on a state conducted by experts who possess every arbitrary right including the death sentence; and Sidney and Beatrice Webb came to believe that a free press was inconsistent with socialism and 'positively dangerous to the community'.[1]

The Platonic ideal of a government by 'those who know' is vital to the appeal of socialism to the intellectual. Meredith, in *The Tragic Comedians* (1880), a novel based on the life story of Lassalle, created a messianic hero Alvan who was irresistible to the heroine by seeming to possess the scientific key to the laws of social history. He claimed to lead the people by the sheer fact of understanding those laws of history: ' "I set them moving on the lines of the law of things. I am no empty theorizer, no phantasmal speculator; I am the man of science in politics. When my system is grasped by the people, there is but a step to the realization of it. One step . . ." ' (ch. 7). That is hardly a parody of what many socialists believed; though not all believed, like Alvan, that only one step was needed. The Victorian socialist more often blended Darwin with Marx, and saw revolution as a continuing process of history and prehistory rather than a single cataclysmic event. The pamphlet that Hyndman wrote with Morris, *A Summary of the Principles of Socialism* (1884), puts the familiar Marxist case for social reform arising out of man's power over nature, leading inevitably to conflict, a process which had begun in the earliest stages of prehistory: 'The first object of every animal, man included, is to feed itself and its offspring' (p. 4). That sentence measures the distance between the rival ideologies: no liberal would accept the primacy of materialism, or speak so unconcernedly of man as a species of animal. Nor, of course, would he speak of

1. Sidney and Beatrice Webb, *A Constitution for a Socialist Commonwealth* (London, 1920) p. 270.

the process of history 'in which the individual is lost in utter insignificance' (p. 6). To reduce history to laws, to deny to man the right of choice and the dignity of being more than a statistic, and to glorify arguments couched in scientific language above all other arguments – these are the hallmark of the new intellectual socialism. If its impulse had been a generous urge to abolish poverty, it very soon became enamoured of its own powers of analysis and of its superior social data. Its genius was to be for detail. Hyndman, who knew both Mazzini and Marx, continued to admire the Italian as a man and as a moral influence; but Marx became for him the 'supreme analytic genius' and 'the Aristotle of the nineteenth century'.[1] To enter into that system was to believe oneself equipped with the unanswerable arguments of the scientific spirit.

But science might lead away from revolution: from Alvan's 'one step' to thoughtful analogies between the progress of society and the progress of the species. It is the characteristically English contribution to socialism to show that Darwin might count for more than Marx. Marx too, in some degree, had been a Darwinian: he had asked permission to dedicate a volume of *Das Kapital* to Darwin, without success. But to minds trained in the gradualism of parliamentary politics and impressed by the vast areas over which, in the Darwinian vision of the universe, biological changes occur, the revolutionary fervour of some continental socialists seemed contrary to the cool scientific spirit. Webb believed that Fabianism, or gradual socialism, was a fact of history deducible from scientific laws. Socialism was inevitable – 'the inevitable outcome of Democracy and the Industrial Revolution'. But 'no philosopher now looks for anything but the gradual evolution of the new order from the old without break of continuity or abrupt change of the entire social tissue at any point during the process'.[2] No Fabian bothered to ask if there were any sufficient reason to suppose that biological and political change are similar; but socialism, for reasons however implausible, had taken a curious and unexpected turn. It had accepted Parliament.

1. H. M. Hyndman, *The Record of an Adventurous Life* (London, 1911) pp. 269, 271.
2. Sidney Webb, *Fabian Essays* (London, 1889) p. 32.

The opposite of socialism, in the terminological sense, was ceasing to be individualism and becoming capitalism. Oscar Wilde, in his 'The soul of man under socialism', which first appeared in the *Fortnightly Review* (February 1891), claimed to believe that socialism was a higher form of individualism; if his argument is to be taken seriously, he was an opponent of what he calls 'Authoritarian Socialism' or 'an industrial-barrack system', and thought socialism of interest only to the extent that it would abolish poverty and introduce a 'far freer, far finer, and far more intensified' individualism than men already possess. It is hard to be certain where the irony here begins and ends; but the modern observer, viewing the socialism–capitalism antithesis at a distance, may wonder if that familiar argument is any less paradoxical than Wilde's. If socialism means state socialism, then it can hardly be doubted that it is very capitalistic indeed, since it concentrates ownership in the single agency of the state. But the antithesis can be explained, if not justified. 'Capitalist' is an earlier word in the language than 'capitalism', and it is doubtful if any examples of capitalism as a name for an economic system are earlier than the 1870s. Ruskin uses capitalist often, capitalism hardly at all. A capitalist is one who possesses capital; Coleridge in his *Table Talk* (27 April 1823) uses it to mean employer; and Disraeli uses it similarly in *Sybil* (1845). It relates more naturally to new industrial wealth than to old landed possession; Bagehot, in an essay of 1857, speaks of 'the capitalists who had created the new wealth'.[1] Dickens uses it extensively, often in the sense of *nouveau riche*: Merdle in *Little Dorrit* is called 'one of England's world-famous capitalists and merchant-princes' (i, ch. 21), and Mrs Merdle, apparently uncomfortable with the word, later refers to 'gentlemen who are what Society calls capitalists' (ii, ch. 15).

Capitalism, in its earliest history as a word, meant no more than the state of owning capital. Clough uses it as a personification in an article of the 1840s, to represent the collective body of those who save and invest: 'Capitalism, who keeps his carriage, will never be able to build mills, unless labour, who

1. Walter Bagehot, 'Lord Brougham', *National Review* (July 1857); reprinted in his *Collected Works* (1968) iii. 161.

barely keeps himself, saves money to help him.'[1] Thackeray uses the word to mean simply ownership: 'The sense of capitalism sobered and dignified' a drunken character in *The Newcomes* (1854–55) (ii, p. 75). The notion followed only later that the existing economy was dominated by those new men who owned and invested largely, that socialism would reduce or abolish their dominance, and that the system they would abolish could be abstracted as 'capitalism', though all these views were familiar before the end of the century. That it was a grave and perverse misnomer seems to have bothered hardly anyone. All developed economies, after all, are based on accumulations of capital, and this is not less true of socialist than of private economies. 'Capitalism' has flourished as a convenient term by which socialists draw attention away from those concentrations of capital power which universally characterize their own solutions.

A grand critique of socialism would be a subject for the historian of the twentieth century. Victorian intellectuals, being only vaguely and imperfectly aware of what total state power could inflict upon mankind, were more often hesitant, puzzled and even tolerant of a doctrine that seemed to arise, disturbingly and yet naturally, in the wake of democracy. Since the people controlled government, why should not government control the economy? And since the poor could now vote, why should they not organize themselves politically in their own interest? Men might see objections to all this, both practical and moral, but they were bound to attend to those objections less as the reality of the suffrage became felt. All class government is evil; the power of the state cannot simply be the same as the power of the people, whatever the constitution; and to confer tyrannical powers on the state, in however virtuous a cause, is to hasten the day of tyranny itself. All these arguments were heard and understood. They helped to hold socialism at bay, as a parliamentary force, until the First World War. But they were heard with less conviction in the face of the possibilities for power offered to organized labour by manhood suffrage.

1. A. H. Clough, *Selected Prose Works*, edited by B. B. Travick (University, Alabama, 1964) p. 212, from an article of 1846.

That organization had progressed fast, both as a fact and in the acceptance of respectable opinion. Those who in the 1850s had called trade unions lawless conspiracies might be ready to tolerate them in the 1860s, though only on the assumption that they could not fulfil their promises to raise wages and improve conditions. By the 1870s, however, trade unions were being congratulated on having done just that. W. T. Thornton, Mill's friend, wrote in 1869 as if the rights of workmen to unite were now generally accepted, though only ten years before many would have regarded them as sinister: 'Everyone now concedes to labourers, for the promotion of their common interests, the utmost freedom of collective action not inconsistent with individual liberty.'[1] That concession was to cost everything. By the mid-seventies the liberation of the unions from legal restriction was virtually complete for a hundred years to come, and the age of their accumulation of power had begun.

Some voices, it is true, were still raised in sophisticated protest, and of a kind more specific than a general distaste for class government and a tyrannical state. Mill, in his *Chapters on Socialism*, attacked the fundamental socialist assumption that a capitalist who receives a return on his investment is somehow cheating the system; the truth is, he argues, that the investor who abandons for a period his own use of his capital in the hopes of a percentual return is performing a social service: 'As long as he derives an income from his capital, he has not the option of withholding it from the use of others.'[2] Socialists often confuse the question whether, having capital, a man should invest and profit from it with the larger question of whether he should possess it at all. But this is merely to muddy the waters of debate. 'Anti-property doctrines', as Mill calls them, tend to be emotional and muddled; it is a pity he did not live to complete these chapters as a book and expose those muddles for all time. As it is, he is clear that revolutionary socialism is a pig in a poke; and though he did not possess direct experience in the matter, he could see at a distance the clear possibilities of socialist despotism: 'Those who would play this game on the strength of their own private opinion, unconfirmed as yet by

1. William Thomas Thornton, *On Labour* (London, 1869) pp. 182–3.
2. J. S. Mill, *Essays on Economics and Society* (Toronto, 1967) p. 734.

any experimental verification, . . . must have a serene confidence in their own wisdom on the one hand and a recklessness of other people's sufferings on the other',[1] a recklessness, he adds, greater than Robespierre's or St Just's. Democracy might be the tide on which socialism arose; but would democracy survive the victory of socialism? This is as near as the Victorians came to the arguments of Koestler and Orwell, and their instances are necessarily out of date. But it is fascinating to watch Mill's analysis verge on that prediction. His fear was shared by others. It is a fear of statism; of monarchy, in the original sense of the word, or government by one man; or of 'Caesarism', a fear already incarnated in France in the two Napoleons. Joseph Conrad, in a letter of December 1885, raised the fear that 'socialism must inevitably end in Caesarism';[2] and there were those who, almost before the age was out, were reaching for the crown. Lenin, in his pamphlet *What Shall We Do Now?*, declared it inconceivable that the working class should ever find a political solution for themselves; they must be led by middle-class intellectuals. After a diet of revolutionary study dosed with Nietzsche, the leader principle itself might take on a scientific gloss, and some foresaw a new age that would give birth to a new race of men. This is the heady side of the scientific spirit in politics: 'Caesarism and science together could evolve Faustian man.'[3] The sources of that view are complex and numerous: Disraeli, Marx, Shaw and Lenin are all ingredients. But then Fascism, compounded as it is of Victorian elements, is the one considerable political dogma of the twentieth century which, as a totality, the nineteenth did not know and could not imagine.

The literary influence of socialism, in the age of its conception and since, must be judged disappointing. In that respect it stands at a grave disadvantage to its ideological rival. Liberalism is fertile in literature. Its corpus of great verse and great fiction within the nineteenth century is arguably the greatest body of political literature in the European tradition: Shelley, Keats, Dickens, Macaulay, Thackeray, Trollope, Mill, George

1. *Ibid.*, p. 737.
2. G. Jean-Aubry, *Conrad: life and letters* (London, 1927) i. 84.
3. Sir Oswald Mosley, *My Life* (London, 1968) p. 325.

Eliot, Browning, Acton, Meredith. This is the intellectual's credo. Beside it, the socialist literary record looks drab: a body of stridently declamatory verse, some passages from Ruskin and Morris, Shaw's plays and prefaces, the novels of Wells and Galsworthy. That is to list what is memorable, and it is mostly later than 1890. The dearth was noticed, and has since been puzzled over, by the faithful themselves: when the Fabians organized a summer school in 1890 on Socialism in Contemporary Literature, Morris gave a paper on Gothic architecture (having modestly declined to give one on himself), Shaw a paper on Ibsen, while another spoke on Zola; and Hubert Bland, according to Shaw's account, 'undertook to read all the socialist novels of the day, an enterprise the desperate failure of which resulted in the most amusing paper of the series'.[1] The paper has not survived, but the nature of the topic must have contributed to the amusement of the audience. There was no socialist novel, to speak of. Englishmen had known socialism for half a century, but no fiction to remember had been born of the dogma.

The failure is curious, and has been noted since. 'Nearly everything describable as socialist literature', wrote Orwell years later, 'is dull, tasteless and bad. . . . In Western Europe socialism has produced no literature worth having.'[2] That is not much of an exaggeration, even on later reflection, unless the more recent literature of socialist protest against orthodox socialism is to be admitted into the count. The internal differences of socialists have produced much more that is memorable in drama and fiction than the struggle of socialism against capitalist oppression. The oddity runs even deeper. Those plays and novels in which the authors proclaim themselves socialists bear with embarrassing clarity the marks of what the censor might call bourgeois sensibility. Many a hero and heroine of Shaw's plays, like Major Barbara and St Joan, celebrate the triumphs of individual will over circumstance more plainly than they illustrate any doctrine of historical inevitability; and Wells's favourite design for his social novels is the traditional Dickensian pattern of a bright young man working his way up

1. Bernard Shaw, *The Quintessence of Ibsenism* (London, 1891), preface.
2. George Orwell, *The Road to Wigan Pier* (London, 1937) ch. 11.

through the ranks of society to win a wife, a position and the plaudits of the reader. One does not need to be a socialist to think all this a very bourgeois fiction. Only Galsworthy's *Forsyte Saga*, in the mass of classic English fiction, enacts with much attempt at consistency the characteristically socialist contentions concerning the corruption of wealth, especially inherited wealth, and the impoverishment of human values that such wealth is supposed to cause; and there the polemical interest is largely confined to the first of the novels, *The Man of Property* (1906). And the inability of English Marxist writers in the 1930s to produce a fiction which was plainly socialist in design and purpose is one of the notorious gaps in literary history. It is not just, as Shaw and Orwell remark, that there is so little socialist literature, but that so much of the literature written by the faithful is so markedly unsocialist.

The Victorian resistance to socialism, then, though never absolute, has a literary as well as a political aspect. Socialism penetrated the world of literature almost as little as it penetrated Parliament, and for reasons not altogether different. The temper of parliamentary institutions favours gradual and piecemeal change. It is a temper unfavourable, on the whole, both to outright conservatism and to revolution, and it is normally unconcerned with utopian solutions. Some socialists accepted all this in the 1880s and have accepted it ever since. But the dogma itself remains irreversibly utopian. It is about a world that is not: about what Morris called 'News from Nowhere'. A liberal novelist or dramatist has a significant advantage in writing about what his readers know. When he illustrates such virtues as manly independence, upward striving and self-help, thousands who read him have lived what he speaks of and have watched thousands more live it too. In a social literature, where issues of accuracy arise, this is a commanding advantage. Great fictions are about individuals, not about the laws of history. That makes the English ideology fertile in great literature, for individuals are what it is about.

[13]

The Sages

The works of the Victorian social critics, or 'sages' – notably Carlyle, Newman, Matthew Arnold and Ruskin – have so far figured in this account only as shadowy adversaries of the English ideology. Their case must now be given fuller weight. The social criticism they wrote forms a curious corpus without parallel before the Victorian age (though Cobbett and the older Coleridge are significant predecessors) and continuously familiar in the English literary scene since. This is a body of criticism of the contemporary world written by intellectuals and for intellectuals in a tone of minority dissent. It seeks to create a coterie of support rather than a national movement. One can imagine a nation dominated by liberals or socialists – but never, in the wildest of dreams, by Carlylians, Newmanites, Arnoldians or Ruskinians. It is non-party. It is composed of books like Carlyle's *Past and Present*, Newman's *Idea of a University*, Arnold's *Culture and Anarchy* and Ruskin's *Unto This Last*. Novelists and statesmen, including George Eliot and Disraeli, are marginally a part of the story, and the mood of the sage occasionally invades the novel or the political oration – when a Disraeli hero is assured of the superior comforts and civilization of the English people in the Middle Ages, for example, or when George Eliot in *Felix Holt* warns her readers against exaggerating the significance of the suffrage, the characteristic tone of admonishment is heard. But the group, apart from its principals, remains hard to identify and almost as hard to name. I shall call them the sages, in recognition of the playful sense of that word and of the title of an earlier study.[1]

1. John Holloway, *The Victorian Sage* (London, 1953).

It is a name to indicate rather than to define. What they were, and what they should be called, remains a puzzle.

The Victorians themselves had no accepted title for the new literary phenomenon. 'Prophet' attracted some,[1] and it could apply at least to Carlyle, that 'Calvinist without a theology' as Froude called him;[2] it carried the right note of Hebrew defiance and woe-prediction, and it suited the Old Testament colouring of Carlyle's more vatic prose. It suited Ruskin less well, however, and Newman and Arnold hardly at all, though a newspaper once called Arnold an 'elegant Jeremiah'.[3] Mill, writing to Carlyle in May 1833, contrasts his friend's prose with his own as the difference between a 'vates' and a 'Logician in Ordinary', and he praises Carlyle as an artist of a language out of tune with the times: 'My word . . . is partly intelligible to many more persons than yours is, because mine is presented in the logical and mechanical form which partakes most of this age and country, yours in the artistical and poetical, . . . which finds least entrance into any minds now.'[4] That was admittedly a poor forecast, and Mill gravely underrated the coming vogue of Carlyle, who had just written *Sartor Resartus* and who was about to strike the taste of a new discipleship, including Dickens's, with *The French Revolution*. His vogue was an impressive one. A hostile reviewer twenty years later was to protest that 'Carlylism' by the 1850s had replaced Byronism in the enthusiasm of certain young men – a shift from the 'despairing-romantic' to the 'despairing-prophetic'.[5] Carlyle was a 'prophet', a member of a 'class of writers called of late Thinkers' who are content to 'address a smaller audience' than

1. William Cory, *Extracts from the Letters and Journals* (Oxford, 1897) p. 376: 'A prophet like Carlyle has a sort of right to lift up his voice . . .'

2. James Anthony Froude, *Thomas Carlyle* (1882–84) ii. 2.

3. Quoted from the *Daily Telegraph* by Henry Sidgwick, 'The Prophet of Culture', *Macmillan's Magazine* (August 1867), who calls the phrase 'tolerably felicitous for a Philistine'. The Sidgwick article is reprinted in his *Miscellaneous Essays and Addresses* (London, 1904).

4. J. S. Mill, *Earlier Letters 1812–48*, edited by F. E. Mineka (Toronto, 1963) i. 57.

5. General Sir E. B. Hamley, *Thomas Carlyle: an essay* (Edinburgh, 1881) p. 37. This review first appeared anonymously in *Blackwood's Magazine* in February 1859, and was promptly reprinted as a volume on Carlyle's death in 1881. George Eliot, in a letter of 1859, approved it as 'not unjustly severe'; *Letters* (1954–56) iii. 23.

poets do.[1] But the puzzle remained a puzzle, for many Victorians. Who were these writers, what was their title to rail and to prophesy, and why did anybody listen to them?

The sages were a species, not a party, and often viewed one another without sympathy. Carlyle is not known to have held a high view of Arnold; and Arnold, who owed much to his example, returned no better opinion. The differences were of temperament rather than of substance, but they mattered. 'A moral desperado', he called him in a letter to Clough;[2] and when he heard he was dead, even death could not mellow his opinion. 'I never much liked Carlyle,' he wrote to a friend in March 1881; he had carried coals to Newcastle by 'preaching earnestness to a nation which had plenty of it by nature'.[3] Rivalry may have sharpened that antipathy; and rivalry was inevitable, since it is almost of the inherent nature of sagehood to claim a unique status. A messiah may have disciples, but hardly colleagues, and the sages could no more unite in a cause than they could write a common programme of action. Newman had set himself apart, in any case, by his conversion to Rome in 1845. Carlyle and Arnold could not make alliance. Only Ruskin could be generous: he wrote *Fors Clavigera* with Carlyle in mind, and called him the one man in England 'to whom I can look for steady guidance'. He even approved Arnold's contention, in *Culture and Anarchy*, that the English aristocracy are barbarians.[4] But these are exceptional tributes. For the most part there could be no unity of purpose among them, and little open meeting of minds. That is not to doubt the deep resemblances that link their views. But disparities of manner and emphasis still set them, in their own age, forever apart. No one could ever confuse Carlyle's syntactic mannerisms and facetious railing with Arnold's urbanity, Ruskin's intense and insistent sincerity, and Newman's high marmoreal rhetoric stamped with all the marks of a classical training. They were not a group,

1. *Ibid.*, pp. 5, 7.
2. Matthew Arnold, *Letters to Arthur Hugh Clough*, edited by H. F. Lowry (Oxford, 1932) p. 111.
3. Arnold, *Letters 1848–88*, edited by G. W. E. Russell (London, 1895) ii. 191.
4. John Ruskin, *Works* (1903–12) xxviii. 22, xxvii. 263.

unless by the hindsight of literary history, nor did they wish to appear as one.

To write as a sage, then or now, is to write as an amateur. Carlyle wrote almost unrelievedly in that role, but for the rest some distinctions need to be made. They had, after all, professional standing in some of what they did: Newman in theology, Ruskin in art history, and Arnold in education. Books like *Lectures on the Present Position of Catholics*, *The Stones of Venice*, and *Report on Elementary Education in Germany, Switzerland and France* do not fall within the limits of this discussion. But others of their works come before the attention of the reader with quite different guarantees and need to be considered in a more questioning light: Newman's reply to Sir Robert Peel in *The Tamworth Reading Room*, Ruskin's social criticism in general, together with his long asides on moral and social questions in works devoted to art and architecture, and Arnold's works on society and religion such as *Culture and Anarchy* and *Literature and Dogma*. To put the matter bluntly, it is simply not obvious that Newman knows what he is talking about when he admonishes a Prime Minister on the state of national culture, or Ruskin when he expatiates on the deficiencies of political economy, or Arnold when he reproves the quality of English life or the doctrines of the churches. To believe what they say, to use such passages as evidence for the state of affairs in the age, or to suppose that they represent any body of opinion whatever, is to reveal the merest historical credulity. Punditry (to give the activity a more modern name) is not truth-seeking or truth-telling. This was plainly seen at the time, and it needs to be seen again. 'He belongs to a class', wrote Cornewall Lewis to a friend in 1838, after hearing Carlyle lecture, 'whose business it is to deny all accurate knowledge, and all processes for arriving at accurate knowledge, and who ask mankind to accept blindly certain mysterious dicta of their own.'[1] That, for a contemporary, is not an unrepresentative view: there were plenty of Victorians who believed that the sages lacked the knowledge to justify the assertions they made. Bridges was to call Arnold 'Mr Kidglove

1. Sir George Cornewall Lewis, *Letters to Various Friends*, edited by G. F. Lewis (London, 1870) p. 102, from a letter of 2 June 1838.

Cocksure'.[1] This is not to say that experts are always or usually right; still less that anyone should be deprived of the right to hold opinions and express them. But again and again the sages can be shown to have misrepresented matters of social concern, whether honestly or not; and prejudice and partisanship are fully within the terms of what they do.

The common features that unite the works of the sages are worth some serious consideration. When intelligent men agree, there is a natural disposition to take them seriously; and when they agree independently of one another that disposition is all the greater. The charges levelled by the sages against Victorian politics and civilization, diverse as they are in tone and style, suggest an impressive amount of common ground. They saw the English path to liberty as a path to anarchy, and they spoke out loudly against it. They declined to occupy any intelligible place on the existing spectrum of politics that stretched from the Radicals to the ultra-Tories; and they refused to have anything to do with the parliamentary system. Novelists in the Victorian age stand as candidates for Parliament, or consider standing: sages do not. This is the true voice of the prosecutor – a voice of protest against the libertarian tendencies of the times which the Conservative Party (Disraeli apart) largely failed to provide. Most Conservatives were too unideological by nature, and too much concerned with competing with the Liberals, to offer a thoughtful opposition to the English ideology. The sages, by contrast, though incapable of influencing the course of events, provide for the age a counterpoise of ideas which would otherwise be lacking.

The historical impulse that unites the sages is not mysterious, and it is shared by others. It is the failure, real or alleged, of the nation to match its material improvement with cultural and moral advance. That is a misgiving shared by many: it was the task of the sage to exploit and exaggerate what for others was a matter of mild and occasional concern. Mill, who had nothing of the alarmist about him, had been saying all this before Newman, Arnold and Ruskin were heard of, and years before

1. G. M. Hopkins, *Letters to Robert Bridges*, edited by Claude C. Abbott (Oxford, 1935) p. 172, from a letter of Hopkins to Bridges of 28 January 1883: 'I do not like your calling Matthew Arnold Mr Kidglove Cocksure . . .'

Carlyle's *Past and Present:* 'The celebrity of England', he wrote in 1835, 'in the present day, rests upon her docks, her canals, her railroads. In intellect she is distinguished only for a kind of sober good sense, free from extravagance, but also void of lofty aspirations.' These are matters 'where man most resembles a machine, with the precision of a machine'. A reflecting Frenchman or German notes in England 'the absence of large and commanding views'.[1] This, in summary, is the vital issue of the sages. They saw their civilization as rich and powerful, but provincial and narrowing. The task was to liberate and to refine. 'We live among the marvels of science', Bagehot wrote in 1857, 'but we know how little they change us. The essentials of life are what they were.' And then his argument repeats Mill's, almost verbally: 'We go by the train, but we are not improved at our journey's end. We have railways, and canals, and manufactures – excellent things, no doubt, but they do not touch the soul.' When a man as solid as Bagehot writes in these terms, and speaks of 'the day after the feast',[2] an important shift in intellectual fashion has occurred.

The sages were contemptuous of parliamentary institutions as such and, as a natural consequence, of all legislative acts in particular. This confers on their writings an air of loftiness. It is not just that the parties are wrong, since all parties are always wrong; or that this or that Act of Parliament is mistaken, since all Acts are so, where they are not merely trivial. Their contempt is profound and pervasive. For Newman liberalism always meant something more than a political party or even an ideology: it meant the whole modern tendency towards secular rationalism, already established inside the Church Establishment and general, almost universal, in intellectual circles by the 1860s. The word 'liberal', he observed bitterly in the *Apologia* (1864), had first been the name of Byron's periodical, then a school of theology; but 'now it is scarcely a party; it is the educated lay world'.[3] Godlessness

1. J. S. Mill, 'Professor Sedgwick's *Discourse*', *London Review* (April 1835); reprinted in his *Dissertations and Discussions* (1859) i. 96.

2. Walter Bagehot, 'Lord Brougham', *National Review* (July 1857); reprinted in his *Collected Works* (1968) iii. 191–2.

3. J. H. Newman, *Apologia pro vita sua,* edited by Martin J. Svaglic (Oxford, 1967) pp. 233–4.

was his own private ground for despising the atmosphere in which he lived; but whether on this ground or another, the sages rejected the state of public opinion and the parliamentary institutions that expressed that opinion. They were anti-democratic: the suffrage had been built on legislative acts passed by deliberative assemblies dominated by the traditional political parties, and that was enough. More than that, the right to vote was involving men by the hundreds of thousands in the mechanical rigmarole of constitutional procedure. Carlyle's contempt for those who imagine wisdom can be attained by counting heads is supreme: his ideal men are heroes who make themselves dictators, like Cromwell and Frederick the Great. The Reform Act, he had once remarked, was 'but a singeing of the dungheaps':[1] it is mankind that needs to be changed, not laws. Democracy, he wrote in the first of the *Latter-Day Pamphlets* of February 1850, is supposed by many a 'kind of "Government" '. They are wrong – it is nothing of the kind:

> Your ship cannot double Cape Horn by its excellent plans by voting. The ship may vote this and that, above decks and below, in the most harmonious exquisitely constitutional manner: the ship, to get round Cape Horn, will find a set of conditions already voted for, and fixed with adamantine rigour by the ancient Elemental Powers, who are entirely careless how you vote.

The winds are ruffianly, the icebergs inexorable, he runs on; though he does not explain why the limiting factors of nature should not constrain the hero-king as much as any legislative assembly. Dictators are not less given to asserting an imagined superiority over nature than other men – rather the contrary. Carlyle's programme is not as practical as he pretends. The shooting of the Levellers is described with such relish in his *Cromwell's Letters and Speeches* (1845), where they are mocked along with 'other misguided martyrs to the liberties of England then and since', that one needs to recall with a sense of effort that the martyrs, after all, died in an enduring political cause, and that Carlylism has never changed anything at all. This is the loftiness that pervades the arguments of the sages, and it

1. J. A. Froude, *Thomas Carlyle* (1882–84) ii. 133.

sets them at a point very remote from the active concerns of political men. Arnold's derision of 'liberal nostrums' in *Culture and Anarchy* is a blander and more understated version of a similar position. Parties and governments are chasing will-o'-the-wisps, he argues; they are failing to be fundamental when they pursue issues like free trade and Irish disestablishment. All this represents the weakest aspect of the sage's case. No historian today could hesitate in his answer if asked whether free trade, or Arnoldian Hellenism, had made more difference to more men, then or since. Lofty as the arguments of Carlyle and Arnold are, and replete with a sense of personal superiority, both moral and intellectual, one is still entitled to ask whether they have any intelligent content, and whether events have justified or failed to justify them.

The contempt of the sages for parliamentary institutions is matched by their distaste for industrialism. Here, indeed, is where their indictment begins: the case against Parliament is born of a sense of despair at the social and human effects of the industrial revolution. *Past and Present* arose out of a visit made by the Carlyles in September 1842 to friends in Suffolk, where the contrast between the St Ives workhouse and the ruins of the abbey in Bury St Edmunds affected Carlyle with a sense of human loss. Some of the contentious medievalism of that book was borrowed by Disraeli two years later in *Sybil*, with its unqualified assertion in the mouth of one of the characters in the novel that the English people were 'better clothed, better lodged and better fed just before the Wars of the Roses' than they were in the 1840s (iii. 5). But the Condition of England question, with its emphasis on poverty, is largely characteristic of the Hungry Forties. There is a significant shift in the writings of the sages, after 1850, from material issues to intellectual and moral: perhaps the modern phrase 'quality of life' sums up their later interests best. Like all who engage in the argument of quality, they assume that poverty has been solved or is about to be solved: no one ever argued about the quality of life who wondered if he could afford to eat or pay the rent. In the later years of the century the arguments of the sages grow luxurious. The talk is no longer of economics, and political economy is condemned not because it has failed but because it has succeeded too well. The English are the richest nation on earth, after all; the economic doctrines that have brought them to this condition are unlikely to be merely bad arguments, though they may with ingenuity be charged under a number of heads: that they are heartless, that they fail to take account of the variety of human experience, notably in aspects other than the material, that they are indifferent to the arts, to leisure and to joy. 'The Knowledge School', as Newman protested in *The Tamworth Reading Room*, 'does not contemplate raising man above himself; it merely aims at disposing of his existing powers and tastes', and leaves him a man, not an angel. That is not a charge that would bother many economists, but it is a charge that, as it is repeated down the years, signalizes the shift of interest towards a new spiritual emphasis.

Arnold represents the point of turn. Born in 1822, and a whole generation and more younger than Carlyle, he is near enough to the Condition of England to invoke instances of poverty when he builds an indictment against authority. But the indictment, though it refers to material issues, does not usually settle upon them for long. In 'The function of criticism at the present time', an essay written as an arresting introduction to the first series of *Essays in Criticism* (1865), he invokes a recent child murder in Nottingham, where 'a girl named Wragg' left the workhouse with her illegitimate child and was arrested after the infant had been found strangled. The workhouse setting links the argument to the older concern for material alleviation; the reference to illegitimacy widens the issue. But Arnold's comments on the case make it sound as if his strictures are directed at none of these matters, but rather at some artistic deficiency in English life. His pain is not that of a reformer but that of an aesthete:

> *Wragg!* If we are to talk of ideal perfection, of 'the best in the whole world', has anyone reflected what a touch of grossness in our race, what an original shortcoming in the more delicate spiritual perceptions, is shown by the natural growth amongst us of such hideous names – Higginbottom, Stiggins, Bugg! In Ionia and Attica they were luckier in this respect. . .

Such aesthetic delicacy seems heartless, in the circumstances, and Arnold's fancy-waistcoated rhetoric offers no comfort to a girl under threat of hanging, or to anyone who cared for her or for those like her. What, after all, has the euphony of English names to do with infanticide? Industrial poverty has already drifted out of the centre of interest; the sages accepted, as they were bound to accept, the reality of a unique and still advancing national prosperity. It was by virtue of this prosperity that their reputations throve. A prosperous nation was now turning its attention towards the refined and inward anxieties that beset the sufficient or luxurious existence.

The sages offer a negation: to that extent the title of 'social critics' is an accurate one. They criticize, but they do not prescribe; not, at least, in terms that offer any prospect of acceptance. This is a rhetoric of despair. Newman does not believe that his people will ever, in any measurable future, submit again to Rome; 'Peter has spoken', but England will not listen; and even if some day she did, as he explained to a Dublin audience in 1852, the civilization and literature of England are forever Protestant. Carlyle's political ideals are a fantasy in the Victorian context: we understand his Everlasting No, but it is hard indeed to attribute any clear sense to his Everlasting Yea. No Frederick the Great could govern such a nation as England, and he knew it. His behaviour was more like that of a German savant than of an Englishman: he composed word-games for his fellow-intellectuals, that is to say, rather than proposals that could be weighed and adopted. Mark Pattison characterized the oddity of the German intellectual situation in a passage that applies to the sages as well: 'Their great authors write a dialect of philosophical slang, which is unintelligible to their own lower classes; and they address themselves, in fact, not to their country, but to each other.'[1] Arnold's Hellenism is a vapour: whatever its relation to Periclean Athens, he cannot seriously suppose it has a chance in Victorian England. Ruskin is not an obscure author, but it is hard to read *Unto This Last* or his later political tracts on the assumption that he hoped governing opinion might change its policies in that direction. In all this, it needs to be emphasized,

1. Mark Pattison, *Essays* (Oxford, 1889) ii. 398, from his 1857 review of Buckle.

the writings of the sages stand in eternal contrast to many novels of the age. Fiction could alter things, and sometimes did: it could certainly be written on the assumption that it might effect change. *Bleak House* is a clear injunction to its readers to see their social relations in a different light, and to act on that new understanding; and the great parliamentary novels of the 1860s and after are very close to the grain of events at Westminster and in the country. They assume that men can inform themselves about the state of affairs and alter them. The novel is about a world that exists. That is just what cannot be said of the works of the sages.

The sages are hostile to the idea of progress. This is at once a cause and a consequence of their despair. To live in Victorian England was to watch progress happening; men were aware of an ebb and flow, but they were above all conscious of a movement that was irresistibly for the better. That view need not be complacent: Macaulay, viewing the England of the 1680s in the third chapter of his *History of England,* concluded by deriding intellectual fashions for finding in the past a golden age, 'when men died faster in the purest country air than they now die in the most pestilential lanes of our towns, and when men died faster in the lanes of our towns than they now die on the coast of Guiana'. But that only pointed to the probability that the Victorian achievement was about to be supplanted:

> We too shall, in our turn, be outstripped, and in our turn be envied. It may well be, in the twentieth century, that the peasant of Dorsetshire may think himself miserably paid with fifteen shillings a week; that the carpenter at Greenwich may receive ten shillings a day; that labouring men may be as little used to dine without meat as they now are to eat rye bread.

All such arguments are anathema to the sages. If living standards are improving, they held, then living standards are not the whole story. If more and more men are participating in the decisions of government, then democracy is merely a shadow. If the power of the state has diminished, then it ought to be increased. If England is rich, she is for all that a cultural desert. She does not know where she is going. 'Many of our recent classics', Acton told his Cambridge audience at his inaugural in 1895, referring to Carlyle, Newman and Froude,

> were persuaded that there is no progress justifying the ways of God to man, and that the mere consolidation of liberty is like the motion of creatures whose advance is in the direction of their tails. They deem that anxious precaution against bad government is an obstruction to good, and degrades morality and mind by placing the capable at the mercy of the incapable, dethroning enlightened virtue for the benefit of the average man. They hold that great and salutary things are done for mankind by power concentrated, not by power balanced and cancelled and dispersed.[1]

The echoing cry of the sage is that everything is getting worse; if men think otherwise, they are looking in the wrong direction. In this school of thought optimism is always superficial, gloom a guarantee of having reflected long, of having deeply felt. That assumption is not new, and not specially Victorian: 'To preach long, loud and damnation', Selden had remarked two hundred years before, 'is the way to be cried up.' The manner of the sermon is wonderfully various. Carlyle is often facetious, even hilarious. Arnold can flash wit at his reader, and revel urbanely in the discomfort of his enemies. And Ruskin can be sweet-tempered as well as hectoring. But in the end their tale is always an indictment: things are bad, they are getting worse, and the apostles of progress are blind and blinkered.

The sages begin in antirationalism, though they are not content to remain there. Their search for truth is a search beyond mere information and, at its most intense, against argument itself in its familiar forms. Carlyle's Clothes-Philosophy, in *Sartor Resartus*, proposes to strip away the outward appearances of things, along with all mechanical reasoning and inert accumulations of human knowledge. Rationalism encourages men to believe the universe is only a machine; then imagination and poetry awake him, and he casts off the repressions of rationality in favour of energy, spontaneity and love. Emerson is said to have angered Carlyle, on a visit to London, for not believing in the Devil, and he showed him slums, gin-shops and finally the House of Commons, asking him at every turn: 'Do you believe in a devil noo?'[2] But Carlyle's 'mirage philosophy',

1. Lord Acton, *A Lecture on the Study of History* (London, 1895) pp. 28–9.
2. *The George Eliot Letters* (1954-56) i. 372, from a letter of 2 November 1851.

as Hamley called it severely, is the extreme antirational case. Antirationalism survives only in mild and modified forms in the writings of the later sages; and before the end of the century Nietzsche had stepped in, with more potent spells, to supply a continuing demand on the part of impatient intellectuals eager to reject the painstaking and the mechanical in favour of the lusts of the spirit.

Newman is only a mild and partial advocate: it is mere liberalism, he held, to suppose that man's reason can achieve truth unaided; but truth is none the less there, validated by a Church which is at once tradition and authority. Ruskin can be resolutely rationalistic: his attack on Mill in *Unto This Last* is little short of logic-chopping. But it is somehow not the kind of logic that invites a reasoned answer, so hot is the conviction that underlies it, and one cannot easily imagine Ruskin changing his mind because new evidence had been offered him. Arnold calls for a 'free play of ideas', but he advocates rather than illustrates it, and his attacks on adversaries are displays of point-scoring rather than examples of candid debate. Whether it is more rational to hellenize than to hebraize would be hard to answer: the distinction is not between the rational and the irrational, but between great arguments and small. Free trade is hebraistic, so Arnold argues in *Culture and Anarchy*, because free-traders are 'mechanically worshipping their fetish of the production of wealth and of the increase of manufactures and population, and looking neither to the right nor left so long as this increase goes on' (vi. 4), whereas Hellenism would mean 'letting our consciousness play freely and simply upon the facts before us'. The meaning of 'freely and simply' can only be interpreted in the light of all Arnold's writings as a social critic, including his advocacy of lofty inaction as an alternative to reform:

> Our main business at the present moment is not so much to work away at certain crude reforms of which we have already the scheme in our own mind, as to create, through the help of that culture which at the very outset we began by praising and recommending, a frame of mind out of which the schemes of really fruitful reforms may with time grow (vi. 5).

But that, a liberal practitioner would be inclined to reply, would not help feed the hungry, clear the slums or solve the Irish question. It is highly characteristic of the sages that they are unconcerned with specific solutions to specific problems. Their loftiness could cause annoyance. 'What should we think,' Elizabeth Barrett Browning asked despairingly as she contemplated Carlyle, of

> a philosopher who went to one of our manufacturing towns where the operatives work from sixteen to eighteen hours a day, and are nevertheless badly clothed, dirty and without sufficient food – and to whom the philosopher, as a remedial measure, suggested that they should get more soul? No – give the fire some more fuel, and then expect more light, and the warmth of an aspiring flame.[1]

The superiority of other lands and peoples, in the arguments of the sages, is a significant tactic. The fashion runs wider and deeper than the social criticism of the age, but here the sages intensified and exploited to their advantage a tendency in Victorian debate. Mill was a francophile: in his essay on Vigny (1838), in a passage that might have been written thirty years later by Arnold, he called the French mind 'that most active national mind in Europe at the present moment'. The Brownings were enthusiasts for Italy. But both Mill and the Brownings lack that edge of hostility for English things that makes a foreign civilization, in the writings of the sages, a calculated reproach to the homeland. Carlyle's Germany, Arnold's France, are models of what England lacks: Germany, in its metaphysical profundities, and France in its centralized and administered culture. It is 'the intelligence of their idea-moved masses' that makes the French superior, Arnold wrote in 1848, years before he developed the idea in a critical essay; they are 'the most civilized of European peoples'.[2] The total economy of the *Essays in Criticism,* if the two series of 1865 and 1888 are placed together, illustrates that opposition: the first eulogizes continental authors of the second rank, the second gently disparages the great names of English poetry, and notably the

1. E. B. Browning, 'Carlyle', which appeared anonymously in R. H. Horne, *A New Spirit of the Age* (London, 1844) ii. 263.

2. Matthew Arnold, *Letters 1848–88* (1895) i. 4–5, from a letter of March 1848.

English Romantics. It is hard to imagine a sage without a foreign enthusiasm. The charge of insularity and provincialism, the claim to have found a man or a book in Paris or elsewhere that will show English civilization to be badly at fault, are marks of the trade that are even older than Carlyle.

In all this the claim for culture is vital, and here the sages stand on a ground that is emphatically their own. The charge of amateurishness or ignorance counts for less here than elsewhere, though it still counts for something: if the sages do not know as much history as Macaulay, as much political economy as Mill, or as much contemporary politics as Bagehot, at least they pronounce on English culture out of an equipment that is not notably inferior to anyone else's. Culture is the grand free-for-all of intellectual debate since the 1850s. On that subject anyone can have a view and express it with confidence. Any literary or political argument can be extended to embrace reflections about the national state of consciousness. Every man, in such a matter, is his own pontiff: it is a game without rules. 'The very silliest cant of the day', wrote one observer, 'is the cant about culture'; it may do for reviewers and professors, but in politics it means 'simply a turn for small fault-finding, love of selfishness, and indecision in action'.[1] It is pedantic nonsense, for some; for others a chance to air a prejudice or put a case.

Could it ever be more? The question here is not whether the sages were amateurs, since in the strictest sense there are no professional analysts of the cultural condition. But even in a field so lacking in frontiers and in established methods of procedure, it is still possible to ask whether the sages were behaving in a manner calculated to advance the inquiry and provide for the future a basis for argument and research. That is putting it as cautiously as it needs to be put. A sociology of thought, to use an ambitious phrase, was only a remote aspiration in the age. Foreign sages like Comte and Marx were devising laws to link history to movements of knowledge and belief, and lonely pioneers like Buckle had occasionally attempted something similar for the English. But the writings of the sages do not aspire to that sort of formality. Theirs is the wisdom of

1. Frederic Harrison, *Order and Progress* (London, 1875) p. 150.

the *aperçu*. Nothing in Ruskin or Arnold amounts to a developed theory of how cultures are formed or changed. When Arnold accuses an opponent of a lack of culture – and those opponents are sometimes men of high intelligence and education – the charge is one to which lucid sense can be attributed only with difficulty. The jibes at Gladstone and Bright at the conclusion of *Culture and Anarchy*, oblique as they are, are still breathtakingly arrogant, and the claim in the 1865 preface to *Essays in Criticism* that England is about to sink into drabness, that 'the world will soon be the Philistines', cannot be based on any serious inquiry into the state of the arts in the England of Dickens, George Eliot, Meredith, Mill and Swinburne. Those names hardly appear in Arnold's essays, which measure the heights and depths of mid-Victorian culture without even considering them. The procedure cannot be seen as a serious one. Whether the sages knew the culture of England in their own age remains an open question, but it is plain that, for whatever reason, they failed to describe it.

How much, then, did the sages know about English civilization in their own age? In contemporary politics their knowledge seems to have been scattered and fragmentary. A reference in a newspaper can fire them, a remark in an essay; but a thorough account of a total work of controversy is unusual. Ruskin's treatment of Mill in *Unto This Last* is an honourable exception here: it may be partial and mistaken, but it is a serious attempt to come to grips with the mind of an adversary. The neglect of the novel is above all remarkable. It was the dominant literary form of the Victorians, and nobody would now attempt an account of Victorian civilization without considering it. The usual Victorian view was not much different: it is uncommon in the age to find contemptuous estimates of the novel as a form, of a sort that Jane Austen had complained about early in the century. Macaulay, an author with a strong sense of his own dignity, defended himself defiantly to his father as an undergraduate against the charge of being a 'novel-reader', and used to converse with his sister in the remembered dialogues of the novels they both loved; he even thought he could rewrite *Sir Charles Grandison* from memory with her help.[1] He quoted

1. G. O. Trevelyan, *Life and Letters of Lord Macaulay* (1876) i. 95, 130–1.

Dickens in speeches and in essays; in his essay on Frederick the Great (1842) he refers to *Oliver Twist* and *Nicholas Nickleby* some three or four years after they had appeared, as if they were a matter of common knowledge; and three years later, in his speech to the Commons on the Maynooth grant in April 1845, he alludes to *Nickleby* again. The enormous sales of the great Victorian novelists forbids one to suppose that any educated opinion was unaware of them. Approving and illustrative references in serious political contexts are not hard to find. Acton tried to convert Gladstone, an older man, from a preference for Scott to one for Dickens and George Eliot, whom he revered as one who could do more than some of the greatest historians – she was capable 'not only of reading the diverse hearts of men, but of creeping into their skin, watching the world through their eyes, feeling their latent background of conviction, discerning theory and habit'.[1] Victorian statesmen were often ready to acknowledge the massive contribution that the novel was making to the study of the times.

The contrast with the sages is striking. Unlike the educated statesmen of the age, most of them held the novel in slight regard. Disraeli, who awkwardly straddles this distinction, was little interested in novels apart from his own; he confessed to Lady Londonderry in 1857 that he wished he could console himself by reading them, as she did: 'I have never read anything of Dickens except an extract in a newspaper.' His remedy was simple: 'When I want to read a novel, I write one,' he once remarked.[2] Carlyle ignores the Victorian novel in the mass of his writings, though he wrote a review of its great ancestor, Scott, in the *Westminster Review* in 1838. Arnold did not read *David Copperfield* until thirty years after its appearance, in 1880;[3] he never wrote at length about any English novelist, and his only essay on any novel whatever is a late and jejune

1. Lord Acton, *Letters to Mary Gladstone* (1904) p. 60. On Gladstone's preference for Scott over George Eliot, which Acton attributes to his idealism, see p. 109. There is a long and perceptive analysis of Shorthouse's historical novel *John Inglesant* (1881) in the same volume (pp. 135–51), written by Acton months after the book appeared.

2. W. F. Monypenny and G. E. Buckle, *The Life of Benjamin Disraeli* (London, 1910–20) vi. 636.

3. Matthew Arnold, *Letters 1848–88* (1895) p. 184, from a letter of 14 October 1880.

article on Tolstoy's *Anna Karenina*, which appeared in the *Fortnightly* a few months before his death. Newman and Ruskin were admittedly more openminded than this; Newman once said he had gone to bed laughing at the opening pages of Trollope's *Barchester Towers* and had begun laughing again when he woke up in the middle of the night;[1] and Ruskin read Dickens, Thackeray, and George Eliot, and claimed to have known the *Pickwick Papers* by heart, 'pretty nearly all, since it came out'.[2] He praises *Hard Times* in a long footnote to the first essay in *Unto This Last*, defending Dickens from the charge of caricature: but that is a rare instance of intellectual exchange between the worlds of the sage and the novelist. Their usual stance is one of mutual rejection. Trollope derides Carlyle in *The Warden* as Mr Pessimist Anticant, 'a Scotchman who had passed a great portion of his early days in Germany', imbibed metaphysics there, and failed to notice that 'in this world no good is unalloyed' (ch. 15). The novelists and the sages are rivals, and the struggle is between those who describe what they see and those who claim to look beneath the surface of things. Carlyle's Clothes–Philosophy is as antipathetic to the social novel as it is to any other art of social description. He claims to look within, and that claim in its very nature hostile is to the social fiction that the Victorians knew.

What did contemporaries think of the claims of the sages? Individual disciples apart, there is a significantly wide consensus of rejection on the part of novelists, statesmen, journalists and others. The serious reputation of the Victorian sage is a fact of the twentieth century, not of the nineteenth. These prophets lacked honour in their own century. Mill sets the tone in his celebrated essay on Bentham (1838): in jurisprudence a master, Bentham was in life a great baby, with 'the empiricism of one who has had little experience' – never rich or poor, ill or dejected, 'a boy to the last'. That is a theme on which the Victorians ring the changes. The sages, they insisted, did not know the world they were living in, whether out of innocence

1. J. H. Newman, *Letters and Diaries*, edited by C. S. Dessain (London, 1968) xviii. 482, from a letter of 8 October 1858, only a year after the appearance of the novel.

2. Letter to *Daily Telegraph* (4 January 1888); *Works* (1903–12) xxxiv. 613.

or out of wilful ignorance. They were easily seduced by new ideas, and especially by foreign ideas. They were word-spinners; they were self-seeking; they could not think. 'I suppose', someone remarked of Arnold, 'he was driven to patronizing Jesus Christ as the only way of earning cash. It is a mean way of getting a living, but hardly baser than making money by tracts and rigmaroles.'[1] Many reviewers are simply derisive. 'When we find', wrote one of Carlyle, 'that the style continues while the thinking is left out, the marvel becomes a prodigy.'[2] Sidgwick, when he read in a newspaper of Arnold as the 'elegant Jeremiah' of modern England, pocketed the phrase for future use and mocked gaily at Arnold's pretensions to criticize English culture:

> It is certainly hard to compare him to Jeremiah, for Jeremiah is our type of the lugubrious; whereas there is nothing more striking than the imperturbable cheerfulness with which Mr Arnold seems to sustain himself on the fragment of culture that is left him, amid the deluge of Philistinism that he sees submerging our age and country.[3]

All this leaves Arnold a figure of fun, and the joke seems to have survived. Forty years later Rupert Brooke, as an undergraduate, refers to Arnold as 'a recurrent figure of most excellent comic value',[4] and his reputation did not revive until enough about the age had been forgotten to enable readers to suppose him accurate. But accuracy, above all, is just what the sages were seen to lack. The myth of *laissez-faire* is attributable to them too, though not only to them; and above all, the myth that seems oddest of all to their contemporaries, that everything was getting worse and would soon end in some unspecified disaster unless some nebulous nostrum like Hellenism were promptly adopted. Many Victorians, conscious of the rising tide of social reform and of standards of living, thought all this merely funny. Everybody, writes Trollope in the conclusion to his

1. William Cory, *Extracts* (1897) p. 532.
2. E. B. Hamley, *Thomas Carlyle* (1881) p. 7, from a review of 1859.
3. Henry Sidgwick, 'The Prophet of Culture', *Macmillan's Magazine* (August 1867); reprinted in his *Miscellaneous Essays and Addresses* (London, 1904).
4. Rupert Brooke, *Democracy and the Arts* (London, 1946) p. 32, from a Cambridge paper written in 1910.

Autobiography, knows what Carlyle thinks about England: 'we are all going straight away to darkness and the dogs.' But how can any sane man believe it?

> We do not put very much faith in Mr Carlyle – nor in Mr Ruskin and his other followers. The loudness and extravagance of their lamentations, the wailing and gnashing of teeth which comes from them, over a world which is supposed to have gone altogether shoddy-wards, are so contrary to the convictions of men who cannot but see how comfort has been increased, how health has been improved, and education extended.

Trollope coins the word 'Carlylism' for the myth of deterioration: 'It is regarded simply as Carlylism to say that the English-speaking world is growing worse from day to day.' Trollope could admit that personal dishonesty might be on the increase, but not social or intellectual debasement in general. This is not a lonely voice of good sense. There were others to report that the sages were not to be believed. R. H. Hutton, reviewing Froude's life of Carlyle in 1882, complained that Carlyle's tone of writing made it impossible to accept that he was engaged in any genuine inquiry. Everything was designed to assert a superiority over the reader, to keep the 'rabble rout' beneath his feet; so much so that it seemed wonderful anyone could 'live so constantly in the atmosphere of scorn'. The effort was costly to him: 'He spends all his energies in a sort of vivid passion of scorn.'[1]

It is easy to exaggerate the attention paid to the sages by their contemporaries. Gladstone, in a private conversation in 1888, said he thought Newman's influence in Oxford had stopped dead with his conversion to Rome in 1845, and that Arnold had always failed to have much influence there; Jowett and T. H. Green, he had heard from Oxford men, 'had counted for much more than Matthew Arnold', who had been 'an influence on the general public, not on the universities'.[2] The rhetoric

1. R. H. Hutton, *Criticisms on Contemporary Thought and Thinkers* (London, 1894) i. 32.

2. W. S. Peterson, 'Gladstone's review of *Robert Elsmere:* some unpublished correspondence', *Review of English Studies* new series xxi (1970) p. 450, from Mrs Humphry Ward's notes on her conversation with Gladstone in April 1888.

of despair had a market, but not principally among the informed. They saw it as the work of the 'too clever by half people', as Bagehot scornfully called irresponsible intellectuals in *The English Constitution* (1867), noting the new harmony between the nation and its parliamentary institutions that had grown up since 1832: 'There is no worse trade than agitation at this time. A man can hardly get an audience if he wishes to complain of anything', and this because Parliament has now achieved 'that precise species of moderation most agreeable to the nation at large'.[1] A rhetoric created during the constitutional trouble of the 1830s and the hunger and class divisions of the 1840s lingered on as a literary mannerism, ill-adapted to an age of manifest political achievement. And at times, one suspects, the tone is overloud because the sage knows he is not heeded.

Events themselves had betrayed him. The sages had thought industrialism and democracy must invite disaster. Instead, the ancient parliamentary institutions of the nation had taken the new strains and sucked new energy from them. Thirty years ago, wrote Bagehot in 1876, celebrating the centenary of Adam Smith's *Wealth of Nations*, 'Carlyle and Arnold had nearly convinced the world of the irrecoverable poverty of our lower classes. The "condition of England question", as they termed it, was bringing us fast to ruin. But, in fact, we were on the eve of the greatest prosperity which we have ever seen, or perhaps any other nation.'[2] The sages had been abandoned by history itself. By the later years of the century, far too many people knew more than they did about the condition of England, and knew it on the most direct of evidence.

But at a profounder level, there were always those who doubted whether the sages could think, and the puzzling and indeterminate status of their writings all conspired to keep that doubt an active one. No one could believe the sages were writing out of special knowledge or professional qualification: the very manner in which they wrote forbade one to suppose it, and the conduct of their argument and cavalier use of quotation

1. Walter Bagehot, *The English Constitution*, edited by R. H. S. Crossman (London, 1963) pp. 179, 173.

2. Bagehot, *Economist* (3 June 1876); reprinted in his *Collected Works* (1968) iii. 117.

all confirmed the doubt. As events failed to justify the jeremiads, doubts spread to question the authenticity of their whole endeavour. Thomas Hardy, writing in his diary in 1891, mused to himself on those two dead prophets, Newman and Carlyle. What, in the end, had they done? They had sought a reputation for wisdom by devices which were plainly unphilosophical. Newman's was 'a feminine nature, which first decides and then finds reasons for having decided. He was an enthusiast with the absurd reputation of a logician and reasoner. Carlyle was a poet with the reputation of a philosopher. Neither was truly a *thinker*.'[1] This, in memorable summary, confirms the growing conviction of the age. To have watched Newman in self-justification, Carlyle's worship of autocratic power, Arnold's lofty contempt for the processes of parliamentary reform, or Ruskin invoking a medieval past unknown to historians of the Middle Ages, was to create doubts of an understandable sort about the efficacy of literary culture itself. Had it been wise to encourage men to believe that a knowledge of literature gives them a licence to pontificate? Arnold, in 'The study of poetry' (1880), had sought to assimilate all human knowledge to the poetic mould: 'There is not a creed which is not shaken, not an accredited dogma which is not shown to be questionable, not a received tradition which does not threaten to dissolve.' But if everything is to be judged incomplete – politics, religion, philosophy and the sciences – without this mysterious component of which the sages claim to possess the secret, then the world will estimate that claim by the accuracy of what the sage may say. Its value must somehow be redeemable: it is, after all, a critique of a given civilization at a given point in history. Viewed in this exacting light, many saw the claim as without foundation.

And the sages had offended more deeply than by inaccuracy. They had rejected the very processes of cool analysis by which questions of accuracy are commonly judged. They had denied the intellectual spirit, and that denial looked all the more sinister by virtue of its advocacy by men of intellect. If the mood were to prove infectious, so some men felt, then an entire intelligentsia might be corrupted by a taste for the irrational.

1. Florence E. Hardy, *The Life of Thomas Hardy* (1962) p. 233.

'It is not good to fall into the mood of Carlyle's or Ruskin's rout,' John Addington Symonds wrote to Robert Louis Stevenson in 1885 – 'the rout of men who dyspeptically belch forth undigested gobbets of the Minor Prophets or the French Socialists.'[1] That dyspepsia might easily prove catching; and if it did, it would be the credit of the whole life of mind that would suffer. That 'usurping personal wilfulness' that Bagehot noted in Carlyle could give men of intellect only a false sense of freedom, like Carlyle's wilful support for Governor Eyre's suppression of the Jamaican rebellion in 1866.

> This strange championship of a purely muscular morality by men of high intellectual reputation will have a very detrimental effect. If this is seen to be the legitimate outcome of literary culture, depend upon it, literary culture will be more distrusted in the world of politics than ever it has been before.[2]

That prediction, at all events, was to be vindicated by events. It was the fine fortune of the Victorians, who had married mind and politics as no men before or since had done, that they did not live to see that future of distrust.

1. J. A. Symonds, *Letters*, edited by Herbert M. Schueller and Robert L. Peters (Detroit, 1967–69) iii. 39–40.
2. Walter Bagehot, *Economist* (15 September 1866); reprinted in his *Collected Works* (1968) iii. 564–5.

Index

Abercorn, 1st Duke of, 32
Abbott, Claude C., 245n
Acton, Lord, 10–11, 13–14, 16 & n, 94 & n, 134n, 213 & n, 239; on Bentham, 38 & n; on class, 187 & n; on consistency, 17–18, 18n; on democracy, 155, 156 & n, 160 & n, 226 & n; on 18th century, 37 & n; on French Revolution, 45 & n; on Gladstone, 126 & n, 127; on *laissez-faire*, 68 & n; on liberty, 19 & n, 20; on morality, 22 & n, 48 & n, 52–3, 54, 55, 57–8, 58n, 61 & n, 90 & n; on sages, 251–2, 252n; on Adam Smith, 81–2, 82n; on socialism, 223 & n
  Henry James on, 8
  History of Liberty, 18 & n
Addison, Joseph, 36
Amberley, Lady, 16 & n
American Civil War, 183, 207, 208
American Revolution, 39–40, 45, 187, 202
anarchism, 16, 219
Anglo-Saxons, 31
Annan, Noel, 75 & n
Anne, Queen, 38
Aristotle, 32–3, 120
Arnold, Matthew, x, 13, 14, 30, 49, 55, 110; on class, 194 & n; on Dickens, 257 & n; on equality, 167 & n, 170; on Hebraism, 19; on race, 199 & n, 200, 202, 206, 207; as sage, 241f
  Culture and Anarchy, 248f; *Essays in Criticism*, 57, 249, 254–5, 256
Arnold, Thomas, 32, 120; on class, 179–80, 180n
Aspinall, A., 113n
Asquith, H. H., 130n
Asquith, Baroness, (Lady Violet Bonham Carter), 116
Athens, 33, 250
Austen, Jane, 8, 87 & n, 256
Austin, John, 169
Aydelotte, W. O., 99n

Bagehot, Walter, ix, x, 9 & n, 13 & n, 48 & n, 49, 64 & n, 95 & n, 110–11, 111n, 115 & n, 116, 235 & n, 255; on class, 181f, 193–4; on Conservatives, 103 & n; on democracy, 157 & n, 158 & n, 160 & n, 163; on equality, 165f; on evidence, 53 & n; on government, 73 & n; on G. C. Lewis, 91 & n; on oratory, 112, 116 & n, 117

Bagehot, Walter—*cont.*
& n, 119 & n; on party, 93; on race, 203–4; on revolution, 45 & n, 46 & n; on sages, 261 & n, 263 & n; on Whigs, 107 n.
English Constitution, 163, 194, 261
Baker, E. A., 39n
Balfour, Arthur, 126, 130n, 216
ballot, secret, 142, 161, 163–4
Barmby, Goodwyn, 219–20, 220n
Barzun, Jacques, 199
Bassett, A. T., 126n
Bentham, Jeremy, 6, 11–12, 11n, 16, 22, 38 & n, 39, 41, 69, 202, 227, 258
Bestor, Arthur J., 220n
Birkenhead, Lord (F. E. Smith), 115
Bismarck, 228–9
Blanc, Louis, 24
Bland, Hubert, 239
Blanqui, L. A., 42
Bloch, Marc, 178 & n
Bolingbroke, Lord, 102
Bond, Maurice F., x
Booth, Charles, 194
bourgeoisie, 194
Brebner, J. Bartlett, 72n
Bridges, Robert, 244–5, 245n
Briggs, Asa, 175n
Bright, John, 95, 117n, 119, 130 & n, 131, 183; Arnold on, 256
Brontë, Charlotte, 27, 139, 201, 205
Brooke, John, 1n
Brooke, Rupert, 231 & n, 259 & n.
Brougham, Lord, 64, 117, 123, 191
Browning, Elizabeth Barrett, 30, 31, 35–6, 36n, 49, 65–6, 174; on Carlyle, 254 & n
Browning, Robert, 22–3, 23n, 30, 65, 206, 239, 254
Bryce, James, 5–6, 6n, 18 & n, 28 & n, 192
Buckle, G. E., 257n
Buckle, H. T., 28 & n, 42, 250n, 255
Burke, Edmund, 35, 38, 39, 41, 93, 106, 113, 116–17, 216; Acton on, 17
Burns, J. H., 161n
Butler, Samuel (*Hudibras*), 194
Butterfield, Sir Herbert, 37n
Byron, Lord, 16, 33, 119, 246

Caesarism, 238
Cambridge, 15, 120, 121, 231
Canning, Charles John, Lord (Governor-General of India), 32
Canning, George, 95, 102, 119
capitalism, 183, 230, 235f
Carlyle, Thomas, 3, 16, 30; on cash-nexus, 50; on 18th century, 36–7; on *laissez-faire*, 68f; on novels, 257; as sage, 241f; on race, 206, 207–8
Chartism, 75–6
French Revolution, 43, 45, 94
Carlylism, 242, 247, 260
Carr, E. H., 211n
cash-nexus, 50
Castlereagh, Lord, 108
Cavendish, Sir Henry, 113 & n
centralization, 12–13, 70f, 229f
Challoner, W. H., 5n
Chamberlain, Austen, 130n

Chamberlain, Joseph, 95, 115, 125, 130
Charlemont, Lady, 42–3
Charles II, 40, 145
child labour, 84
Christianity, 49f
Christian Socialism, 220–1, 223, 230
Churchill, Sir Winston, 85 & n, 115; on race, 200; *Savrola*, 138, 139
Cicero, 117–18, 119
Civil War, English, 27, 40
Clarendon, Lord, Edward Hyde, 40
Clark, Sir G. N., 42n
class, 174–97
class war, 99; and transport, 190
clerisy, 60–1, 162
Cline, C. L., 188n
Clough, Arthur Hugh, 49 & n, 65 & n, 235–6, 236n, 243 & n; on *laissez-faire*, 73 & n
clubs, 143–4
Cobbett, William, 11, 114, 241
Cobden, Richard, 42 & n, 197, 216; on socialism, 227 & n
Cole, G. D. H., 175n
Coleridge, S. T., 60, 69, 70n, 104, 235, 241
collectivism, 229f
Communism, 38, 70, 219–20
Comte, Auguste, 20, 54, 255
Condition of England, 248–50
Conington, John, 95
Conrad, Joseph, 152, 214, 238 & n
Conservatives, 15, 101–5, 245; and Disraeli, 148, 217
Contagious Diseases Act, 71
Corn Laws, 115, 216
Cook, E. T., 19n, 231n
cooperation, 220, 230
co-ownership, 230
Copernicus, 40
Cory, William, 242n, 259 & n
Cotgrave, Randall, 40
Creighton, Mandell, 58 & n
Crimean War, 46
Croker, John Wilson, 101, 107, 108n
Cromwell, Oliver, 247
culture, 255f
Crossman, R. H. S., 261n
Cunningham, William, 221
Curzon, Lord, 118–19, 119n, 127, 131n

Dalhousie, 10th Earl of (Governor-General of India), 32
Dalton, Hugh, 231
Darwin, Charles, 56, 59, 212, 233f
death duties, 170–1
Defoe, Daniel, 36, 137
democracy, 1, 38, 61, 80, 149, 155–73, 225f; in fiction, 135, 155–73; and the sages, 246f
Demosthenes, 117, 119, 131
De Quincey, Thomas, 96 & n, 109 & n
Dessain, C. S., 258n
determinism, 20–1, 86f, 234
Dicey, A. V., 21–2, 45 & n, 74, 80; on class, 183f, 193; on collectivism, 227–8, 228n
Dicey, Edward, 74 & n
Dickens, Charles, x, 5, 8, 13, 14, 48, 156, 207, 238, 242, 256; on colonies, 214; on Parliament, 114, 139–42, 144
Barnaby Rudge, 159
Bleak House, 7, 140, 143, 251
Child's History, 39, 142

Dickens, Charles—*cont.*
  David Copperfield, 4, 140, 143, 251
  Edwin Drood, 141
  Great Expectations, 6, 29, 63, 140, 189, 214
  Hard Times, 50–2, 79 & n, 139, 140; Macaulay on, 224–5; Ruskin on, 258
  Little Dorrit, 63, 72, 89, 96, 140, 216, 235
  Martin Chuzzlewit, 140
  Nicholas Nickleby, 257
  Oliver Twist, 66, 257
  Our Mutual Friend, 70–1
  Pickwick Papers, 7, 140, 145, 164, 195; Ruskin on, 258 & n
  Tale of Two Cities, 36, 39, 44, 45–6, 159
Dilke, Sir Charles, 218 & n
Disraeli, Benjamin, Lord Beaconsfield, 13, 15, 39, 92, 102, 135, 138, 143, 144, 163, 241, 245; on class, 193; on empire, 213, 217; on equality, 166f, 191–2; on novels, 257 & n; his oratory, 113, 115, 118–19, 125f; on Peel, 122; on principle, 18–19; on race, 204–5, 206, 209; Trollope on, 100–1
  Coningsby, 30, 43, 129, 133, 138f, 153 & n, 155, 176, 204, 206, 209
  Endymion, 102, 129–30, 204
  Sybil, 139, 145f, 176, 191, 235, 248
  Vivian Grey, 147
Dod, Charles R., 92, 98n, 105n
Donothingism, 69, 75, 83
Durham, Lord, 163
Edel, Leon, 8n
Edgeworth, Maria, 3–4, 3n, 77–8
  Castle Rackrent, 200
  Harrington, 204
  Patronage, 138–9, 145
education, 58, 60, 71, 73; and class, 190–1
election addresses, 93
Elgin, 8th Earl of (Governor-General of Canada, Viceroy of India), 32
Eliot, George, x, 24 & n, 30, 48, 49, 51, 54, 135, 145, 150, 201, 238–9, 241, 253 & n, 256; on Carlyle, 242n; on morality, 55f; on race, 205–206; on state welfare, 70 & n; on sociology, 180–1, 181n, 194; on truth in art, 3 & n, 4 & n; Acton on, 257 &n
  Adam Bede, 6, 65
  Daniel Deronda, 65, 205
  Felix Holt, 7, 64 & n, 139, 140, 156, 158, 164, 241; Holt's Address, 182–3
  Middlemarch, 56f, 63, 66, 87, 205, 214
  Romola, 6 & n
  Scenes of Clerical Life, 4
  Silas Marner, 6
Elliot, A. D., 106n
Elliot, H. S. R., 63n
Emerson, R. W., 29, 122–3, 124, 209; and Carlyle, 252–3
empire, 198–218
Engels, Friedrich, 5 & n, 9, 211 & n
Enlightenment, 35–9, 187, 219
equality, 164–73, 174f; economic, 224f; racial, 198f

Escott, T. H. S., 119n, 126 & n, 138n
evolution, 59
Eyre, Governor, 207, 263

Fabian Society, 224, 230, 231, 232–3, 239
Factory Acts, 14, 71, 75f, 84, 98–9, 227
Falkland, Lord, 102
Fascism, 23, 238
Faverty, F. E., 199n
Fichte, 202
Fielding, Henry, 36, 37–8
Figgis, J. N., 18n, 61n, 223n
Fisk, Wilbur, 124 & n
FitzGerald, Edward, 206
Foot, M. R. D., x, 93n, 102n, 131n, 217n
Forster, W. E., 73
Forster, E. M., 214
Fourier, 230
Fox, Charles James, 113, 117
France, 30, 35f, 45, 163, 209–10, 254; its fiction, 66; its equality, 166f; its political terms, 94
Francis, G. H., 116 & n, 123–4, 213 n
Frederick the Great, 36, 247, 250, 257
Freeman, E. A., 31, 198 & n, 204 & n, 205
French Revolution, 11, 12, 27, 36, 39f, 81-2, 159, 164, 169, 202
Froissart, Jean, 29
Froude, J. A., 27, 242 & n, 247n, 252

Galsworthy, John, 177, 239, 240
Gardiner, A. G., 106n
Gash, Norman, 99n
Gaskell, Elizabeth, 3n; *Mary Barton*, 3, 5, 66, 139, 180, 193, 201
gentleman, 143, 195–7
George I, 37
George IV, 36
Gibbon, Edward, 35–6, 111
Gilbert, W. S., 59
Gilmour, Robin, 79n
Gladstone, Mary (Mrs Drew), 17n, 18n, 82n, 156n, 192n, 257n
Gladstone, William Ewart, x, 10, 13, 15, 20, 23 & n, 32, 48, 49, 55, 92, 95 & n, 105, 106, 142, 143, 155, 161, 164–5, 210, 216; on class, 192n; on consistency, 17 & n, 54; on democracy, 61; on empire, 217 & n; on equality, 166f; on 18th century, 38 & n; on novels, 257 & n; on oratory, 115, 119, 124f; on party, 93 & n; on sages, 260 & n; on socialism, 221 & n, 223; on Tories, 102 & n; Acton on, 16–17, 126; Arnold on, 256
Godwin, William, 16, 202
Goethe, 30
Gordon, General, 213
Gordon, Riots, 159
Goschen, Lord, 106 & n
Greece, 31–4, 57, 63, 206, 207; its oratory, 117–18; Greek quotations, 119–20
Green, John Richard, 31, 109 & n.
Green, Thomas Hill, 260; on gentleman, 196 & n; on novels, 7 & n; on 1689, 42 & n; on paternalism, 90 & n.

Grote, George, 32, 33, 53, 57, 58 & n, 62n, 163–4
Grote, John, 62 & n
Guedella, Philip, 95n, 221n

Haggard, Rider, 201
Haight, Gordon S., x
Halévy, Elie, 101n, 108n
Halifax, Lord (Charles Wood), 76–7, 76n
Hallam, Henry, 41
Hamilton, 11th Duke of, 32
Hamley, Sir E. B., 242n, 253, 259 & n
Hammerton, J. A., 3n
Hanham, H. J., 2n
Hansard, 112, 114f
Harcourt, Sir William, 106 & n
Hardie, Keir, 222
Hardy, Florence E., 8n, 193n, 201n, 262n
Hardy, Thomas, 6, 8, 86, 193 & n; on region, 201 & n; on sages, 262 & n; *Jude*, 66; *Tess*, 66
Harrison, Frederic, 75, 117 & n, 255 & n
Hastings, Battle of, 33
Haubtmann, Pierre, 211n
Hegel, 219
Heine, Heinrich, 30
Hellenism, 14, 19, 31–4, 206, 207, 248, 250, 253, 259
Henderson, W. O., 5n
Herbert, Sidney, 33
historical novel, 5f, 27
Hobbes, Thomas, 11, 102
Hobhouse, L. T., 230
Hodgson, W. B., 79 & n
Holland, Lord, 107
Holloway, John, 241n
Holyoake, G. J., 110 & n
Homer, 33
Hopkins, G. M., 245n
Horace, 34, 118, 119
Horne, R. H., 254n
Houghton, Walter E., x
House, Humphry, ix
House, Madeline, x
Hume, David, 35, 41, 59, 71 & n, 102
Huskisson, William, 95, 102
Hutton, R. H., 66, 87 & n; on Carlyle, 260 & n; on class, 183, 192–3
Huxley, T. H., on *laissez-faire*, 71 & n, 73, 85–6; on race, 207–9, 209n; *Evolution and Ethics*, 59
Hyndman, H. M., 224, 228, 233, 234 & n

Ibsen, Hendrik, 239 & n
ideology, 9f
imperialism, 213 & n
India, 214, 215; Macaulay on, 215–16
individualism, 63, 219, 224, 235
industrial novel, 139
industrial revolution, 42 & n, 169–70; and sages, 248–50
Ireland, 15, 34, 74, 102, 108, 200–1, 213

James II, 41
James, Henry, 8 & n, 139, 142, 152
Jean-Aubry, G., 238n
Jeffrey, Francis, 82 & n
Jennings, L. J., 108n
Jephson, Henry, 115n, 124
Jews, 203–6; and socialism, 210f
Johnson, Samuel, 147; on gentleman, 196

Jordan, H. D., 115n
Jowett, Benjamin, 32, 120, 260
Joyce, James, 142

Keats, John, 238
Keynes, Maynard, 74
Kingsley, Charles, 27, 139, 192
Kintner, Elvan, 36n
Kipling, Rudyard, 207, 214
Knox, Robert, 205
Koebner, Richard, 213n
Koestler, Arthur, 238

laissez-faire, 50, 68–90, 157, 227, 259
Lambert, R. J., 71n
Lansdowne, Lord, 110
Lassalle, Ferdinand, 211, 220, 223, 229, 233
Laurence, R. V., 18n, 61n, 223n
Left, 93f
Lenin, 11, 57, 238
Leroux, Pierre, 24n
Lewes, G. H., 205
Lewis, Sir George Cornewall, 32, 44, 53, 85; on Carlyle, 244 & n; on class, 193
Use and Abuse of Political Terms, 91 & n, 95–6, 96n
Lewis, G. F., 244n
Liberals, 16, 105–11; Wells on, 229 & n
Liberal-Conservatives, 98 & n
Lichtheim, George, 211n
Liddell & Scott, 32
Livy, 34 & n
Lloyd George, David, 115, 210
Locke, John, 11, 35, 39, 40–1, 187
Londonderry, Lord, 101
Lowell, Abbott Lawrence, 2n, 99 & n
Lowry, H. F., 243n
Lubenow, William C., 71n
Ludlow, J. M., 220–1, 223 & n

Macaulay, Thomas Babington, 16, 27, 29, 38, 63 & n, 80 & n, 94–5, 94n, 111, 137 & n, 138, 156, 238, 255; on America, 4; on class, 179 & n, 190, 194 & n; on Dickens, 4 & n; on Disqualified, 99 & n; on education, 58 & n; on gentleman, 196 & n; on India, 215–16; on *laissez-faire*, 68f, 83–4, 84n; on Liberals, 108 & n; on novels, 256–7, 256n; on Parliament, 1 & n; on progress, 251; on reform, 41f, 42n, 101; on socialism, 224–5; on Thackeray, 4 & n; on Tories, 103 & n; on Whigs, 106–7; his oratory, 112 & n, 114, 116n, 117, 118 & n, 123–4, 130
McCulloch, J. R., 69, 81; Jeffrey's review, 82 & n
MacDonagh, Oliver, 38n
Macgregor, D. H., 68n
Mackintosh, Sir James, 41, 46, 94, 107
Maine, Sir Henry, 86, 156
Malthus, T. R., 69
Marat, 40
Marathon, 31, 32, 33, 38
Marcus Aurelius, 57
Marshall, Alfred, 74–5
Martin, Kingsley, 121n
Marx, Karl, 9, 54, 55, 74, 88, 176f, 183, 192, 194–5, 219f, 223f, 233–4, 255; and Jews, 211 & n

Marxism and literature, 23, 177, 238–40
Masson, David, 96n, 109n
Masterman, Neville C., 223n
May, Sir Thomas Erskine, 2, 24–5, 25n, 93 & n, 134n, 155 & n 157, 226n; on socialism, 222–3
Mayer, J. P., 158n
Maynooth grant, 257
Mayor, J. B., 62n
Mazzini, Giuseppe, 202, 234
Meredith, George, 3 & n, 8, 97 & n, 135, 139, 187–8, 188n, 239, 256; *Tragic Comedians*, 220, 233, 234
Mill, John Stuart, x, 8–9, 9n, 12 & n, 13–14, 20, 25, 30, 48, 49, 54, 78 & n, 90 & n, 94 & n, 96f, 97n, 120 & n, 238, 255; on Bentham, 202, 258; on class, 176, 181f; on clerisy, 21 & n; on Conservatives, 15, 103–4; on cooperation, 61–2, 62n; on France, 37 & n, 46, 254, 256; on democracy, 158, 160f; on Greece, 33 & n; on G. C. Lewis, 91; on Liberals, 108 & n, 109f; on history, 28 & n; on ideology, 10 & n; on individuals, 87–8; on nationalism, 202; on race, 207–8; on revolution, 46 & n; on Rome, 34; on sages, 242 & n, 245–6, 246n; on socialism, 221, 225f; and Ruskin, 253
  Chapters on Socialism, 229 & n, 237
  On Liberty, 56–7, 70, 83, 165, 185, 225
  On Representative Government, 88, 160f, 185
  System of Logic, 60, 87–8, 97, 100
  Thoughts on Parliamentary Reform, 186–7, 187n
  Utilitarianism, 38, 55
Millar, John, 177–8
Milner, Alfred, 78
Mineka, F. E., x, 12, 21n, 94n, 185n, 242n
Mirror of Parliament, 114, 140
Missolonghi, 38
Mitford, William, 32, 33
Mommsen, Theodor, 28, 228
Montesquieu, 187
Monypenny, W. E., 257n
morality, 9, 11, 22, 26, 48–67; and social forces, 86f; and Parliament, 145
Morley, John, 30n, 227 & n
Morris, William, 207, 223, 231, 239, 240
Mosley, Sir Oswald, 212 & n, 238 & n
Mulhauser, F. L., 73n

Namier, Sir Lewis, 1n, 113n
Napoleon I, 10, 27, 45, 62, 213n, 238
Napoleon III, 24, 166, 213, 238
nationalization, 171, 230, 235
Nettleship, H., 30n
Nettleship, R. L., 90n
Newcastle, 5th Duke of, 32
Newcastle Programme (1891), 93
Newman, John Henry, Cardinal, 14 & n, 17, 49n; as sage, 241f

Niebuhr, B. G., 34 & n
Nietzsche, 238, 253
Nightingale, Florence, 33
Nonconformity, 100
novel, as historical evidence, 2–5; historical novel, 5f; industrial novel, 139; parliamentary novel, 133–54; regional novel, 200–1; social novel, 3f; novel of ideas, 147; and the sages, 256–8

objectivism, moral, 52f
oratory, 112–32; Dickens on, 140–1
Orwell, George, 39, 238, 239 & n, 240
Ostrogorsky, Moses, 92
Owen, Robert, 88 & n, 89, 210, 219, 220, 221, 230
Oxford, 32, 37, 120
Oxford (formerly *New*) *English Dictionary*, x, 94

Page, F., 136n
Paine, Thomas, 16, 61
Palmerston, Lord, 15, 16, 32, 48, 105, 106, 115, 116n, 121 & n, 216
Parliament, 1–2; the parliamentary novel, 133–54; and the sages, 245f
party, political, 91–111
Pater, Walter, 35
paternalism, 70f, 89f
Pattison, Mark, 30 & n, 95, 250 & n
Peacock, Thomas Love, 147
Peel, Sir Robert, 9 & n, 71 & n, 73n, 93, 107–8; on gentleman, 196; his oratory, 115 & n, 116n, 117, 119 & n, 122 & n, 244
Peters, Robert L., 35n, 263n
Peterson, W. S., 260n
Pitt, William, the younger, 120, 121, 131
Plato, 32
Poor Law, 14, 71, 75, 227
Positivism, 117
progress, 251–2
proletariat, 194–5
prostitution, 65–6, 71
Proudhon, P.-J., 24, 210–11, 211n
prudery, 65–6, 226
Prussia, 30, 228–9
public libraries, 71

quotation, classical, 118–20

race, 198–218; and socialism, 210f
Radicals, 105f; Mill on, 96–7
Rae, John, 222 & n
railways, 190
rank, 174–97
Reade, Charles, 27
Reeve, Henry, 106
Reform Acts, 22, 38, 41f, 108f, 124, 135, 140, 152–3, 182f, 191–2; Carlyle on, 247
Reid, Andrew, 23n
Reid, Loren, 126n
Renaissance, 35–9
revolution, 11, 39–47, 61; 1689, 16, 39–47, 124
Ricardo, David, 3n, 4, 69, 80–1, 81n, 185; Toynbee on, 77–8, 78n
Richardson, Samuel, 37–8
Riehl, Wilhelm, 54, 180
Right, 93f

Rights of Man, 11–12, 61
Risorgimento, 30 & n, 44
Roach, John, 15n
Roberts, David, 72 & n
Robespierre, 40, 238
Robbins, Lionel, 75, 81n
Robson, John M., x, 229n
Roebuck, J. A., 109–10
Rome, 28, 31–4, 194; its oratory, 117–18
Rousseau, J.-J., 35, 37, 194, 200
Ruskin, John, 13, 30, 35, 50, 235, 238; on equality, 231–2, 232n; on Mill, 19 & n, 256; on revolution, 44–5, 45n; on Scott, 4; as sage, 241f
Russell, Bertrand, 16 & n, 219 & n, 223–4
Russell, G. W. E., 194n, 243n
Russell, Lord John, 105, 123
Russell, Patricia, 16n

sages, 241–63
St John-Stevas, Norman, x, 9n
Saint-Simon, Comte de, 176
Saville, John, 175n
Schmidt, H. D., 213n
Schneewind, J. B., 161n
Schueller, Herbert M., 35n, 263n
Scotland, 200–1
Scott, Sir Walter, 4, 5, 6, 7, 26, 27, 39; on region, 200–1; Disraeli's debt, 147–8; Gladstone's, 257n
Seeley, Sir John R., 215, 216 & n, 217
Selden, John, 252
Senior, Nassau, 69, 76
Shakespeare, William, 32
Shaw, G. Bernard, 233, 238, 239 & n, 240
Shelley, P. B., 16, 202–3, 238
Sheridan, R. B., 113
Shorthouse, J. H., 257n
Sidgwick, A., 15n
Sidgwick, E. M., 15n
Sidgwick, Henry, 15 & n, 54, 55, 221–2, 222n, 242n, 259; on Clough, 65 & n
Silver Fork novels, 147
slavery, 14, 56, 207f
Smiles, Samuel, 51–2, 60, 69, 88–9, 195, 196
Smith, Adam, 69, 70, 76–7, 80f, 102, 177, 185, 213 & n, 261
Smollett, Tobias, 200
Smythe, George, Viscount Strangford, 102n
Snow, Vernon F., 40n
Social Democratic Federation, 224
socialism, 22, 81–2, 219–40; and literature, 238–40; and race, 210f; and social conditioning, 54, 88–9; and the State, 230f
sociology, 54, 180–1, 255
Solon, 57
Sophocles, 119
Southey, Robert, 104
Southgate, Donald, 108n
Spencer, Herbert, 59; on *laissez-faire*, 73–4, 74n
Spinoza, 57
Sraffa, Piero, 3n, 78n
Stanley, A. P., 109
Steele, Sir Richard, 36
Stephen, James Fitzjames, 15n, 156 & n
Stephen, Leslie, 37–8, 38n, 109n; *Science of Ethics*, 59
Stevenson, Robert Louis, 263
Stowe, Harriet Beecher, 207
Stalin, 11, 210

Stanhope, Lord, 131
Storey, Graham, x
Stubbs, William, 2, 24 & n, 26 & n, 31, 37
subjectivism, moral, 52f
Suez Canal, 217
Super, R. H., x, 156n
Svaglic, Martin J., 246n
Swift, Jonathan, 36
Swinburne, A. C., 30, 256
Switzerland, 169
Symonds, John Addington, 35 & n; on sages, 262–3, 263n

Tell, William, 30
Tennyson, Alfred Lord, 55, 59, 86, 190
Thackeray, William Makepeace, 4, 7, 13, 27, 65–6, 66n, 142, 174, 238
Henry Esmond, 6, 38
Four Georges, 36
Newcomes, 139, 236
Pendennis, 139, 189
Vanity Fair, 63, 145
Thiers, M. J. L. A., 130
Thomas, P. D. G., 113n
Thomson, James, 86–7
Thornton, A. P., 213n, 237 & n.
Thucydides, 32, 179, 180n
Tillotson, Geoffrey, 14n
Tillotson, Kathleen, ix
Tocqueville, Alexis de, 13n, 14, 42–3, 43n, 109 & n, 124–5; on class, 190 & n; on democracy, 155 & n, 158 & n, 160n, 164; on gentleman, 195–6, 196n; on Wellington, 121–2; and Mill, 225
Todd, Alpheus, 2 & n
Tolstoy, Leo, 29, 258
Tories, 96, 101–5, 130
Toynbee, Arnold (1852–83), 42, 77 & n, 80, 189
trade unions, 62, 82, 236f
Traill, H. D., 127 & n
Travick, B. B., 49n
Trevelyan, G. M., 30n ;
Trevelyan, George Otto, 4n, 42n, 44 & n, 80n, 108n, 118n, 123–4, 124n, 137 & n, 194n, 256n
Trollope, Anthony, 5–6, 13, 51, 92, 135–6, 136n, 138, 139, 144, 149–54, 191, 238; on Carlyle, 258, 260; on Conservatives, 103, 104–5; on equality, 144f, 171f; on oratory, 123, 127; on Whigs, 105–6; on women, 196 & n; Hutton on, 87 & n; Newman on, 258 & n
Barchester Towers, 36, 97, 258
Duke's Children, 143 & n, 145f
Palmerston, 121 & n
Prime Minister, 143, 144f, 164–5, 171, 224
Ralph the Heir, 136, 164
Thackeray, 38
Warden, 175, 258
Way We Live Now, 6, 52, 100–1, 138, 142, 144
Tupper, Martin, 32–3, 33n, 127 & n
Two Nations, 147, 176–7

Utilitarianism, 12, 38, 55

vaccination, 71 & n
Victoria, Queen, 48, 95 & n, 221 & n, 224–5
Vigny, Alfred de, 33 & n, 96, 97n, 254
Vincent, J. R., 108n

Virgil, 34, 118, 119
Vizetelly, Henry, 114
Voltaire, 39

Waller, R. D., 3n
Walpole, Spencer, 105n
Ward, Mrs Humphry, 260n
Washington, George, 36, 40
Waterlow, Sir Sydney, 8n
Watson, George, 175n
Webb, Beatrice, 125 & n, 176 & n, 194, 229, 233 & n
Webb, Sidney, 212, 233 & n, 234 & n
Weber, Max, 176
Wedderburn, A., 19n, 231n
welfare state, 70, 172–3, 227–8
Wellington, Duke of, 56, 95, 101, 103, 116n, 118, 121-2, 130, 143, 144
Wells, H. G., 133, 139, 142, 229 & n, 232, 239–40; on race, 211
Whigs, 12, 15, 16, 38, 39, 84, 105–7; on revolution, 39f, 110; De Quincey on, 96
Whips, 92–3
White, R. J., 156n
Wilde, Oscar, 235
William III, 39, 41, 106
Wood, Charles, Lord Halifax, 76–7, 76n
Wordsworth, William, 26, 29, 104, 188–9
work, 49f, 208

Zionism, 205
Zola, Emile, 239

Lightning Source UK Ltd.
Milton Keynes UK
UKOW041617221012

200991UK00001B/204/A